THE CRIMINAL CODE

OF THE

GERMAN EMPIRE

TRANSLATED

WITH PROLEGOMENA AND A COMMENTARY

BY

GEOFFREY DRAGE, B.A.
OF LINCOLN'S INN
SOMETIME JUNIOR STUDENT OF CHRIST CHURCH, OXFORD

THE LAWBOOK EXCHANGE, LTD.
Clark, New Jersey
2005

ISBN-13: 978-1-58477-593-5
ISBN-10: 1-58477-593-9

Second printing 2007

Printed in the United States of America on acid-free paper

THE LAWBOOK EXCHANGE, LTD.
33 Terminal Avenue
Clark, New Jersey 07066-1321

Please see our website for a selection of our other publications and fine facsimile reprints of classic works of legal history:
www.lawbookexchange.com

Library of Congress Cataloging-in-Publication Data

Drage, Geoffrey, b. 1860.
The criminal code of the German Empire / Geoffrey Drage.
p. cm.
Originally published: London : Chapman and Hall limited, 1885.
Includes bibliographical references and index.
ISBN 1-58477-593-9 (alk. paper)
1. Criminal law--Germany. I. Title.
KK7975.51871.D73 2005
345.43--dc22

2005000818

THE CRIMINAL CODE

OF THE

GERMAN EMPIRE

TRANSLATED

WITH PROLEGOMENA AND A COMMENTARY

BY

GEOFFREY DRAGE, B.A.
OF LINCOLN'S INN
SOMETIME JUNIOR STUDENT OF CHRIST CHURCH, OXFORD

LONDON: CHAPMAN AND HALL
LIMITED
1885

Richard Clay and Sons,
BUNGAY, SUFFOLK,
and Bread Street Hill, London.

DEDICATED

WITH PERMISSION TO

Professor Rudolf Gneist,

MEMBER OF THE PRUSSIAN COUNCIL OF STATE, OF THE PRUSSIAN

HOUSE OF DEPUTIES,

OF THE SUPREME COURT OF ADMINISTRATIVE JUSTICE

AT BERLIN, ETC., ETC.,

SOMETIME RECTOR MAGNIFICUS OF THE ROYAL UNIVERSITY AT

BERLIN, MEMBER OF THE IMPERIAL PARLIAMENT, ETC., ETC.,

AS THE FIRST-FRUITS OF HIS TEACHING AND ADVICE,

BY HIS AFFECTIONATE PUPIL

THE AUTHOR.

PREFACE.

THE interest excited by the approaching codification of our English criminal law has emboldened me to publish the present work in the hope that it may be of use to students.

Whatever merit the Prolegomena and the Commentary may possess is due to two of the most celebrated Professors in the University of Berlin, Dr. Gneist and Dr. Berner.

The works of the latter, especially the tenth and thirteenth editions of his 'Lehrbuch des Deutschen Strafrechtes,' have been made the subject of my most careful study, and there is not a page of mine in which his influence cannot be traced.

The debt I owe to the former is even more extensive. I attended the lectures of Professor Gneist on this and other legal subjects during part of one and the whole of another semester. To the fascination of his eloquence in public and his kindly encouragement in private is due what little success may attend this or any subsequent attempt of mine to explain the law of the German Empire.

The text from which the translation is made is that of Doctor Rudorff, of whose notes I have made frequent use.

The difficulties which such a work involves will be understood by every lawyer and scholar, and I cannot hope to have attained the golden mean between a free and a literal rendering, but if the work with all its imperfections should lead to a better appreciation in England of what is perhaps the most successful of modern Criminal Codes I shall be content.

On one or two points I have consulted Sir James Stephen's 'History of the Criminal Law of England,' but I have studiously avoided all reference to English Criminal Law as beyond the scope of this work.

It remains for me to thank Sir Edmund Hornby, late Chief Judge of the Supreme Consular Courts in China and Japan, and Mr. J. E. Vincent, of the Inner Temple, for reading through the proofs of the Prolegomena and Commentary, and Mr. Tancred Raven, of Lincoln's Inn, for reading through the whole of the MSS. and proofs, and for their many excellent criticisms and suggestions.

G. D.

1, The Cloisters, The Temple,
March 20th, 1885.

CONTENTS.

FIRST PART.

OF THE PUNISHMENT OF FELONIES, MISDEMEANOURS, AND MINOR OFFENCES IN GENERAL.

SECOND PART.

OF THE INDIVIDUAL FELONIES, MISDEMEANOURS, AND MINOR OFFENCES, AND THEIR PUNISHMENT.

PAGE

ERRATA.

Page 59, line 7 from foot, *before* misdemeanours *insert* attempted
,, 59, line 3 from foot, *for* § 243 *read* § 253
,, 59, line 2 from foot, *insert* unlawful compulsion on the part of officials by the misuse of official power, *instead* of the words after § 339
,, 194, line 21, *for* power *read* force
,, 216, line 10, *for* entices *read* incites

THE GERMAN CRIMINAL CODE.

HISTORICAL PROLEGOMENA.

THE criminal law of all nations passes through three stages, in which its object is successively revenge, a fine for the disturbance of society, and a just requital. The German law forms no exception to the rule. In its earliest form it is based on the fact that the people is uncivilized, and not yet firmly settled in newly-conquered territory. Man depends on himself, and helps himself. There is no authority, save that of the gods, yet the theocratic element is weak; religion is only called in to hallow the execution of military criminals, traitors, and deserters. The first bonds of union are those of the family and the village community; the first constitution is founded on the basis of relationship and neighbourhood; later the *civitates* develop and gather strength, and the nation is at length united under the Carolingian Empire, the fountain from which the middle ages drew their ideas on all questions of statesmanship and public law. Down to the end of the 15th century we can trace how crime is first met by feud (*faida*), then by a public fine (*fredum*), and lastly by a public penalty (*vindicta publica*).

Revenge, or feud law, is founded on the idea that injuries to person and property concern the injured person alone. He feels the necessity of satisfaction, but over-estimates the damage which has been done to him, and carries his revenge too far. This leads the original offender to retaliate, and the quarrel is taken up by the clans. War is then waged by the injured and his clan against the injurer and his clan. Eventually the elders (*seniores*) intervene and peace is made. The fact is expressed by a payment in money or in kind[1] (*compositio*). The feud however remains, and like relationship runs in the male not in the female line;[2] it exists between the *gentes* between whom the money paid *fide compositâ* passes but not between two sons of the same father. The next step is to make *compositio* compulsory. As soon as society has reached a certain stage of development, and has magistrates, the injurer is compelled to answer and do justice, under pain of outlawry. As an outlaw he must leave the country at once, and, being unprotected, may be slain by the injured person or his friends. If he answers to the charge he will be defended, and if condemned, will have to make three different payments: first, the value of the property taken, or of the man slain, for every injury at this stage does not necessitate a feud; next, a mulct as an acknowledgment of the wrong done; and thirdly, dues to the community and the magistrate for the expenses of the trial (*fredum*). Such is the list recited in the 'Leges Bavarorum,' which also contain the amount to be paid for every injury, fixed according to the rank of the injured person. The third step brings us to a public criminal law, which recognizes crime as an injury to society, and to the king as its head, to be met with a suitable punishment; and on the demand of the injured person the penalty is exacted by public means, death being the punishment

[1] L. Sax. 2, 5. Compositionem persolvat vel faidam portet. Berner, p. 55.

[2] L. Angl. vi. 5. Ad quemcunque hereditas terræ pervenerit et ultio proximi.

for all the greater injuries. The king's peace takes the place of the peace of the village or the mark; a breach of the peace is an attack on the authority of the monarch, not merely a disturbance of the community. The weak point is that accusation is not compulsory; without an accuser the law has no power to intervene, and hence there is no protection against the worst offenders. The Capitularies attempt to compel an official prosecution, but with the fall of the Empire its laws fall also.

Just at this time Christianity begins to influence law and custom in direct antagonism to the dominant ideas. Stress had hitherto been laid merely on the outward and visible act, the Church attaches more importance to the will. According to the layman, the killing of a man by chance is to be punished with the same fine as murder;[1] according to the churchman, he who is angry with his brother without a cause is in danger of the judgment. It is from the union and amalgamation of these two points of view that the modern ideas of crime and its punishment have developed. The law exacted the outward equivalent of the action; the Church was filled with the consciousness of her mission to extinguish sin and improve the human race; sin and crime are the same thing. But this was not all. The Church, not content with laying down general principles, went further and took part in enforcing them. Under the Capitularies she had acquired a right to the *fredum* paid for certain crimes and in the confusion of the times which followed the death of Charlemagne began to assert a jurisdiction of her own. In her courts was laid down for the first time the principle of the equality of all before the law.[2] She enacted the *treuga Dei* from

[1] L. Angl. x. 8. Qui nolens sed casu quolibet hominem vulneraverit vel occiderit compositionem legitimam solvat. C. 21. Ex consilio autem velut ex facto aliquem teneri Augustinus probat.

[2] Can. 6, Causs. 26, 7. Sacerdos pœnitentiam imploranti

Wednesday evening till Monday morning, and included therein all holy-days. Within this period the exercise of feud, nay even the levying of a distraint, was forbidden under pain of excommunication. In a like spirit was conceived the idea of the right of sanctuary, with the same penalty for its violation. Above all the Church set her face against mutilation and the other brutal penalties of the age, and declared that her object in punishing was to produce penitence and improvement in the criminal.[1]

At the same period Roman law began to exert its influence north of the Alps, but the system of *compositio* was hard to oust. Instances occur in which the system of *vindicta publica* had been substituted for the *compositio* as early as 595 A. D. by Childebert, and yet is only allowed to stand as an alternative in the Capitularies of 802 and 813. The confusion was at its worst in the 10th century; but after the Crusades, with the increase of civilization came also limitations of feud law. The feud must be made public, and is only allowed to those who have the right to bear arms, that is, the upper classes. *Compositio* is more rarely used, barbarous public punishment becomes the rule. The Sachsen Spiegel marks a step forward, dividing crimes into two great classes according as they are committed: "*zu Hals und Hand*," or "*zu Haut und Haar*." The first class included the seven capital crimes of the Carolingian law, and for these death was the sole penalty. The offences which fell under the second class involved fines and nothing more. Thus the poorer classes came badly off, while the richer could still appeal to arms if they wished

absque personarum acceptione pœnitentiam secundum leges injungat.

[1] Can. 1, 2, 3, 7. Causs. 23, 5, cap. 5. Clericis in sacris ordinibus constitutis ex concilio Toletano judicium sanguinis agitare non licet, unde prohibemus ne aut per se truncationes membrorum faciant aut judicent inferendas.

to do so. The rival principles were still at work; on the one hand the system of *compositio*, on the other the *vindicta publica;* the payment for crime no less than the punishment of subjective guilt. Other countries surmounted the difficulty, thanks to their strong centralization. In France the House of Capet, in England the Normans, gradually ousted feud law, improved the procedure, and provided for official prosecution. In England this had taken the form of presentment, first by the coroner's jury, and then by the grand jury summoned by the sheriff; in France that of the inquisitional procedure. But in Germany, as in Italy, there was no legislative power. The states of the Empire were too far developed to allow the emperor to give laws. The result was that the practice of the criminal court took the place of legislation; the influences which had worked imperceptibly were now publicly recognized; the courts adopted the Roman and the canon law; for although men would not hear of laws from the emperor or the pope of the time being, they did not object to being ruled by those laws which former emperors and former popes had, or were said to have, enacted. Hence, soon after the worst period, that of the Interregnum in the 13th century, we find the old code being made the subject of careful study by the Glossatores, Gandinus in the 13th, Aretinus and Bonifacius in the 15th century; but the great work which was the result of the movement was the Speculum Juris of Durantes (1271). Unfortunately the *Schoffen* or lay assessors who administered the law were not learned in the *novum jus*, and hence had recourse to the presiding judge; but even this functionary was not always able to explain it to them. The right of holding courts of law had been granted to all who could afford to maintain them, and the result was that in the outlying districts the lord of the manor appointed the first man he could get, without much reference to his capacity. The courts did not do the work provided for them, secret societies took the law into their own hands, and the same period which saw the introduction of the procedure of the canon law into the law courts, saw also the Vehmgerichte in full force.

In spite of all the troubles of the times, both civil and ecclesiastical, the idea prevailed that the law should be laid down in a manner intelligible to the "*Schoffen.*" With this view a series of popular works were written on the Roman law. The most important were the 'Spiegel der wahren Rhetorik,' by Friedrich Riederer, published at Freiburg in 1493, the 'Klagspiegel' of Sebastian Brandt, and the 'Layenspiegel' of Ulrich Tengler, published at Augsburg in 1506 and 1509 respectively. The principle which animated these writers was that there is only one law, that of Rome, from which all German law and custom is a stupid deviation. At the same time an attempt was made to amalgamate the two, which only added to the existing confusion. The way for a new departure was paved in 1495 by the Universal Landfriede, a prohibition of all private self-help, to enforce which was instituted the Imperial Chamber of Justice. Besides these measures Maximilian I. attempted to transform the Vehmgerichte and adapt them to general use. In addition to his imperial legislation, Maximilian enacted the Malefizordnung for part of the Tyrol in 1499, a code which was imitated by the Halsgerichtsordnung of Radolfzell in 1506, and the Malefizordnung of Laibach in 1515. In all these laws the system of public punishment without the alternative of fine prevailed exclusively, and at the same time the system of official prosecution on the model of the procedure in vogue in the ecclesiastical courts. But the penal code for the whole Empire was put off from year to year, and it was soon found that the new Imperial Court did not work well. Repeated complaints against its injustice induced the court to appeal to the Imperial Diet. The Diet passed resolutions in 1498 at Freiburg, and in 1500 at

Augsburg, for the preparation of a draft code, and probably would have gone on doing so without effect had not one of the most remarkable men of the age assisted in solving the problem.

Johann Freiherr von Schwarzenberg was born on December 24th, 1463, and died on October 20th, 1528. His education was apparently no better than that of the noblemen of his time. He did not even learn Latin, but he became acquainted later on with the works of Cicero, which his learned friends translated for him. The translation he converted from loose into elegant German, and to this practice has been attributed the unusual facility with which he wrote his own language. As minister (*Landhofmeister*) of the Bishop of Bamberg he was entrusted with the task of drawing up a new penal code. This he did, and in 1507 his code was made law under the title of the Bambergische Halsgerichtsordnung, commonly known as the Mater Carolinæ. This work includes the criminal law and the criminal procedure. It was intended especially for the information of the "*Schoffen*" and unlearned judges, and to restore harmony amid the general confusion. The code fulfilled its object excellently, and was adopted as early as 1516 by the Markgraf of Brandenburg, in the Brandenburgische peinliche Gerichtsordnung, generally known as the Soror Carolinæ. In 1521 it was laid before the Reichstag, and again in 1529, but the excitement of the Reformation engrossed men's minds, and it was not till 1532 that it was passed, with but few alterations, under the title of the Penal Law and Procedure of the Most Serene, Mighty, and Invincible Emperor Charles V., and the Holy Roman Empire. It is generally known as the Constitutio Criminalis Carolina, or more shortly by the letters C. C. C.

The first part of the new code deals with criminal procedure, the second with the details of the criminal law, and the conclusion contains a series of general definitions. The C. C. C. is the foundation of all criminal law and procedure in Germany, but does not embrace the whole of the criminal law, and rather contains directions for the right application of the legal axioms which it lays down. Viewed in this light it is not touched by the objections raised against it in the course of the 18th century, and does not pretend to perfection. To these admirable general definitions succeeding generations have been able to add but little, and its negative services were immense. It removed once and for all the law of *faida* and *compositio* and reformed the law of evidence which was perpetually bringing matters to a deadlock. The new system was based indeed upon torture, but there was no other way open to the legislator, who at least did what he could to regulate its application.

The appearance of the Carolina coincides with an era in history. Up to this time Church and State had been in a condition of continual warfare, but a change had come over the spirit of the combatants. At first it was in the Church that all that was deep and intellectual was found. It was the Church which introduced the principle of subjectivity into the doctrine of imputability and gave crime and punishment a deeper meaning. The Church, as the warden of all the learning of the middle ages, ruled the State. But gradually the State absorbed the intellectual principle, and the Church became thoroughly superficial and thoroughly dead to the inner life; the sale of indulgences was the triumph of that very maxim which the Church had combated in the system of *compositio*. The greater intellectual lights, Huss and Savonarola, Galileo and Vico, were not only repulsed but persecuted by the quondam protectress of the arts and sciences. This tendency culminates in the Reformation, which, at any rate, as far as Germany is concerned, separates Church and State once and for all.

Henceforth both recognize the territory which is peculiarly their own. The State has to do with man's outward action, and must here be supreme; ecclesiastical law will play for the future a subordinate part; the Church has to deal with man's inner life, and with this the State will not interfere. The modern conception of *dolus* and *culpa* attests the influence of the old German and of the canon law, the objective and the subjective points of view. The same is true of the modern conception of punishment. The punishment of the Church in the middle ages is penitence with a view to improvement, and the standard is not the greatness of the crime but the possibility of amendment; on the other hand, the State punishes without the slighest reference to the state of mind of the criminal. The object of later ages has been to unite these two points of view harmoniously.

The Imperial legislation, which ought to have developed German criminal law, came almost to a standstill after the enactment of the C. C. C.; on the other hand, the states of the Empire were not slow in adopting the Imperial code. The laws they passed were in many cases like that of Hesse in 1535, slavish repetitions of the Carolina. In no case was any improvement made; all that was bad was retained, and above all, the secret written form of procedure and the torture. Malblank is wrong in saying that the C. C. C. was ignored; it was used in practice, but did not attract so much attention as it would otherwise have done for two reasons. The first was that the religious and political questions of the day were all-engrossing, the second that the learned men who should have assisted the process of the law's development only understood the *corpus juris*. The jurists of the 16th century had no liberal education; they had no knowledge of the science or history of legal ideas; they were under the spell of foreign law with its learned dress and its connection with classic literature—

that law they would have adopted entirely, had not the existence of a native code been secured by the enactment of the C. C. C. The form and contents of the Carolina were German; they therefore set to work to remove this reproach. Gobler in 1543 gave to the world a Latin translation, Remus in 1594 a Latin paraphrase. Bigelius in 1588, and Musculus in 1614, strove with mistaken zeal to find texts in the Roman law to support its regulations.

With the 17th century came indeed a change. It was the beginning of a period of transition, and was accompanied by all the confusion which is the characteristic of such a time. The Reformation had removed mountains of superstition and prejudice, but much still remained of the old Adam; this is testified by the extraordinary penalties for blasphemy and witchcraft, which now became the subjects of special legislation; and here the Protestant lands were far behind their Catholic neighbours. It was on these that Grotius (1625), Hobbes (1642), and Puffendorf (1660) exerted a salutary influence, and their social contract theories were soon to be applied by Thomasius to the criminal law.

It was now the fate of the C. C. C. to meet with an intelligent exponent. If explained a century earlier, before it became antiquated, by a school like that of the Saxon jurists, the code would have exercised quite another influence on legislation. Now, when too late, Moller, Berlich, and above all Carpzow, applied to it the erudition which alone could give vitality. Carpzow, who was born in 1595 and died in 1666, was the most influential lawyer of his time. He was not clever or original, but his 'Practica nova rerum criminalium' and his 'Decisiones' are thorough and clear.

His severity and practical knowledge may be estimated from the fact that he is said to have passed 20,000 sentences of death at Leipsic. His faults lie on the surface, and have been pointed out by his chief antagonist, Oldekopp. He lays down no general principles, is blindly obedient to tradition, even childishly superstitious, and his disquisitions are disfigured by casuistry. But for all that his authority was supreme in Germany, because, like Schwarzenberg, he understood the needs of the age. His works were translated and used in the Netherlands, in Italy, and in France.

From the beginning of the 18th century the criminal law becomes the subject of careful study. Lectures are delivered on it in the universities by Beyer (1711) and Gärtner (1729); these are followed by a series of systematic manuals, of which that of the Freiherr von Böhmer (1733) is the most important, although it never attained to the authority enjoyed by the works of Carpzow. The Carolina appeals in every case to Roman, canon, and German law to supplement its deficiencies, but till Matthæus and Böhmer no one had the art to use these subsidiary sources aright. The progress of humanity was another source of reform; the penalties laid down in the Carolina were barbarous to a degree; an enlightened age could not put up with torture and mutilation. The result was that in default of other authority the judges began in perfect good faith to reform the common law, by explaining away its severity. The greatest ingenuity was here called into play. It is said in all seriousness by the biographer [1] of a judge of this period: "The departed Meister gave proof of the benevolence of his heart throughout his criminal decisions, and possessed in a high degree the power of bringing his excessively indulgent principles into harmony with the laws so discreetly, that one never observes a violent deviation from them, and yet he attained his object in every case."

Here, then, theory and practice separate from each other; practice becomes more and more capricious;

[1] Malblank.

each court has its own peculiarities. The common law exercises only a negative influence; it becomes a *jus varium* and *incertum*, the judge thinking that he is there not to administer but to improve the law. At this point it was evident that the legislature must intervene, but there was no organ by which a new code could be passed. The Estates of the Empire were only an assembly of delegates who spent their time in fighting about questions of precedence; the Estates of the different divisions of the Empire had ceased to be summoned; no state had an intelligent body of public servants on which it could rely. While the local laws were eluded in the same way as those of the Empire, we have a series of special laws issued by the different princes to meet particular cases, which bear all the marks of unripe extempore legislation. They are as cruel as capricious. Take, for instance, the edicts issued by Frederic William I. of Prussia from the year 1720 onwards.

An edict in 1720 decrees the *pœna culei* [1] for child murder, an edict in 1723 the penalty of death for fraudulent bankruptcy, an edict in 1725 death by strangulation for all gipsies found in the country, and an edict of 1728 the penalty of death for theft. But the gem of the whole collection is an edict issued in 1739, which runs to this effect:—"If an advocate or procurator, or any other similar individual, shall venture to have delivered to his Majesty *immediate* memorials with reference to lawsuits or other matters dependent on his pleasure, or also if any of them shall stir up (*aufwiegeln*) persons to hand over to his Majesty *immediate* memorials, it is the will of his Majesty that such an one be then and there hanged without any mercy, and that a dog be hanged by his side." It seems hardly credible that the edicts in Brunswick and other states were even worse. Such a state of things was only to be

[1] The offender was sewn up in a sack with a dog, an ape, a cock, and a viper, and so drowned. Cf. Juvenal, Sat. 8, 214. Digest. 48. 9. 9.

remedied by ripe legislation, and for this the works of the eloquent foreigners Voltaire, Beccaria, and Filangieri paved the way.

It is noteworthy that two Germans, Globig and Hufter, won the prize offered by the Economical Society of Berne for the best outline of a new criminal code. This was in 1770; the so-called period of enlightenment (*Aufklärungs-Periode*) had begun. Its services were great, and must not be depreciated because purely negative. If much that was good was involved in the general destruction, the loss is fully counterbalanced by such reforms as the abolition of the burning of heretics, of witches' trials, of the rack, and the other barbarous penalties attached to some of the smallest offences.

If this great school of thinkers was negative in practice it was more so in thought; with history they would have nothing to do; law, custom, and the use of the courts they would not give themselves the trouble to study; they perceived as little as their adversaries, the historical school a quarter of a century later, that philosophy is but the essence of history, and that therefore philosophy and history must go hand in hand. However, all their faults are more than counterbalanced by their merits; they awakened the century to a sense of its duties, and the question whether the age had a call to legislate is answered by the fact that legislation was necessary. Legislation was called for by every consideration which law and policy could dictate, and came from the states which alone were capable of it. The smaller states had no councils, and no body of public servants able and willing to attempt the task. It fell to the lot of the absolute rulers of the three larger states—the enlightened despots, as they have been called—to begin the course of legislation which culminated a century later in the criminal code of the German Empire.

The first to appear was the Codex Maximilianus of Bavaria, on October 7th, 1751. It was the work of Freiherr von Kreittmayr. The criminal part of this code is far inferior to the civil; its character is best indicated by the fact that it contains the penalty of death for heresy, and also for such witches as have carnal communication with the devil; for others a milder punishment is devised. Of a similar nature is the Constitutio Criminalis Theresiana, published on December 31st, 1768. It is orthodox, bigoted, and cruel, and was followed in 1787 by the short code of the Emperor Joseph II., which tried to hold the balance between the old and the new ideas, and, like most compromises, must be pronounced a failure.

In 1780 appeared the Prussian Landrecht, which contained all the reforms demanded by the spirit of the age. The criminal code is contained in the second part, chapter twenty, and, although a little inclined to be theoretic and *doctrinaire*, it marks a real progress. It confuses, it is true, matters of administrative with matters of criminal law, and attempts to inculcate religion and virtue, a province which is clearly not its own, and is in its details not free from casuistry. On the other hand, it proved useful and practical, and remained in force till 1851, when the Rhine jurists took it in hand, but except in the matter of form it cannot be said to have been very much improved by them.

In 1803 Austria issued a new code, which is simple, clear, and short; better in form and more elastic in its penalties than the Prussian Landrecht, it showed its excellence by remaining in force for half a century.

The last of the codes of the despotic period was published by Bavaria on May 16th, 1813, during the time of the Confederation of the Rhine. The work of Feuerbach, and worthy of its author's fame, it is clear, logical, and classical in its diction, but did not prove a success in practice. The definition of *culpa* was too wide, that of *conatus* too severe. The generalizations led to such severity in the application of the law that five-sixths of the decisions made under it had to be reconsidered.

The second series of codes were the production of the smaller states after the July Revolutions. Once in possession of a constitution, the people naturally demanded to be governed by a *jus certum*. Saxony had begun a code in 1824 under the despotism and this was completed by the two chambers in 1838. The code of Wurtemberg, passed in 1839, is remarkable from the fact that the chambers refused the services of Wächter on the ground that he was too learned. In Hanover all difficulties were peremptorily settled by King Ernest Augustus, and the code contains some antiquated provisions in favour of the sovereign. This became law in 1840. Other codes were made by Brunswick 1840, Altenburg 1841, Darmstadt 1841, Detmold 1843, Baden 1845, Nassau 1849, Thuringen 1850. That of Baden is noteworthy from its excessive mildness.

The third great series of codes is formed by the Revisions. These took place in Prussia 1851, Austria 1852, Saxony 1856, Bavaria 1861. The revised Prussian code, on which the present Imperial code was to a large extent founded, was introduced into the new provinces of Hanover, Schleswig Holstein, Frankfurt, Nassau, and Hessen-Homburg in 1867.

The smaller states continued to issue codes of their own: Oldenberg 1858, Reuss 1861 and 1868, Lubeck 1863. The list is closed by the criminal code of Hamburg, which was hastily put together and published in 1869, although it was known that the General code was in preparation. The latter was passed on May 25th, 1870, and came into force on January 1st, 1871 for the North German Confederacy, and on January 1st, 1872 for the newly-constituted German Empire.

Of the sources from which the Imperial code was drawn,

two are by far the most important—the Common Law of Germany and the Prussian code, which was practically an adaptation of the Code Pénal. At these we must now for a moment glance, not forgetting that each one of the codes of the different states was not without its influence on the evolution of the final result.

The common criminal law of Germany was abolished for Austria, Prussia, and Bavaria, in the 18th century, and for most of the smaller states in the 19th century, by the enactment of their several codes. Formally, as a matter of public law, the common law ceased to exist at the dissolution of the Holy Roman Empire in 1806. With the Empire fell the Imperial legislature and the Imperial courts. As far as the common law existed in the supreme courts of the German Confederation it existed as the law of the separate states. Thus it existed till the end in Mecklenburg and Schauenburg-Lippe, and, as we have seen, till very late in Holstein, the electorate of Hesse, and Hamburg. Practically speaking it was much the same in each of the states in which it prevailed, and in the universities, and by jurists generally, was held in the highest honour and carefully studied. The four chief sources of the common law were the Roman law, the canon law, Imperial laws, and the law made by custom, the judges, and jurists generally. When the Carolina appeared Roman law was already adopted throughout Germany to supplement the want of legislation; so far from excluding it, the C. C. C. acknowledges its value as supplementary. The Roman law as such was for the most part useless for mediæval Germany; the kernel was extracted by the Glossatores, and their reports were taken on trust till the middle of the 17th century, when Antonius Matthæus made it his especial study. In the compilation of Justinian are scattered here and there rules of criminal law; but a consistent treatment of the whole subject is only to be found in the Institutions, Book

IV. chapters i.—v. and xviii. The first five chapters treat chiefly of *obligationes ex delicto*, the 18th chiefly of criminal procedure. But the principal source of Roman criminal law are the Books XLVII., XLVIII. of the Pandects, the *libri terribiles* of the middle ages, which in the words of Justinian himself, *omnem continent severitatem pœnarumque atrocitatem*. Lastly, we must mention Book IX. of the Codex.

With regard to the criminal law of the Church, we must remember that the prohibition of an act by canon law did not make it a crime, and that the penalties of the canon law do not belong to the system of the common law. Canon law divided crimes into three classes: *delicta ecclesiastica*, such as apostasy and heresy; *delicta mixta*, such as blasphemy, forgery, and the like; and *delicta clericorum;* but the division soon became antiquated. Canon law as a whole has rather a mediate than immediate influence on the common law. In the general axioms of the criminal law the best ideas as to imputability and criminality are to be traced to this source, and many particular enactments, especially with regard to adultery. The most important part of the canon law for our purpose is to be found in the Fifth Book of the Decretals of Gregory IX. Of the Imperial laws, by far the most important is the C. C. C., but there are also other criminal enactments which were passed by the Estates of the Empire. These are to be found in the Imperial police ordinances, the Imperial mint ordinances, the regulations as to the public peace, the orders contained in the Recesses of the Empire (*Reichsabschiede*) and in the Golden Bull.

The criminal ordinances enacted by the German Confederation of 1815 form no part of the common law. They became, however, part of the law of the particular states, in so far as they were adopted by the several legislatures.

Since the reception of the foreign law Germany had

been particularly dependent on the lawyers and judges. The *communis opinio doctorum* and the *usus fori* were not misused till the time of confusion in the 18th century. Then each court had its own rules, each judge his own interpretation, each jurist his own opinions; and all these variations became part of the common stock. It was not till the works of Böhmer appeared that any unity was introduced into the system. He was followed by Feuerbach, Wächter (1825), and Köst-tin (1855), the work of the last being perhaps the most successful treatment of the subject as a whole.

The Prussian code was the result of much labour. From 1825 to 1840 the reform of the criminal code contained in the Landrecht was in progress, but no advance seemed to be made. At length Frederic William IV. appointed Savigny as minister, and much was expected from his industry and ability. After the Council of State had been engaged under his directions for two years (1843-5) a draft was issued, and being unfavourably received, was revised in 1846, and again in 1847. At each revision the Rhine jurists, who were enchanted with the Code Pénal, introduced more and more from that quarter. Although constitutional difficulties stood in the way of the new code, it was eventually passed under the new constitution in 1851. The form was excellent, the weak points being those of the French code. As a whole it was too severe, the circumstances with which it had to deal differing from those of France after the Revolution. Too much stress was laid on the subjective side of crime; *conatus* and participation are not the same thing as the crime itself. Lastly, throughout the French code reigns the passion for excessive fines and confiscation, a passion inherited from the Roman law itself. On these foundations the German code was based. Article 4 of the North German Confederation pledged the Legislature to compile one criminal law, and in 1868 the Reichstag and Bundesrath undertook the task. The first draft, which was drawn up by the Prussian Ministry of Justice, appeared in July 1869, and was on the whole unfavourably received. The second draft was published in December of the same year as the result of the labours of the Commission of the Federal Council. This was submitted to the Federal Council and the Federal Parliament from February 4th to May 25th. It passed these bodies successfully, and was published on May 31st, 1870, became law for the North German Confederation on January 1st, 1871, and on the accession of the South German States, was passed anew as the criminal code for the German Empire, coming into force on January 1st, 1872.

For the new Imperial province of Alsace-Lorraine some special provisions were made by the laws of August 30th, 1871, and July 14th, 1873, to adapt the code to the local legislation, and, further, with regard to procedure, the competence of martial courts, and one or two unimportant offences. The code was revised in 1876. The most important additions are the Arnim paragraph § 353 *a*, the Duchesne paragraph § 49 *a*, § 4 as to treasonable acts committed by state servants abroad, § 229 *a* as to injuries to the person, and an extension of the responsibility of the clergy to their writings. The code is arranged to fall into an introductory law, an introduction, and two main divisions.

The introductory law is concerned with the territory over which, and the questions on which, the code is to be enforced. It is to be law for the whole German Empire. All other criminal laws are null and void when they treat of the same subject as the code. But other laws still hold on matters as to which the code gives no directions. These are chiefly questions of administrative law, such as the provincial regulations with regard to hunting, fishing, and the maintenance of roads, Imperial laws as to taxes, the post, and the mint, and laws to enforce discipline on the servants of the state. When the legislation of the empire is silent local criminal law still holds good, and new rules may be made; but the ground which these new rules may cover is strictly limited. The local enactments may only refer to questions which lie outside the code; they may only inflict penalties up to two years imprisonment, including dismissal from office and pecuniary fines; they must observe in all respects the general rules as to attempt, participation, &c. laid down in the code. In conclusion the local legislatures must provide regulations for the transition from the old code to the new.

The introduction to the code itself, which is divided into twelve sections, was separated from the general part in the Prussian code on the ground that it referred to all three classes of crime, that is, to minor offences (*Uebertretungen*) as well as to felonies (*Verbrechen*) and misdemeanours (*Vergehen*), and not to the last two alone. But as in the Imperial code the general part lays down rules for the treatment of all three classes of offences, there is no reason why the introductory definitions should not have been placed in it. As it stands, the introduction deals with the triple division of offences, and the applicability of the code in respect of time, place, and certain privileged persons. The general part is divided into five paragraphs concerning penalties, attempt, participation, reasons which exclude or extenuate guilt, and the concurrence of several criminal acts. The second part deals with the particular offences.

PHILOSOPHICAL PROLEGOMENA.

THE existence of a penal code implies an advanced stage of political development, and that the state has taken upon itself three separate series of duties—the protection of the rights of the individual to life, health, freedom, honour, and property, the maintenance of public order, and the maintenance of public morality in the visible sphere of action.

The criminal code is the menace which the ruling body finds it necessary to employ to compel those duties which it feels entitled to call upon the individual citizen to fulfil. History traces the evolution of the criminal law *pari passu* with that of the state; philosophy points out the object of the state and its organization, and why a system of penalties is necessary to maintain it. These last two problems were never solved in the middle ages; belief took the place of philosophy. The state and the penal law were held to be the institutions of God, and further inquiry seemed unnecessary. The Reformation shook this belief to its foundations, and subjected the matter to a searching and sceptical examination. A century later the foundation was laid for a new view by Hugo Grotius (1625), Hobbes (1642), and Puffendorf (1660). These writers derive both the state and the penal law from the nature of man. According to their view the state is merely an institution for the advantage and security of the individual. The penal law is part of the activity of the state to attain this object. This view laid the foundation for the relative theories, so called because they deduce the necessity of punishment from utility, that is, from an end which lies outside the punishment itself. Among the Romance nations this idea had a great success. Rousseau founded on it his theory of the social contract, according to which the state is the result of *pacta unionis, subjectionis,* and *ordinationis:* the agreement is such that the slightest modification of its terms breaks it up and restores the state of nature. A sovereign body thus founded cannot alienate or divide its rights without violating the contract between itself and the persons who constituted it, and thus becoming *ipso facto* dissolved. It is the erection of anarchy into the ruling principle of the state. This view was taken up and advocated with extraordinary eloquence by Beccaria and Filangieri. All legal and political institutions were capriciously treated. In the impulsive desire for progress, all that was historical was thrown over, nothing but perfection would do. This could only be found in the subjective mind of the thinker, which must refuse to take into account the objective existence of the idea. Under this view prizes were offered for the best draft of a criminal code.

When these ideas became popular in France they led to the Revolution; in Germany they were only taken up by the philosophers, and cannot be said to have reached the lower classes. The most important if not the earliest advocate of this view was Fichte, who published his 'Naturrecht' in 1795. According to this writer the state rests on the social contract, and the object of the state is mutual security. This contract is the basis of every individual right; whoever breaks it has no rights, and becomes an outlaw. He must be so treated and expelled the state, which only exists for those who preserve the contract. But this is more than the security of the citizen requires. If then a method can be discovered by which we can attain that end with equal certainty, we need not expel the criminal. Hence the contract of atonement (*Abbussungsvertrag*), which runs to the following effect. All promise all, so far as it is compatible with the security of the state, not to exclude them from the state because of their misdeeds, but to allow them to make atonement in another way. The better to attain this object, the state attempts to deter criminals by threatening a penalty. If this has had no effect, it seeks so to arrange the execution of the penalty that the criminal may be thereby reformed. The reformed criminal then returns to the state, because by his example future crime will be prevented. Fichte gave the relative theory in all its strength, but he was not a popular writer; others therefore popularized his statement, laying stress on different points in it, according to their individual talent and inclination.

The theory that the state punishes in self-defence found a zealous supporter in Martin. The state on his view has a right to exist because men are bound to live in the state by their moral needs. From the right to exist follows the right of self-maintenance. Every crime is an attack against the life of the state, and consequently endangers it. Hence the state has the right to impose on the author of this danger an evil, which will avert the danger, namely punishment. This view is open to several objections. In the first place, punishment and defence cannot be mentioned in the same category; punishment can only be applied after, defence is used before the injury has been done. A crime which has been already committed is not a mere danger, but an injury already done, and not merely an injury to the individual, but one to the state also. Moreover, out of a hundred crimes which may be committed there will hardly be one which absolutely brings the state to the danger on which Martin founds his system of severe penalties.

The reform of the criminal was next advanced as the sole object of punishment. The supporters of this view respect the human being in the criminal, and refuse to use him merely as a means; they therefore propose through punishment not so much to deter others as to preserve the criminal from a relapse. This object is more effectually attained by reform than by terror, for it is notorious that habitual criminals are most common in countries where the severest penalties are inflicted. The desired results can only be attained by a mild punishment which does not stir up hatred and the desire of revenge in the mind of the criminal. If reformation is the chief object with which we punish, capital punishment cannot be permitted. There is obviously much that is true in this view, but the weak point is that according to it punishment is inflicted because reform is necessary, but it does not give the reason why this reform should be effected by means of punishment. Besides, what are we to do in those cases where reform is impossible? How are we to graduate the standard of improvement? How are we to estimate the difference between the reform produced by ten years' and that produced by one month's imprisonment?

Another school of thinkers laid stress on the deterrent effects of punishment. This seemed to be the most practical view and influenced legislation more than any other. According to Grolman, not only must there be no illegal action, but also there must be no illegal will. The civil law compels compensation, and thus annuls the illegal action, but the illegal will must also be eradicated, and this is the function of the criminal law. Seneca is quoted to support this view, *nemo prudens punit quia peccatum est sed ne peccetur.* The criminal is not punished for the action, but for the disposition. But the disposition is not the province of law, but of morality. It is contrary to common sense to punish a man for future crimes which he may commit, instead of for past crimes which he has committed. Logically, according to this view the punishment should precede the crime. Besides, Grolman gives us no adequate standard as to the amount of punishment necessary to render the illegal will harmless. How many persons must be punished to deter the public?

The change in the mind itself is the ground on which Feuerbach founded the menace of punishment by law. The state must secure the rights of all. It must therefore find means to hinder crime, for when once crime is committed the harm is done. Now every crime arises from the moral impulse to do wrong. We must then overcome this impulse by the threat of the penalty. The law must be so arranged that the threatened evil shall be greater than the present good and the desire for it. The will thus undergoes psychological compulsion. The object of punishment is to threaten, the object of the execution to carry out the threat. The only ground for punishment is the danger of the state, and this is insufficient. The security of the state can be otherwise attained by education and other such means. All crimes do not spring from the moral impulse, as Feuerbach assumes; some are from necessity. The threat does not in reality overcome the desire, because the criminal always hopes to escape; and even were this not so, he rarely knows the code so well that the threat of the particular punishment can be said to be balanced against his desire to commit the crime. This last objection Feuerbach proposed to remedy by publishing the code, so that all must know it, and by teaching it in the schools. This would only teach the young what crime is, a fact of which they are as a rule happily ignorant. We are also not told what the average man is, and where he is to be found, and what is to be the standard of threatening. In his anxiety to reach this imaginary person, Feuerbach made an almost Draconian code, under which five-sixths of the penalties had to be remitted. Indeed the objections to his theory are so obvious, that it is wonderful that even his eloquence and talents could give it currency for twenty years.

According to Bauer the state has three means of enforcing its will—popular education, police, and the criminal code; the last named is necessary to supplement the first two. The warning of the criminal code should influence not only the sensual, but also the moral side of human nature. It should deter the sensual impulse by the thought of the penalty affixed; it should vivify the moral consciousness of the guilt of the crime, and impress on the citizen the duty of prudence in action. The legal threat justifies the execution of the penalty as soon as the crime is committed. The threat itself is justified by the fact that no one's freedom is thereby impaired. In the same manner one might justify threatening the most trivial offence with death, and the execution of the penalty on the ground of the threat.

Klein recognized with the material injury, which crime inflicts, and for which the civil law gives compensation, an ideal injury. This is the result of the bad example, the diminished reverence felt for the law, and the public alarm. This ideal injury the criminal makes good by suffering a punishment. But it is obvious that the ideal injury is not the crime itself, but a more or less accidental consequence thereof which is sometimes altogether absent.

The relative theories contain in most cases an element of truth; the fault in each is that it does not look for the basis and justification of punishment in the equity of punishment itself. Beyond this the actual end can be better attained in each case by other means. In no case is a standard given by which we may mete out punishment. The relative theories approach the truth in so far as they found the justification of punishment on the crime already committed; they deviate therefrom in so far as they base it upon future possible crimes.

Not only are these theories inconsistent with one another, but they are opposed and corrected by the so-called absolute theories. These are based on the view that the state is not the result of the caprice of man, but rests on a moral necessity. It does not depend upon the individual whether he will enter the state; he is rather compelled to do so by his moral nature, being *φύσει πολιτικὸν ζῷον*. Besides, the state, like all that is moral, does not exist purely for utility and outward social ends. It is an end in itself. Apart from all questions of utility, it satisfies by its social and ethical existence a moral need in the nature of man. From this point of view it follows that the criminal law, like the rest of the institutions of the state, rests on a moral necessity. Punishment is inflicted because it is just, not because it is useful either to the individual or to the state.

This theory was first based by Jacobi and others on the moral consciousness. According to them punishment rests on a moral feeling which condemns all injustice; of this no scientific proof need be given. This is the first reaction against the utilitarian view of punishment, if one may so call it, and goes too far. According to Jacobi, sin punishes itself within, but without it cannot be properly punished; we should then require something like a system of rewards to act as supplementary. Law and morality are here confused, and no standard given by which the judge who sees merely the outside can punish.

After Jacobi came Kant and his school with a still more untenable view. Punishment is always inflicted because a crime has been committed. Its basis must lie in the past, man cannot be used as a means for the future. The necessity of punishment rests on an absolute law of practical reason which we need not prove logically. The penal law is a categorical imperative. The penalty rests on the same basis as the state. Each man must limit his freedom by the like freedom of all others. Punishment has to do with the outward act, not with the idea. The double basis of the natural law and the categorical imperative is important, because this was the rock on which the whole theory was wrecked. Jurists asked which of the two foundation-stones was the most important; the answer was, the law of nature. The result was that Kant's followers, and among them Feuerbach, fell back into the relative theory that punishment must be inflicted to preserve the state.

Further, Kant is not always clear as to the standard of punishment. Equality would appear to be the fundamental principle. But this is not to be carried out to the letter, except in the case of murder; here no inner equality is possible, for there can be no comparison between life, even the most miserable, and death; penal servitude for life itself is far from adequate. As to the details, Kant is often in difficulties; for instance, he lays down that marriage is ordained by law, therefore a bastard is an outlaw, and any one may kill him. Kant's penal system as a whole is open to the objection that it forms no organic part of his system. It contradicts his view both of the state and of law. His state is the social contract state, and originally intended for the security of the individual alone. Law is the result of the initiative of the individual and the expressed will of the people. How then is the activity of the state in the criminal law an end in itself? How is the criminal law itself the result of a superior necessity? Obviously a relative theory would have here been more logical.

Zacharia attempted to translate Kant's theories into a practical form. Each crime is an encroachment on the rights of another; hence the criminal must have his own freedom limited to the same extent to which he has limited that of the injured person. All penalties must therefore be reduced to imprisonment. In estimating the length of this only the outer injustice done must be considered. Where the injured person has been wholly or temporarily deprived of his freedom, this can be immediately translated into the penalty; but where an artificial estimate has to be made, the question must be asked whether the effect of the crime cannot be reduced to money. Here a certain relation of money to time must be laid down about in the ratio of daily wages. When the crime has been estimated in money, the question must be put, how long would a daily labourer have to work to earn this sum? and for this period, whatever it be, the offender must be imprisoned. The weak points of this theory lie on the surface. Freedom is used by Zacharia to mean the sum total of all man's rights when he declares every crime to be an encroachment. It is used to mean only the right not to be imprisoned when he deduces the punishment of imprisonment from his definition of crime. The theory is, however, important, in that it shows an attempt to pass from the abstract idea of requital to a material equality between crime and punishment.

Zacharia had drawn attention to the outer side of crime; he was followed by Henke, who laid stress on the subjective point of view. According to the latter the measure of punishment can only be laid down after improvement has begun. Guilt as such is incommensurable. It is by the improvement which punishment has effected that one can see whether it has reached its limit. This would lead to lifelong imprisonment for the smallest offences. Besides, a criminal code would be useless; each case would have to be considered on the ground of the promise of improvement of the criminal.

Hegel gives a logical basis to the criminal law. He begins by distinguishing morality from law. With regard to his thoughts and feelings a man is responsible to himself: this is the sphere of morality. The state has only to do with the outer will, which is regulated by a reasonable nature which leads to law. Law is the expression of reasonable universal opinion. As man is free he can do wrong and break the law. This wrong may be civil, in which case he infringes the individual rights of other persons: this he must make good after a civil action. The wrong may be criminal: here not only the subjective, but also the objective side of the law has been broken. Here we have a contradiction of the universal reasonable will which made the law, a contradiction which must be shown to be illogical and negatived. This is done by punishment, which is the negation of the negation of universal reason. The province of the criminal law is thus limited to a violation of positive legislation. Law has only to do with the outward will, and only punishes immorality so far as it is visible in action.

The state is the subject of the criminal law, because it is the ordinance of the state which has been broken, otherwise we should return to the primitive state of feuds. As to the standard of punishment, Hegel rightly lays down that it is not equality, but relativity. Punishment varies according to the nature of the crime, and will also vary according to the different stages of culture which a nation reaches. Within these limits there is room for all that the relative theories urge with regard to improvement, deterrence, and so forth.

Stahl translates the reason of Hegel into the will of God, and on this basis repeats the Hegelian system word for word. In human life we must see the will of God working justice. The state is the reflex of the will of God. Man's justice is an imitation in the outward world of the justice of God. This justice must be maintained and vindicated when it has been violated. This can only be done by setting at nought the criminal will; the standard of punishment is according to the greatness of the violation. This construction would only suit a period in which, as in the middle ages, the Church is supreme.

The great service rendered by the absolute theories is due to Hegel. Since his time the idea has never been lost sight of that punishment is based on the offence itself, and that the necessary presupposition of the application of punishment is its justice. Later thinkers have gone further, and tried to unite the relative and the absolute theories on the ground that no state ever did content itself with using punishment merely as a requital. The point of view from which these theories start is that the state is not really an end in itself; man is not here for the sake of the law or the state; these rather exist for man. Utility is indeed subordinate to justice, but both work together for the development of individuality, which is the highest object of the state. This standpoint appears more or less clearly in the theories which combine the absolute and the relative points of view. Some thinkers lay more stress on utility, and some on justice, as the object of punishment.

Abegg holds that punishment must emanate from justice alone. It must be meted out according to the crime. The mere measurement of guilt necessitates a consideration of all the points on which the relative theories lay stress; for the greater danger of the act and its evil influence on others are merely signs of deeper guilt. Justice pure and simple, if properly carried out, satisfies all the utilitarian ends which have any claim to be noticed.

J. U. Wirth points out that punishment is inflicted not only by the state, but also by the family, the school, and the Church. Accordingly he defines punishment generally, and then distinguishes the special branch of state punishment. Punishment generally speaking has two objects: the offence must be nullified objectively in the person and subjectively in the will of the offender. Objectively he is imprisoned, fined, and so forth; subjectively he is improved or deterred from further crime. The punishment which the family, the school, and the Church inflict is primarily subjective and secondarily objective; conversely, the punishment which the state inflicts is in the first instance objective, and only in the second instance subjective. Just retaliation often involves a regard for the subjective side of the crime. Just retaliation must exert its influence against the habit, and therefore improve; on the other hand, the desire to improve or deter the criminal involves the modification of the retaliatory punishment. It is impossible really to try to improve the criminal if we do not take into consideration his subjective condition. However, the standard of punishment must not be altered for subjective ends. If punishment has reached its highest limit the state must not add a further penalty, even if the penalty already inflicted has neither improved nor deterred the offender.

Other writers have taken up the other point of view, and in many cases have gone so far as to make justice practically subservient to utility. The most moderate and perhaps the ablest representative of this school is Ortolan who gives the following theory.

Good deserves to be repaid with good, and evil with evil. This is so generally felt to be the case, that moral pleasure or pain is always felt as the triumph of good or evil. So strong is this feeling, that all nations agree in believing in a future life where compensation will take place, and each individual will be judged according to his works. It is on the strength of this feeling that the absolute theories are founded; but the absolute theories do not show that it is the duty of society to estimate and inflict these penalties. Punishment must above all be just, but the infliction of just penalties is only so far the duty of society as the objects of society demand it. Hence, in considering punishment, the court has two points to keep in view, justice and utility. Punishment must not exceed what is just, nor yet what is suitable.

The theories of Abegg and Wirth give on the whole the right relation between justice and utility; on the other hand, the view of Ortolan, which is followed by

Hélie, lays too much stress on the side of utility; but they are all far from perfect. Abegg only gives any weight to the claims advanced by the relative theories when these claims are founded on justice. But the objects assumed by the relative theories are of themselves perfectly justifiable. They must be realized not only so far as justice demands, but so far as justice allows. Wirth goes so far as to class retaliation with improvement and determent as an object of punishment. But punishment is from its nature identical with retaliation; the satisfaction which results from retaliation can be called an object of punishment, retaliation itself cannot. Wirth also makes the mistake of seeking the improvement exclusively in the criminal, and the determent exclusively in the rest of the world. It may be intended to realize the improvement chiefly in the criminal, but it is certainly intended to deter the criminal no less than others from future offences. Further, Wirth does not give the ideas of improvement and deterrence a distinct influence on the standard of punishment itself. Retaliation is the only standard. Improvement and determent are to be attained in the manner of inflicting the punishment. Ortolan mistakes the duties of the state. It is the duty of the state above all to enforce law, and it is not so much immoral acts as criminal acts that the state suppresses with the help of the penal law. These criminal acts are punished by the state to realize the justice which it is incumbent on the state to maintain. Utilitarian considerations are only of secondary importance; they must not be raised, as Ortolan has raised them, to a position coequal with justice. Justice is to be enforced for its own sake alone, and not in so far as it is useful. The state is an institution to be preserved for itself no less than for the individual. Punishment is the retaliation appointed by law as necessary for the maintenance of society; it must be founded on justice and be relative to the crime. Within these limits there is room for other considerations. Punishment restores the right and amends the wrong. Fundamentally it is retaliation, but it is not merely like for like, nor does it consider the matter merely externally. It is proportional to the criminality of the will as manifested in the outward act. Further, we punish not only the injury done to the individual, but the infraction of the universal will as manifested in the law. Science can only lay down general rulės to be modified by circumstances, which vary according to time, place, and nationality.

The immediate result of retaliation is satisfaction, and this is the first object of punishment. If this be so, retaliation must strike the consciousness as such. To bring this to pass is the duty of the state; a duty which it can best fulfil by maintaining different establishments, and inflicting different penalties for different crimes.

To satisfaction we must add improvement and determent as subordinate ends; these three taken together will work for the defence of the state and the law. We have then several objects by which the character and standard of punishment must be influenced. It is not enough that the satisfaction should be obvious, that punishment often does consider the objects of the relative theories; for instance, the danger of the crime as heightening the guilt, as Abegg has shown, or that, as Wirth has pointed out, justice often includes in its claims the realization of improvement and determent. Each and every one of these objects must be realized as far as justice will allow, for they are ends which the state has in view, and can only be subordinated to justice itself.

The difficulty then arises, that while justice requires one definite standard, improvement and determent may require quite a different one. But this admits of a solution. We must remember that in the ethical as well as in the physical world, a certain difference in quantity brings about a distinction in quality. Generosity to excess becomes prodigality, valour becomes foolhardiness. A certain limit must not be passed. It is the same with justice. A certain amount of bodily pain is necessary for the punishment to attain the quality of just retaliation. Too much would make it revenge, too little would reduce it to connivance. On the other hand, between revenge and connivance there is room left for free play. Between these limits the judge can increase or diminish the amount of punishment. The legislator has wide scope in affixing the penalty to the class of offences, the judge has the same power with regard to the particular offence. Within these limits justice allows improvement and determent. Just retaliation may require a maximum and a minimum, but there is considerable room left for the influence of the relative theories. Views with regard to the criminal law will always vary according to the social and political circumstances; in times of peace and contentment there will be more inclination to the absolute, in times of trouble and revolution to the relative theories. Before 1810 lawgivers were on the whole independent of philosophy, although security and determent were prominent objects, especially in the Prussian Landrecht and the Austrian penal code of 1803. The Code Pénal (1810) fluctuates between the standpoints of utility and abstract justice, and scientific writers in France were from the troubles of the times more inclined to relative than to absolute theories. The Bavarian code of 1813 is the realization of the theory of Feuerbach. Since 1838 the ruling idea has been a combination, the so-called "justice theory." Advocates of this idea were all powerful in the composition of the Prussian code, and hence no great stress was laid on improvement and determent. The Imperial code has made a step in the direction of the relative theories, by recognizing an adaptation of the English ticket-of-leave; but the whole composition of the code, together with the limitation of the time to be served before the conditional release, is inspired by the absolute doctrine of great punishment for great crimes, and small punishment for small offences. Experience has shown that the desire on the part of the lawgiver and judge to improve the criminal meets with but little success. Legislation in Germany may now fairly be said to be on a level with the social and political circumstances of the day, and further progress will doubtless be made in the direction above indicated when crime has so far diminished as to give society the confidence to call for a milder system.

THE COMMENTARY.

CRIME was defined by Kant as an action which the law threatens with punishment. Crime is therefore positive, and constituted by a positive command of the law. It is dependent on the penal law, beyond the provisions of which acts may be wicked and immoral, but cannot be criminal. The fact that crime is an act implies that the will has been active and has made a decision, and hence arises the question of imputability. Again, the decision was in a particular direction, namely, contrary to the penal law, and this involves guilt. Here the question arises, was the guilt direct or indirect? are we dealing with malice (*dolus*) or negligence (*culpa*)? Further, the act may be inchoate or complete, and it may be the work of one or more than one person.

In the first place then a crime is an act determined by the will, and therefore freedom of action is a necessary condition. This was formerly denied by many eminent thinkers. A man, they held, is the slave of his education and circumstances; he acts whether he will or no. Therefore he must be lightly punished; we must try to influence him by stronger motives, and improve or deter him from relapsing into crime. As a matter of fact man really has a freedom of choice. It is true that there is an impulse to do wrong; but man is not a beast, that he should follow every impulse; the fact that he is a man implies that he is reasonable as well as animal, and that he can overcome his animal nature. We can trace this double nature in the development of the will on which Hegel has insisted. In childhood man's will is immediate, it is only defined by the impulse to do what he likes, there is no idea of duty. The reflecting will arises from deferred satisfaction of the impulse: man begins to choose the best means to the end. It is here that he becomes the object of criminal law. He is no longer the slave of impulse, he has the power of choice and might have chosen otherwise. At the last stage, that of the reasonable will, the criminal certainly never arrives. Here the will is really free: man remembers all his duties, weighs them, and acts on the decision. The criminal allows his moral freedom to be overcome by other impulses. We must have then a man capable of willing as the basis of imputability.

This enables us to deal satisfactorily with two points which have perplexed early writers. Beasts cannot be made the subjects of criminal proceedings, as they were in certain cases in the canon law. Further, a juridical person cannot commit a crime. The personality we attach to the state, the parish, and other similar bodies is clearly a legal fiction, true personality can only exist in men. A crime if committed by such a body is in reality only punishable as committed by such members of it as took part in the action. The idea of a juridical person arose from a fiction of civil law; the state as the possessor of property is treated in the Pandects as the subject of rights.

We require then a human being capable of willing, and, further, an action done and a relation proved between the action and the man, namely, that of author and act. Imputability is out of the question where the subject is incapable of willing. It is equally out of the question where there is no act done. *Delicta putativa* and attempts with insufficient means are thus put out of court. Thoughts and intentions, unless expressed by will, are outside the province of the criminal law:

cogitationis pœnam nemo patitur. Faults of omission are only punished in combination with a former action, as in the case of non-performance of official duties. Omissions are punished under minor offences as part of the police regulations, which are part of administrative rather than criminal law.

Lastly, where there is no voluntary connection between the action and its author there can be no imputability. It is so in instances of *vis absoluta, vis major naturæ* and *casus;* in the two latter it is the force of nature, in the former the overpowering force of another, that produces the connection. In all of these man acts merely as a natural object, and not as a reasonable being. In fact, from the point of view of the criminal law, he does not act at all.

The subject of an action must be capable of willing; the subject of a criminal action must further have a knowledge of what he is doing, and be able to measure his duty like a reasonable man. Therefore youth, madness, and unconsciousness exclude imputability.

The will of the child, as Hegel has pointed out, is immediate and subject to every impulse. The ideas which children have of right and wrong they do not understand. As Rousseau says, they retain the words, the ideas fly back. They have no idea of duty. This lasts till the seventh year; thence to puberty is a doubtful period. The Romans, with their practical common sense, left it to the judge to decide *in concreto* whether the child was *doli capax;* the presumption being that this was probable or improbable according as the child was *infantiæ aut pubertati proximus.* This sensible standard was spoiled by the pedants, who mapped out the years between the two limits, and brought them under one or the other head. The canon law followed the Roman law, and added that even when imputability was proved, the minor should be more lightly punished than the major. The C. C. C. laid down that youths under fourteen must not be condemned to death for theft, a provision which extended in practice to all criminals under fourteen, both sexes alike. The fact that all the proceedings were in writing, led to a love of such hard and fast rules as saved the trouble of hearing witnesses. Later this immunity led to the formation of bands of juvenile thieves. Hence the new codes adopted a different standard. Bavaria in 1813 made eight years the limit, Austria (1803) and Wurtemberg (1838) ten years; Saxony (1838) and the later codes of Hanover (1840), Darmstadt, and Baden (1846) twelve years; Brunswick (1840) and Saxony (1855) fourteen years. Up to this age crime was not imputed, and instead of criminal punishment, the offenders were kept in a reformatory under supervision.

The Code Pénal (1810), which was followed by the Prussian code (1851) and the Bavarian code (1861), provides no minimum, but, on the other hand, a higher maximum, sixteen years. The question of imputability in offenders of less age is left in the first instance to the discretion of the public prosecutor, in the second to the judge and jury. The North German Parliament combined both systems. Up to the twelfth year it is presumed, on the report of the Prussian Medical Commission, that crime should not be imputed; from the twelfth to the eighteenth year it is doubtful. In the first period criminal prosecution is excluded; no criminal proceedings are taken. If proceedings are taken under a mistake as to the age of the accused, they are cancelled, and no decision is given. Regulations as to the reformation and supervision of the youthful offender are left to the different states; this duty is, however, recognized by the Novella of 1876. From the end of the twelfth to the end of the eighteenth year criminal prosecution must be commenced and carried through, but it is necessary to decide whether the accused possessed the will which the law requires. This fact the judge can alone decide, and his decision must be recorded in a judgment. The judge in acquitting the accused decides whether he shall be left to his family or consigned to a reformatory. In minor offences he is intrusted to the care of his family, that is, the family must exercise a supervision which the police will superintend. The length of his stay in the reformatory is decided not by the judge, but by the officials of that institution, because it is not a question of punishment, but of improvement. But reason for his release can be found in the opportunity of disposing of him satisfactorily, as well as in an improvement observed in him.

The offender will be set free at the latest in his twentieth year, and in spite of the condemnation he will be treated as if he had been acquitted. He has not therefore to pay the costs, nor must the condemnation be reckoned against him. Older theorists added two cases to that of simple childhood—the so-called second childhood, and the case of deaf mutes. The former has been much exaggerated, and is if anything a mild form of imbecility. The case of the latter has been much altered by the improved education invented for and extended to them. Deafness combined with dumbness hinders but does not altogether prevent intellectual development. Whether deaf mutes have the quickened intelligence necessary to imputability or not must always be decided *in concreto.* Up to twelve years of age they are protected by the general provisions of § 55. From twelve years onwards to the end of life they are subject to the rules laid down for the prosecution of other persons from twelve to eighteen. An especial inquiry must always be held with regard to this imputability. If it is denied they are acquitted, if affirmed, judgment is given with the allowance for extenuating circumstances which would be made in the case of persons under eighteen. Still the judge must often even here be influenced by the consideration of the general condition of the deaf and dumb, which would be likely to affect their whole conduct.

Madness may be divided into insanity, imbecility, and monomania. Insanity is a positive illness which changes the appearance of the outer world. As Kant has said, it is the incapacity to distinguish the subjective from the objective. The insane hold their ideas to be true, and act upon them; for instance, a man may believe he is hammering in a nail when he is killing another. This state precludes imputability. The attempt of the insane to act in their own world cannot be made subject to the rules of the real world. The accused must be proved to be insane, and for this proof we must have experts. The insane may have lucid intervals, and in these are liable for their actions. We must here distinguish from insanity some of the illnesses which medical psychology has discovered. Some passions, for instance, grief, drive a man to the verge of insanity, but even in the worst fits he retains the power of distinguishing the subjective from the objective. Imbecility is an unusual weakness of the intellect and organs, which may be due to old age, weak or backward development. Old age diminishes the power of the intellect, and in some persons the intellect is never fully developed. But so long as the power of decision remains, the loss of power can only be taken into consideration as an extenuating circumstance. Further, when men cease to be able to choose the means to the object, they can no longer be held liable, but this is very rare. Cretinismus is the name we give to the third class. Here man sinks back to the condition of a beast. Instances are found in Switzerland and elsewhere. Such a state must be considered in extenuation of the act, and the offender must be sent to a reformatory.

At the beginning of the century, and even now in many quarters, the belief is held that man is not responsible for his actions. Hence a mania has been discovered for almost every crime under the sun, and thus, as has been well said, the virtuous alone are left as the subjects of the penal law. Some persons have undoubtedly a greater inclination to crime than others, but unless it can be proved that the mania has taken away the power of will and choice, it cannot be admitted even as an extenuating circumstance. No one with a clear view of what morality in general and his particular position in life demand, commits a crime. It is no defence to say that his consciousness was overshadowed, it must be proved to have been entirely obscured.[1]

Unconsciousness (*Bewusstlosigkeit*) includes all transitional states of mind, not due to illness, which exclude imputability, and especially anger, sleep, and drunkenness. In Roman law the father may under certain circumstances slay the adulterer whom he finds *in flagrante delicto* with his daughter. In the Carolina, crimes committed under the influence of anger were visited with milder penalties. The common law of Germany in practice allowed a great latitude of decision. As a matter of fact anger does not deprive a man of consciousness as a rule. The angry man generally chooses his end and the means thereto. In these cases anger may be ground for a mitigation of the punishment, but nothing more. But there are also occasions in which a man is so blinded with anger that he no longer understands his duties or the consequences of his actions, and this he shows by his behaviour. It is also possible for a man to commit injuries in his sleep; this is as a rule *casus;* but when a mother overlays her child, the question must be asked whether there was no negligence on her

[1] This is a point of peculiar difficulty.

Cf. 1. 'Mental Pathology and Therapeutics,' by W. Griesinger, M.D. Translated from the German by C. Lockhart Robinson, M.D., and James Rutherford, M.D. Second Edition. London, 1868.

2. 'Responsibility in Mental Disease,' by Henry Maudsley, M.D. Fourth Edition. London, 1881.

3. 'Stephen,' vol. ii., 125 and foll.

part. In the analogous cases of delirium, somnambulism, and epilepsy we have merely instances of *casus*, and here there can be no question of imputability.

With regard to drunkenness a great variety of opinions have been held at different times. The Roman law punished the drunken man with a milder penalty; the canon law left the offender unpunished, but visited him with the censure of the Church; the Carolina is silent on this point, and since then both theory and practice have varied.

For our purpose drunkenness may be divided into three stages: in the first the consciousness still retains its continuity; in the second consciousness indeed remains, but has become so fitful that mistakes are inevitable as to things which are at other times obvious; in the third the man has become thoroughly unconscious: here, sleep as a rule supervenes. In the first stage a man is always liable for his actions; in the second he is sometimes; in the third he is hardly ever responsible. Each case must be decided *in concreto*. Was the man so far conscious as to know he was doing wrong? Do his acts betray a definite purpose? If a man has committed a crime in the unconsciousness of fully innocent drunkenness, imputability is out of the question even if he has only reached the second stage. If, on the other hand, he has made himself drunk *dolo malo*, with the express object of committing a crime, he is liable so long as the end is still in his mind. But there are circumstances in which his liability extends further. If the action was committed before he was drunk, and only came into effect while he was drunk, he is liable: this is most often the case when a man has a duty to fulfil, and gets drunk with the purpose of sleeping till it is too late. He is equally liable when he gets drunk without the express intention of committing an offence, but with the knowledge that his drunkenness may lead him to do so. This is the distinction between drunkenness *dolo malo*, and drunkenness *culpa*, for which the Prussian Landrecht has been attacked.

In considering the question of drunkenness generally, we must remember that here is no case of full freedom of choice, for in full freedom, as Hegel tells us, no one commits a crime. The question is, could the accused have willed or chosen otherwise? If so, he either did or did not choose as he ought to have done. He is guilty or not guilty, there is no third answer possible. If he did wrong and could have done otherwise, he must be punished. With regard to the evidence, there must be no presumption either for or against the accused. It would be to put a premium upon drunkenness to lay down, as the codes of Baden, Wurtemberg, and Darmstadt did, that all crimes committed in a state of drunkenness induced for that end, either *dolo malo* or *culpa*, are to pass unpunished, and it is astonishing that an attempt should have been made to fix such an interpretation on the Imperial code, which is clear enough as it stands.

Besides cases of persons who are not liable because they cannot will their actions, there are others of persons who can will actions against the criminal code, but to whom their actions are not from a variety of reasons imputed.

The sovereign cannot be subject to the criminal law. The very idea of responsibility is excluded in his case wherever the Roman law has any authority by the meaning of the word *imperium*. In the middle ages the belief was held that kings were responsible to God alone, but in Germany the Church and the great princes found it to their interest to declare that the body which elected the Emperor could also judge and dethrone him. Hence the Sachsenspiegel makes provision for a prosecution of the Emperor, which as a fact never took place. The reigning nobility under the Emperor claimed the right of being tried by their peers only, a form of procedure which was never found practicable after the death of

Henry the Lion. In modern times men have seen that the sovereign cannot fulfil his public duties unless he is irresponsible, they have therefore substituted the responsibility of the Ministry for that of the Crown in all public actions. No provision is made in the criminal law for the contingency of the commission of crimes by the sovereign such as murder, but in most of the German states the laws of the ruling house or the constitution permit the appointment of a regent under such circumstances. This would be proposed by the *agnatus proximus,* or failing him by the Ministry, and would be considered by the family council, or, as is more generally the case, by the chamber or chambers. In Prussia the chambers would sit together and decide by a majority.

Besides the possession of sovereignty, there are other grounds which prevent us from imputing crime to persons in the full possession of their faculties. Such are the command of the state, the permission of the injured person, the necessity of self-preservation, the right of self-defence, error, *casus* and *vis.*

In the first case, a right which the state has cancelled cannot be injured. The state used to cancel all right whatsoever under the old system of outlawry, and also under Roman law and the Carolina in certain cases of anger. The important instance in modern legislation is that in which the state gives a definite command. The official who does his duty in the most extreme case, whether his office be that of soldier, of judge, or of executioner, is shielded by the state. In ancient times the right of the soldier to slay the enemy resulted from the fact that a stranger had no rights. In modern times this right is limited to the actual combatants. In the case of the criminal condemned to death, it must be observed that he is not, as Feuerbach held, an outlaw, for he can be reprieved, and further he can be murdered. Condemnation to death only deprives a man of his right to live as against the universal will which the state has to carry out by means of its organs. Hence, any chance individual has no right to despatch him; if he does he is liable to the usual penalties of murder. In the case of official duties, as a rule such immunity only extends to actions within the competency of the office. It is conceivable that such actions may be immoral, in which case it is the duty of the inferior to appeal to his superior, and, failing relief, to resign, but he cannot be punished for acting within his powers. When the command is absolutely binding, and is delivered in the legal form, then, *is damnum dat qui jubet dare, ejus vero nulla culpa est cui parere necesse sit.* But even this has its limits; even a soldier's obedience is not unbounded. The military code for the German Empire lays down that the soldier will be treated as an accomplice if he is shown to have known that the command of his superior involved an action which had for its object a felony (*Verbrechen*), or a misdemeanour (*Vergehen*) against the codes for soldiers and civilians.

The phrase *volenti non fit injuria* applies only to the narrow circle of goods over which a man has free power. Even here the person who gives the consent must be capable of volition, and his consent must be given before the act has been completed. The result is, that so far from being able to consent to any act which affects the rights of others, whether these be the rights of the family, the community, or the state, the individual cannot even dispose of some of his private rights, if such rights are a condition of man's moral nature. Where he renounces such rights, his own personal rights can no longer be injured, but those of the state are not affected by the renunciation, *jus publicum privatorum voluntate mutari nequit.*

With regard to suicide, be it remembered that neither the state nor his fellow-men have any legal claim that the individual should retain his life. The individual has duties to fulfil towards the state so long as he lives, but he has no legal duty to live. By suicide he injures his own rights alone; but such actions the state merely cancels, and does not punish, as in the case of a man who sells himself. Attempted suicide might be punished in the interest of public morality, but the mental condition of such persons prevents such punishment. A third of the suicides which are committed are due to diseases of the brain, and it is always difficult to demonstrate that the man was in full possession of his faculties. When the act has been completed the spirit of modern penal codes does not admit of any penalty being inflicted on the body. Attempted suicide, on the other hand, requires far more an ameliorating than a penal treatment. The Roman law punishes attempted suicide only in the case of soldiers. The canon law excludes such persons for two months from the sacrament, and when the suicide is complete refuses a Christian burial. Old German law ordains for the suicide an insulting burial (*Eselsbegräbniss*). The common law decrees that when suicide has been committed to avoid confiscation, confiscation shall nevertheless take place. The new codes do not punish suicide at all. Once suicide is exempt from punishment, the accessories thereto are from the nature of participation exempt also. But we must remember that the suicide is only suicide so far as the individual himself is concerned; a second person who assists or drives him to the act is not an accessory but a murderer. The murder of one who consents to it is undoubtedly to be punished. Suicide is immoral although exempt from punishment. Even if the individual refuses to continue his life, the universal will which, in the public interest, has ordained laws to protect life, cannot recognize this refusal. But the usual penalty should not be inflicted, as it is only the universal will, not the individual will also, which has been transgressed. Hence the Imperial code lays down that the man who has been moved to kill another by his earnest and express request will be imprisoned with labour for not less than three years.

Necessity [1] may be divided into two great classes, the right of self-preservation and the right of self-defence. Necessity in the first case (Nothstand), and the impunity which results from it, are limited by most of the German codes to cases where life and limb can only be saved at the expense of the right of others. The later codes of Austria, Bavaria, and Prussia do not define necessity, but extend it to cases in which honour and property are at stake, an extension which the Imperial code does not countenance.

The cases which fall under the right of self-preservation vary. There are sometimes cases in which, morally speaking, it would be better to sacrifice oneself; but the state pardons those who do not, because unable to demand moral heroism. But there are also cases in which the non-sacrifice of the right of others, so far from being an unusual piece of morality, would be the height of madness. Here a man not only may but ought to avail himself of the right of necessity. In the first case the injured party may oppose the infringement of his rights, in the second he may not. Here the Imperial code distinguishes the necessity of self-preservation arising from a threat, and the irresistible force of man or nature against which opposition is impossible. Such force must be real, and where it takes place the case is not one of necessity, but lies outside imputability. On the other hand, the threatening mentioned in the code does not remove imputability, for the man can choose between the two courses, but it constitutes necessity. Necessity, as we saw, involves danger to life and limb, and the law demands presence of mind in the ordinary man. The danger may be relative to the crime, that is, a greater danger may be necessary to compel a greater crime, and *vice versâ*, but the danger must be such as

[1] Imperial code, §§ 52-4.

may be at once realized. Lastly, the danger must threaten the man himself or his near relations. In necessity the code sees only an excuse, not a right; a criminal act committed for the safety of a stranger will not be allowed to go unpunished. The conflict which necessity involves is one between self-preservation and duty, and although it is morally better to sacrfice oneself, self-preservation is allowed except where the duty is official. For instance, soldiers in time of war will, according to the military criminal code, be punished with death for flying or encouraging their comrades to do so. When it is lawful, the act of necessity must be the only means of safety, and must not exceed what one might reasonably do, to attain that end.

Besides self-preservation, a man has also a right of self-defence (Nothwehr), that is, a right to defend himself and his property, not being obliged to suffer injustice. This was the spirit which animated the middle ages. The attack against which force is used must be an illegal one. Subjects have no right of retaliating against the magistrates, nor children against their parents, so long as the one and the other act within the law. The right of self-defence must be used outside certain limits, up to which no retaliation is allowed. The attack must be absolutely commenced or threatening imminently, for, as the C. C. C. observes, a man is not obliged to wait with his self-defence till he is struck. If it is laid down that the danger must be imminent, there is no need of the further proviso that there must not be time to summon the help of the magistrate. The danger need not be unforeseen, nor the injury irreparable, neither does it matter if the person attacked could avoid it by flight.

Self-defence against injustice extends to every right—to the defence of life and limb, of health, of property, and of honour. This is recognized by the Roman law, *ut vim atque injuriam propulsemus, juris gentium est.* The Carolina recognizes it only to a limited extent;

the common law and the new codes have extended it further and further, till the Prussian and Imperial codes have authorized it against every illegal attack whatsoever. The most important rights which come into question here are those of the person, of property, and honour. Under the first we include all assaults on life, liberty, and freedom. The Roman law made special provision for the release of the woman who should slay a man in defence of her honour. In the case of attacks made upon property there need be no proportion between the worth of the property and the force used in its defence. The limit of the force to be used depends not on the worth of the right to be defended, but upon the necessities of defence. As with property so with possession; *recte possidenti ad defendendam possessionem inculpatæ tutelæ moderatione illatam vim propulsare licet, sed hoc confestim non ex intervallo.* If he can obtain possession of that which has been taken from him on the spot, he shows he has never really lost it, and can still defend it.

The new codes only allow the right of self-defence against insults where violence is used in the assault. From the German point of view, this right should be extended as far as possible in questions of honour. Insults committed directly by word of mouth, and indirectly in writing, cannot be excluded from consideration.

Before the assault is actually made, self-defence is premature and punishable. When once it has been made, the injured party, or a third person, is justified in using force in defence of the right, but only so far as is absolutely necessary. Excessive force constitutes not a specific crime, but a *novum delictum,* in which the extenuating circumstances are very strong. When once the assault is complete and successful the right of self-defence ceases; and also when the right attacked has been victorious, any further violence that may be used is punishable. But in judging of excessive force, the whole character of the individual on whom the assault was made must be considered. No hard and fast rule can be laid down, but excessive force used during the struggle is more venial than excessive force used either before or after it. Above all, it must be remembered that passions are roused in the struggle for which the party attacked is not to blame, and which are often uncontrollable. The Imperial code names the negative passions of confusion, fear, and terror, not the positive ones of anger and the heat of the fray. But the last-mentioned can often be included under confusion, and such is the intention of the lawgiver. Persons acting in self-defence may, however, nevertheless be called upon to compensate for injury done. When a man has been killed by another acting in self-defence, the codes of Bavaria (1813), Wurtemberg, Brunswick, and Hanover require the fact to be notified to prevent suspicion falling on the person himself, or on others, and also in the interests of public order.

Vis major naturæ, vis absoluta and *casus* are also sufficient reason to prevent the imputation of an action. In *casus* the result of an action could not possibly have been contemplated. In *vis major naturæ* and *vis absoluta* man acts under irresistible force, and there is no question of choice on his part.

The error which under the Imperial code prevents an act being laid to a man's charge is one of circumstance. Ignorance of the civil law is permissible, ignorance of the criminal law is not. The ignorance which the criminal law allows a man to plead is one of circumstances, which belong to the *corpus delicti,* that is, of circumstances which constitute or increase criminality. In the first case no imputability is possible. In the second the increase of criminality must be subtracted. In these cases intention or negligence is assumed. The code then requires a knowledge of the circumstances which make the act a crime, and only lays down general rules. It thus disposes of the case of a man who attempts to commit a crime, and finds it impossible. *Delicta putativa* are not punishable legally, because the law has to do with actions, not thoughts; morally, such offences are as wrong as wrong can be. The code assumes a knowledge of the criminal law, because in a civilized nation the general outlines of right and wrong are well known. The principle is that *probra quædam turpia sunt naturâ, quædam civiliter et quasi more civitatis.* The Roman law made an exception as to *incestus,* because it is hard to expect all men to know that it is incest to marry relations up to the sixth degree. Modern legislators, however, have seen that this would be a dangerous precedent. It is a simpler principle to assume a knowledge of the law. There can be no doubt that the greater crimes which fall under the ten commandments are known. The minor offences are part of the administrative law, and with regard to them it is not a question of guilt, but of care on the part of the public. Intermediate cases like those of marriage between remote relations under the Roman law can safely be left to the jury.

After reviewing the grounds which exclude criminality we now reach positive ground. Acts directed against the criminal law may be direct (*dolo*) or indirect (*culpâ*), that is, they may be malicious or negligent. In malice there are three stages to be observed. In the first the subject has a desire which it wishes to satisfy, and the mind is called into activity. The satisfaction of the desire is the motive of the subject. At this point there is deliberation as to the means, and nothing more. In the next stage the subject has reached the intent to commit the crime. In the third the intent makes itself apparent by action on the outer world with more or less energy, that is, with more or less malice. The rise of malice in the mind is then the progress from motive to intent, from intent to malice. To the outer world the first thing visible is the malice manifested in the action.

This activity is the realization of the intent, and from the intent the subject obtains the satisfaction of the desire. The criminal law has only to do with the will in so far as it is manifested to the outer world. The second stage in which the crime is willed is morally as bad as the act, but with this the law has nothing to do. Malice takes as many forms as there are laws to be broken. It is expressed by the Latin terms *propositum, fraus, voluntas, consulto, sponte, sciens prudensque, sciens dolo malo.* It is the intent to commit an act against the criminal law with the knowledge of its criminality. Abstract definitions are, however, always open to objection. It is better to state the question concretely in several paragraphs as the Imperial code has done. Malice has been divided into several kinds according to the development we have noticed. In the first place, the progress from intent to *dolus* may be peaceful, or hastened by anger; *dolus* can be *dolus premeditatus* or *impetus.* For premeditation it is not necessary that the will should exist a long time before the execution, but the act must have been weighed. The length of time between the germination of the malicious will and execution may be taken as a sign of premeditation, but it is by no means always the real measure of the depth of the malicious will. In *impetus* the stages run into one another, but the limits between it and premeditation are often hard to trace. An action may be planned in a moment of anger and carried out long after; this is a case of premeditation. It may be planned long beforehand and carried out in anger; this is *impetus. Impetus* changes the character of the guilt; for instance, murder to homicide. Thirdly, an action which was resolved on after consideration ceases to be unconditionally premeditated if anger is aroused in the course of execution.

The intent to commit a crime may be intent to do a certain distinct act, in which case it is called *dolus determinatus.* But in the course of deliberation an alternative may occur to the mind, in which case it is *dolus generalis.* If the objects range themselves one after another in a distinct series, in which the first is unconditionally and the next conditionally desired, we have a case of *dolus determinatus* and *dolus indeterminatus* joined. The value of these distinctions is however open to doubt. In practical law they are of no use at all, for at the moment of execution only one intent is present. It is impossible to stab alternately or eventually; either one or the other is intended, and the intent is seen in the action. The difficulties of proof are such that to bring home the malicious intent is often the *crux* of criminal proceedings. As the written documents naturally did not assist the discovery, it became the habit in practice to presume malicious intent, and hence the mistaken distinction between *dolus directus* and *dolus indirectus.* In the former malicious intent was proved, in the latter it was presumed.

Such presumptions, however, are against the spirit of the German criminal law. It is always possible to draw a conclusion *in concreto;* on the one hand from the whole nature of the action, the means applied, and so forth, and on the other hand from the circumstances of the case viewed as a whole, the time and place of the deed, and the words spoken before and after it was done. When the accused declares that the consequences of his act went further than he intended, the objective necessity and the subjective probability must be closely examined. Above all, the life of the accused must be subjected to a careful scrutiny; for, to take an obvious instance, an habitual criminal is less likely to have committed an act under the influence of passion than a good man who has hitherto had nothing against his character.

Negligence (*culpa*) is the commission of an act with the knowledge that it may infringe the criminal law but without the intention of infringing it. Formerly *culpa* was held to be a mistake which might have been avoided if the usual care which we expect from an ordinary citizen had been used; in other words, a fault in the intelligence, like the want of the *diligentia* of an ordinary paterfamilias in civil law. Berner holds it to be a want of good-will, but this is rather the province of morality. It is rather a positive fault of the will to look on right and wrong as equivalent. The negligent man knows that he can do harm by his action; he does not will the harm but he does the act.

It is a mistake to put negligence as a form of every kind of crime. All crimes cannot be ranged under *dolo* and *culpa*. The nature of theft, fraud, and forgery exclude the idea of negligence, and an attempt arising from negligence (*culposus conatus*) is a contradiction in terms. The concrete treatment of negligence in the Imperial code shows clearly the three points of view under which it is punishable. *Culpa* is punished in the first place in actions which are dangerous to the public—injury to life (§ 222) and limb (§ 230), and bankruptcy (§ 283). Further, negligence is punished when it takes the form of an official misdemeanour; a penalty must be attached to breaking the oath of office (§ 163), allowing prisoners to escape (§§ 121, 347), the non-fulfilment of contracts of delivery in time of war or necessity, and illegal execution of sentence. In minor offences negligence is met by a fine which is imposed as an indemnification. In certain cases the police may inflict a fine of from one to three shillings, and if the offender feels himself aggrieved he has the option of going into court. These cases amount nearly to half a million yearly, and form far the most important instance of *culpa* in practice. Negligence is punishable in the series of misdemeanours which we have noticed, but never in felonies. In one case of negligence only is a penalty of three years' imprisonment with labour provided (§ 222), but this is hardly ever inflicted.

The history of *culpa* is interesting. In early Roman

law it is not recognized at all, and it is not important till the time of the Emperors, when the graver correctional cases are placed under the jurisdiction of the *præfectus urbi.* With the Germans of the middle ages the result of a man's acts was held to be far more important than his will, and it was not till the 18th century that any distinction was made between *dolus* and *culpa.* Then the more enlightened jurists saw that a refusal to punish the faults of the mind involves a refusal to punish faults of negligence like malicious offences. The result is that the new codes only punish *culpa* when the law formulates an express delict, that is, in acts which involve danger to life and limb, in official offences, in bankruptcy, and in minor offences.

From this point of view it is easier to discuss the divisions of *culpa.* It has been divided into conscious (*luxuria*), when the offender acts with the knowledge of the possibility of doing harm, and unconscious, when he has no idea that it is possible, but yet might have had if he had taken the matter properly into consideration. In both of these cases the offender deceives himself by his own fault: in the former he does not consider the consequences from inadvertence, in the latter he turns his attention away from inadvertence. Conscious and unconscious *culpa* may combine in cases where there are many consequences to the careless act, some nearer and some more remote. The criminality of a negligent action rises in proportion to the number of serious consequences it involves.

Till the 19th century *culpa* was divided into *lata, levis,* and *levissima,* according as the result seemed probable, possible, or improbable. These divisions are capricious and of little practical use. Each case must be decided *in concreto* with reference to the age, knowledge, and character of the offender. Feuerbach distinguished from *culpa* a *culpa dolo determinata* on the following rounds. A criminal act is often intended which results in another criminal act which was not intended but which was or should have been foreseen as possible. These are cases of what is called ideal concurrence. In former times the opinion was held that the second effect which was not intended, should be reckoned as malicious, and not as negligent, because of the *dolus* of the first. Such cases are to be solved *in concreto* by considering what was the man's intent in doing the act. Lastly, sometimes the same person performs two actions, the first with criminal intent, and the second without, of which the second brings about the result which the first was intended to produce. This is possible more particularly when the offender imagines that the first action has taken place. Here, according to Berner, a verdict of *culpa* is possible.[1]

Every crime requires a certain will and a certain act; when these are both present the crime is consummated. There are only three cases in which the Imperial code allows the so-called effective repentance to avail the criminal. In perjury it is considered as a ground for moderating the penalty; in cases where an oath has been incautiously sworn, or arson committed, it is ground for exemption from punishment. With this complete stage we have to contrast the imperfect stages of *culpa* and *conatus*, negligence and attempt. In the former the will is imperfectly developed, in the latter the action. In the former more has happened than has been willed; in the latter more has been willed than has happened. *Conatus* can only be conceived as intentional; an attempt is impossible without the intent to make it.

Under the Roman law attempt was not punished at all in *delicta privata*, whereas in *delicta publica* it received the full penalty of the crime. On the other hand, in early German law attempt was not punished at

[1] In the example given by Berner, A thinks he has killed B and throws him into the water to hide the body. It turns out that B was only killed by the effect of the water.

all. The Italian jurist Clarus and the Glossatores, following the Roman mode, laid down that *conatus* was only to be punished in *delicta atrocia*, and then with the full penalty. Schwarzenberg was the first to see that the full punishment should only be inflicted when the crime had been consummated. The Carolina punishes *conatus* only in *delicta atrocia*, and then in the words of the Latin paraphrase, "*si quis non extrinsecus tantum et remotis factis ut adparatu telorum, veneni mala preparatione, ... sed proximis quæ ad perfectionem criminis pertingunt.*"

This was clear enough, but in practice the Carolina was misunderstood. Attempt was divided into various degrees, and applied to all manner of trifling offences. The first reform was due to the Code Pénal, which enacted that only the commencement of the execution is criminal, and further that *conatus* is only to be punished in felonies (*crimes*), and not in misdemeanours (*délits*) or minor offences (*contraventions*). These provisions were introduced into the Prussian code of 1851 by the jurists from the Rhine provinces, who had found them work well in practice. It was however soon recognized that they went too far, and hence the Imperial code, while adopting the same general definition of attempt, lays down that it is criminal in felonies always, in misdemeanours only where it is expressly stipulated, and that the punishment to be inflicted will be a fraction, not the whole, of the penalty attached to the attempted crime.

The most important of the nineteen cases in which misdemeanours are punished are, § 120, freeing a prisoner or assisting him to free himself; § 141, enlisting men for foreign service, or inducing them to desert; § 150, coining; § 160, inducing persons to commit perjury; § 242, theft; § 243, extortion; § 263, fraud; § 339, compelling persons to act contrary to their oath of office.

To constitute an attempt three things are necessary: intent, an outward act, and continued malice. In every attempt there must be visible action, which the new codes denominate the commencement of the execution. There can be no attempt made with threats, although the threat itself may be an attempt to commit another crime. Further, the intent is an intent to commit a particular crime; there cannot be qualified attempt, as Feuerbach asserted. If a man in an attempt to commit one crime commits another, it is one offence not two because the man had not a qualified but only one will. It is an attempt, and must be punished as such; the injury done must be considered as an aggravation of the offence in determining the penalty.

The intent must be followed by the outward act, and here we must distinguish what is merely preparation from what is actually the commencement of the deed itself. The question arises, to which of the two does attempt with insufficient means or on a mistaken object belong? Is it *conatus* to shoot at a shadow, or to use sugar as poison by mistake instead of arsenic? Till the time of Feuerbach it was held and rightly held that there is nothing in such cases *proximum ad perfectionem criminis pertingens*, no commencement of execution, as the modern codes have it. But it was Feuerbach's opinion that the peasant, who prays to God to strike his neighbour dead in the belief that this is the surest means of effecting his object, must be punished by the law. This leads us back to the old conflict between law and morality, with which came the idea of the distinction between absolutely and relatively insufficient means; the use of the latter constituting attempt, the use of the former a *crimen putativum*. This view was however soon put out of court when it ceased to be defended by the eloquence of Feuerbach, and no voice was raised in its favour till the decisions of the Supreme Court of the

Empire at Leipsic on May 24th and June 10th, 1880. The bench, departing from its duty as an interpreter of the law, posed as an authority on the philosophy of law, and by its awards threw the practice of the courts into a state of doubt and confusion. The so-called absolutely insufficient means are otherwise generally recognized as beyond the province of the criminal law. When on the other hand the means are relatively insufficient, *conatus* is undoubtedly criminal; for instance, when a man employs poison but not enough to kill his victim. The limits between what seem to be absolutely and what seem to be relatively insufficient means can only be judged *in concreto.* Further, the means may be sufficient, but the object may not be actually present, or may be mistaken. Where the object is mistaken, and a man shoots at a shadow, the law has no jurisdiction, though the action is morally as bad as it can be. But where the object is merely absent as when a thief puts his hand into an empty pocket, he is, as the Prussian courts have held, undoubtedly guilty of an attempt.

The third requisite of *conatus* is continued malice. Attempt is exempted from punishment when the offender of his own free will desists from the intent. A person cannot be said to desist who breaks off his act to get a better tool but he may be said to desist if he gives up the idea for the present. No punishment is inflicted for two reasons. In the first place, as a matter of public policy it is advisable to give the criminal the hope of impunity as long as he can prevent the consequences of his act; in the second place the penal law has nothing to do with the inner world of the man's mind till it is shown in a commencement of the actual crime. The new codes, with the exception of that of Darmstadt, do not lay down whether fear or repentance alone should determine the man to desist. Such a course would involve an examination of the man's mind, which is beyond the province of law. The practical point to insist on is that, on which the Imperial code lays stress, that the man must desist without being prevented by circumstances over which he has no control.

Two stages are to be recognized in attempt because for certain crimes a result is necessary. A man may have done all he can but the result has not been reached. On this ground we may distinguish *conatus perfectus* and *conatus imperfectus.* In the former a man does not do all he thinks necessary, nor yet all he could do, but he commits the last act of consummation without effect. He may have given a man poison but the man dies from the effect of an accident before the poison has had time to work. The codes of Baden, Wurtemberg, Hanover, and other states laid stress on the criminal's doing all that was necessary on his part; the Saxon code of 1855 attached importance to the offender's doing all that he considered necessary. The former is too narrow, the latter is too wide. In the former it would not be attempt but consummation that would take place; in the latter the question of what is taking place in the criminal's mind is raised. A middle formula is recognized by the implication in the Imperial code. The attempt is complete when the offender has committed without effect the act which should have effected the crime. This is also the definition at which the Prussian code points. The French code in the pride of logic punishes *conatus perfectus* with the full penalty of the attempted crime; the Imperial code attaches only a fraction of the full penalty to attempt. The former is more practical, the latter is more just. At the same time the latter often opens a great door to chicanery from the intricate situations to which crime sometimes leads.

The question then arises, should a man who attempts to withdraw from *conatus perfectus* be exempted from punishment? Mere inactivity is obviously insufficient. In that case causation would take its natural course, and the effect would come to pass or not from reasons over which the offender had no control. The offender must to escape punishment go a step further, and actively hinder the effect of his action. The codes of Hanover, Darmstadt, Baden, Thuringia, and Saxony (1855) punish *conatus perfectus* in the ordinary way when the offender has prevented his act from taking effect. The codes of France (1810), Prussia (1851), Bavaria (1861), under these circumstances allow a perfected attempt to go unpunished. The latter are doubtless right, and are followed by the Imperial code, with the provision that the effect must be hindered of the offender's own free will, and before the act has been discovered. The act must be that of the offender himself; but the Supreme Court at Leipsic has decided that in the case of arson it is enough if he call some one who puts the fire out.

Conatus perfectus is only possible with a small number of offences. *Conatus imperfectus* is a stage which is possible in every offence. It embraces all the cases where the criminal has not attained his object. Formerly it was divided capriciously enough into three degrees: *conatus proximus,* when the attempt reaches the final act though that act is not consummated: *conatus remotus,* when the final act is not reached: and *preparatio delicti.* These degrees had each their measure of punishment, but they rest on no real basis, and the third of them belongs to the province of morality. The Imperial code however in the interests of public security trenches on the province of morality in certain cases, and makes the *preparatio delicti* a *delictum sui generis* in coining, and treason against the Emperor or the sovereigns of the different federal states. This departure from the general rule may be defended on the ground of the public welfare, and further by the fact that in these cases the *preparatio delicti* is much more plainly manifest as the action of the will on the outer world than in any others.

Hitherto we have taken for granted that the crime has been committed by one person but it is also possible that two or more may combine for criminal purposes. The common law of Germany here distinguishes three classes: the *auctor*, who wills the crime, and is its actual cause: the *socius*, who by his assistance intentionally furthers the act, which another has willed: the *fautor*, who comes in after the act has been done.

The *auctor* has the full will to commit the offence and is the full cause of it; but this relation is also possible for several persons, who are called *co-auctores* in regard to the crime. The common law divides these *co-auctores* according as they act with or without agreement, as they are physical or intellectual, and according to the measure of their activity.

When more persons than one come to a common decision to commit a crime and carry their decision into execution, it is called a conspiracy (*Romplott*). If there is no commencement of execution, as a rule no punishment can be inflicted. If it is executed wholly or partially, the question arises, how are they to be punished? The common law on this point rested not so much upon actual legislation as upon the development in theory and practice of several dangerous doctrines. The full penalty was to be inflicted on each participator even when he was prevented from taking part in the execution because in a conspiracy each was said to be the abettor (*Anstifter*) of his fellows. As a rule this is not true; the absence of one man would not as a rule prevent the existence of the conspiracy, but if it can be proved that the absentee was the head of the band he may be punished as abettor. Even when the plot was not executed it was held that the conspirators were to be punished for an attempt, but this is nothing *quod ad perfectionem criminis pertingit.* Lastly, it was held that when a series of crimes were agreed upon by a band of men, they were liable for attempt, even where the individual actions were not yet settled. This is quite against the idea of *conatus*, and for such unions in themselves the Imperial code has no penalty, but theft and robbery, when executed on these principles, become felonies instead of misdemeanours. It is only in high treason that conspiracy is punished even when there has been no commencement of the execution. Under the military penal code an agreement to commit treachery in war is punished with not less than five years' penal servitude.

Secondly, the common law punished the *co-auctores* according to their activity; this is obviously met by increasing the penalty, and there is no need of a special clause to that effect. But in respect of riot (*Aufruhr*, § 115) and breaches of the peace the Imperial code makes an exception with regard to the ringleaders.

Lastly the common law dealt with the *auctores* according as they were physical or intellectual, thus including the two *auctores* who are defined by the Imperial code, the accomplice (*Mitthater*) and the abettor (*Anstifter*). The code enacts that if more persons than one agree to carry out a criminal action, each will be punished as an accomplice. Each of these persons must take a physical part in the execution, and the character of the crime he commits depends on his personality. Thus, when a mother joins with another person in killing her own child at or soon after its birth, she is guilty of child murder and the other person of an ordinary murder. Lastly each has the full responsibility of the act which he has willed in common with the rest. He has done all that was necessary on his part for the act; the help of the rest he has received and used as he would have used the forces of nature. In abetting or intellectual participation the position, from which the Imperial code proceeds, is noteworthy. Mediæval German law only punished joint action on the ground that action on the outer world was necessary and that there was no such action as abetting because the person abetted is a free agent. The Roman and the canon law introduced a fairer view, which was eventually sanctioned by the Carolina. The Code Napoléon went to the other extreme, and punished intellectual participation, even when the criminal was merely asked to do the crime, and no more. The middle point of view adopted by the Carolina is that, which the Imperial code has sanctioned. Abetting must be looked on as authorship in spite of the want of outward action. A mere request is, however, insufficient; active motives must be provided for the crime.

Under the Imperial code *socii* (*Gehülfe*) may be instigated or abetted as well as *auctores*. But instigation will never be criminal till the person instigated has committed the criminal act. It is first criminal when the offender has begun to act. The *socius* and his activity are outside the execution but the *socius* is not liable to punishment when he has given his assistance, if the criminal does not act upon it and begin the crime. Abetting is possible in all three classes of criminal action, but assistance to a minor offence does not involve liability to punishment, and to instigate a man to give such assistance does not involve a penalty. The crime is the act of the abettor, not of the *socius*. The abettor of an abettor is the mediate abettor of the criminal and, if several persons join in abetting, each will be punished as an abettor. Instigation is the product of intention. It determines the criminal to do the crime by acting on his will with various motives, whether they be presents or promises, threats, misuse of power, error, or other means. Instigation incurs no penalty if it fails except under §§ 85, 110, 111, 159, 160. To make the abettor responsible the criminal must have done the misdeed; hence where there is no criminal there is no instigation liable to punishment; but where the criminal has died or disappeared, his abettor is none the less to be punished. The liability of the abettor begins with the commencement of the execution, and goes as far as the action. He is further responsible for mistakes of the offender and for the means which the latter chooses, in so far as the choice of the means is the result of his advice. The abettor does not free himself from punishment by merely declaring his change of mind; he must actively interfere to prevent the offence, either by giving information in time, or hindering it in some other way.

In the question of *societas*, as in that of *auctoritas*, we can distinguish the objective, the subjective, and the intermediate points of view, each of which has been held at different times. According to the first, the physical author is the chief offender, the *socius* subordinate; according to the second, the physical author is acting from a criminal motive of his own, the *socius* from that of another; according to the third, which the Imperial code adopts, the important point is neither the outward action nor the inward will, but the character of the act. Hence the authorship of the crime is separated from the assistance thereof by the question whether the act done formed part of the execution of the deed or not. But it must also be observed that in the *socius* the will does not go as far as the commission of the crime. If the man really wills to do the act he is an *auctor*, even though in the execution he occupy a subordinate part.

The Prussian code tried to define *societas* clearly and *in concreto* by giving the various acts of assistance. On the other hand, the Imperial code does not attempt a definition, but only distinguishes between physical and intellectual assistance, and only requires knowledge of the crime and a relation to the action. The assistance must have been rendered to the offender himself and for the commission of the crime. It can come into play at any time before the offence is actually committed. Before the act is done any help that may be given is only liable to punishment if the act is carried out. The help must be given wittingly by word or deed. The chief assistance in the crime is often hard to distinguish from joint execution of the crime. The Imperial code has deliberately avoided definition. That is generally held to be assistance, without which the man who gives it knows the crime could not be committed, and such assistants are treated as joint authors of the crime. The *socius* is only punished in the case of felonies and misdemeanours, not in the case of minor offences.

Besides the division into principal and subsidiary, *socii* may be divided into those who have promised their help beforehand and those who have not, and lastly into *socii generales* and *socii speciales.* This last division involves a difficulty. *Socii speciales* are offenders whose peculiar status qualifies the nature of their offence. It has been held that the status of the *auctor* determines the nature of the crime for all who take part in it; that is for instance that the man who instigates a son to murder his father is a parricide. It has also been held that the crime is defined for each participator by his status. To take the same instance as above, the instigator would be guilty of a common murder. The Imperial code unites the two points of view and, where the peculiar status of one participator constitutes or removes the criminality, his position is the standard by which it is judged: a non-official, who is a party to an offence, which is constituted a felony purely by the official position of his accomplice, is guilty of a felony. Where on the other hand the peculiar position of one of the participators raises or diminishes the penalty, each participator is judged according to his personal status :—the man who assists a parricide is guilty of a common murder.

It was generally held among jurists from the time the Prussian code appeared that instigation to felonies is punishable. Since 1875 arose the question, should assistance to such instigation be punished? In that year a Belgian coppersmith named Duchesne wrote to the Archbishop of Paris to offer to murder Prince Bismarck. To meet this case Belgium immediately added an article to her criminal code, which was at once adopted by the German Imperial legislature in article 49 *a*. The actions which this section threatens with punishment are invitations to commit a felony, acceptance of such an invitation, the proffer of oneself for the commission of a felony, and the acceptance of such a proffer. The misdemeanour is consummated when the invitation or proffer is made and before it is accepted. These offences can be neither attempt nor participation, for the assumption is that they are not yet accomplished, and hence they are *delicta sui generis.* As soon as the crime is committed the *delictum* becomes absorbed in participation, and the penalty thus increases with the offence.

The third section of the new paragraph involves the distinction between offers and proffers by word of mouth or in writing. The former are of themselves exempt from punishment except where any advantages are added to them, that is to say, they will not be punished where they are pressed with threats, force, or any such means. The latter are to be punished in every case. There is no action by which these offences can be recalled, although that is otherwise possible, even in cases where an attempt at felony has been consummated.

In conclusion we come to the third member of the division, which the German common law lays down, that is the *fautor* or accessory after the fact. The *fautor* is one who takes part in an offence which has been already committed, that is, he cannot be a participator. In fact *favor* is not a kind of participation, but for the safety of the public it includes a series of *delicta sui generis*. *Favor* was limited in the common law to the concealment of a criminal, receiving stolen goods, not hindering or not informing against treason, coining, and blasphemy. In practice *favor* was extended to all great crimes. The modern codes have removed this abuse, and the Imperial code punishes *favor* in general, receiving stolen goods, and not hindering treason where it can be done without danger.

Such being the nature of crime, the further question arises, what are the penalties with which the criminal law threatens it? A penalty is a necessary evil to be inflicted on the offender for his crime; it must be relative to the crime, and within this limit we must keep the objects of the relative theories in view. In Roman law penalties were divided into capital and not capital, according as they affected the *caput* of the citizen. It is no model because of the great desire it betrays of confiscation. The canon law is an improvement, in so far as it makes the amelioration of the criminal its object in punishing. The early German criminal law was cruel at first, but gradually improved under the influence of foreign law, canon law, and the enlightened character of the 18th century. It divided offences from the objective side according as they affect the life, person, honour, freedom, and property of the injured party. A new departure in a practical direction was taken by the Code Pénal, which has left its mark on all modern legislation by its division of crime into three classes of felonies (*crimes*), misdemeanours (*délits*), and minor offences (*contraventions*). The first included all offences which involved imprisonment for more than five years, the second all fines above fifteen francs and imprisonment up to five years, and the third fines up to fifteen francs and arrest up to a week. These provisions were too hard, and were modified in the Prussian, and still more in the Imperial code, by the extension of the two lower classes. The chief penalty in the first class is the much-debated capital punishment, which was executed with much barbarity in the middle ages. In the 18th century Beccaria declared for the abolition of the penalty of death on the ground that no one can contract away to the state his right to live, a view which the relative and absolute theories showed to be untenable, finding a surer basis, the former in determent, the latter in logic. Later thinkers, however, pointed out on the one hand that great criminals always expect to escape, and that the impression made by a public execution is the contrary to that which is desired, and on the other hand that the negation of the negative will is as well effected by imprisonment for life as by death. The fact is, that the question depends on the state of civilization at which the nation has arrived. In higher stages of development there will be less atrocious crime, and less inclination to proceed to extremities in punishing the offender; but capital punishment will always be enforced where it is felt to be necessary for the existence or security of society.

In the abstract several objections may be raised against this penalty. It does not fulfil the conditions we require of a good form of punishment. If frequently enforced it has a bad and not a good effect on the people; it cannot be divided, and therefore gives rise to difficulties when the guilt is not that of one man alone; and above all errors can in this case never be remedied. Further capital punishment is not required by justice nor can it be regarded as a religious command, for although Moses speaks for it, the spirit of Christianity is against it. When scientific thinkers advocate the enforcement of this penalty, they generally do so merely on the retaliatory principle of an eye for an eye and a tooth for a tooth. But it is no more possible to find an equivalent for a life than for a limb. Further, it is not demanded by the idea of satisfaction. The people may demand blood for blood, but the legislator must not yield to the desire for revenge; besides, satisfaction is nobler and truer exactly in proportion to the absence of this vindictive spirit. If the security of the public and the determent of the criminal are our objects in punishing, it may be said that as a rule capital punishment goes too far. A repeated offence is put out of question, but the public security and the determent of the criminal are provided for in almost the same degree by the punishment of imprisonment. Amelioration is almost put out of question, though it is true that criminals are often first awakened to a sense of their condition when the sentence of death has been passed upon them.

The last relics of the old barbarous system were removed in Prussia in the reign of Frederic William III., in Bavaria and Hanover a decade or two later. In 1848 the National Congress at Frankfort voted the abolition of capital punishment, except in cases under the military or naval regulations. It was abolished in a host of minor states including Wurtemberg, Kur-Hessen, Darmstadt, and Brunswick, but in most of these districts it was re-enacted in the reaction which followed. Anhalt and Nassau persisted till the Prussian code was passed (1851), and in two states, Oldenburg and Bremen, this penalty did not again pass the local legislature.

Saxony abolished capital punishment in 1868, and hence it was not at first adopted in the code of the North German Confederation. In the debate in the Reichstag Prince Bismarck spoke for the retention, Herr Lasker for the abolition, of the penalty in question, and the latter carried his motion by a small majority, but the tables were turned by the refusal of the Federal Council to sanction the proposal. When the bill returned for the third reading, a small majority sanctioned capital punishment for murder in general, for attempted murder of the Emperor and the rulers of the federal states, and for certain treasonable actions when a state of siege has been proclaimed. The penalty is executed by beheading in the presence of two members of the court of first instance, one of the public prosecutors, a clerk of the court, one of the officials of the prison, and twelve persons to be chosen by the parish committee. A clergyman and one of the counsel for the defence will be allowed to attend, but no other persons without the permission of the presiding official.

The corporal punishment, which was frequently inflicted under the Carolina because it was indispensable, included torture and mutilation. Torture and mutilation disappeared in practice in the 18th century and corporal punishment in the narrower sense was abolished in the 19th century by the new codes of Nassau (1809), Brunswick (1827), Baden (1831), Darmstadt (1841). In most of the other states it was abolished after 1848, but it prevailed in Hanover till the introduction of the Prussian code in 1868, in Austria till November 1867, and in Saxony till October 1868. It has been urged that it should be retained for certain classes, but this infringes the basis of all justice, the equality of all before the law. Further its effect is different on different people, on the strong and the weak, on the honourable and the dishonourable. Above all, as Savigny urged, it makes improvement impossible in cases where there are any vestiges of honour or self-respect left. It should no doubt be avoided as far as possible, even in establishments for convicts, for it has a bad influence on the officials no less than on the criminals, in whose mind it raises the ideas of hatred and revenge. At the same time it is impossible to lay down absolutely that no such punishment should be used. In inflicting this penalty the criminal law can only be said to have a purely relative end in view, that of preventing certain brutal crimes by a punishment of the same nature. But when members of society behave like beasts, the legislator in other countries, if not in Germany, will feel justified in treating them as such in the interests of the body whose security they have endangered.

Punishment involving dishonour played a prominent part in the middle ages. In the common law such penalties may be divided under three heads—the shameful, the insulting, and the degrading.

The first class included the fines inflicted by the Church—recantation, apology, and the publication of the verdict of condemnation. Most of these were abolished in Prussia in 1811. There still remains the reprimand which the Imperial code recognizes for persons between twelve and eighteen years of age, in cases of misdemeanours and minor offences of a particularly trivial character, and the publication of the condemnation. The insulting penalties are a relic of the symbolic punishment of the early middle ages and include branding and the pillory, and in earlier times crowning with straw, riding on the ass, together with drumming or ringing out of the place. Such penalties are only for the amusement of the masses and punish the better class of criminals far more than the worse; they are therefore rejected by the new codes, although branding was still inflicted under the Bavarian code of 1813. The third class involves the loss of certain rights, public and private. Persons, who had been convicted of certain offences, were not allowed to hold office in the state or commune, nor yet to vote at elections. Further they might not act as advocate or guardian nor give evidence. Convicts were also deprived of the rights of nobility, a provision which could only hold so long as the nobility formed a body recognized by the state. Such persons further lost the right to exercise their trade, a provision which is now recognized as undesirable, unless by misuse the man has shown himself especially unworthy of it, because he is thereby reduced to theft or some other criminal mode of living. In the case of a particular office a man might be deprived of it and incapacitated from further service or he might be transferred or degraded.

The new codes have excellent provisions on this subject; they enact clearly what rights may be lost, and of these rights what may be recovered, and under what circumstances. It is an advantage if the dishonourable punishment can be made visible without the brutality attaching to ancient practices like that of branding. This was possible in Prussia in 1813, when the national cockade was the sign of patriotism. Hence it was decreed that condemnation for any *delictum*, which involved the loss of civil privileges, made a man incapable of wearing it. A few years later the cockade went out of fashion and in 1848 it became the badge of a party. The enactment, which is repeated in the Imperial code, thus lost its meaning, all the more so because there is at present no recognized German cockade. The Code Pénal divides crimes into those which involve infamy and those which do not, placing under the first head all those which are punished with more than five years' imprisonment. The authors of the Prussian code saw the injustice of this hard and fast distinction, for while some of the greatest crimes arise from an exaggerated sense of honour, penal servitude always involves dishonour to the mind of the lower as well as of the upper classes; the Prussian jurists therefore introduced modifications which were carried further in the Imperial code. Under the latter the civil privileges, of which a man may be deprived, are divided into two classes, those which are lost once and for all, and those which may be recovered.

The privileges which are obtained from public election, and all offices, orders, and titles, are lost irrecoverably. The privileges of which a man may be deprived temporarily, or recoverably, are those of wearing the national cockade, serving the state, enjoying honours and titles, acting as witness, guardian, curator, or member of the family council. These privileges may be lost for periods of from two to ten years on a sentence of penal servitude. Under the Prussian code there was here no alternative. Parricides when sentenced to death are also sentenced to lose their civil privileges. A citizen may also be deprived of these privileges for a period of from one to ten years, when he is sentenced to imprisonment with labour for more than three months, if the law expressly enacts it, or if the sentence be a mitigation of penal servitude on account of extenuating circumstances. Confinement in a fortress, arrest, and fines can never involve this loss, which is now as a rule only temporary, and not *ipso jure* connected with any condemnation, requiring a sentence to itself. However condemnation to penal servitude of itself incapacitates a man for the military, naval, and civil services, and the judge is obliged to deprive a man of the second class of privileges when he has convicted him of perjury, aggravated procuring, or usury of the worst kind. When an officer is sentenced to more than three months' imprisonment with labour, he may further be sentenced to lose his capacity for holding public office for periods of from one to five years. In such a case he loses the office he holds at the time. A person may lose his office and retain his capacity to hold it when sentenced to imprisonment with labour for libel on a sovereign (§ 95), and with imprisonment in a fortress under §§ 81, 90, and 94. This punishment comes into force as soon as the sentence has been pronounced, but the term for which it is inflicted is reckoned from the time when the term of imprisonment has been legally completed.

Lastly when a German citizen has been condemned abroad for offences, which would have involved the loss of his civil privileges in Germany, fresh proceedings must be instituted and the whole case discussed and decision given whether he should lose his civil privileges or not.

Punishment may further involve the loss of freedom

under the C. C. C., either in the negative form of banishment or in the positive form of imprisonment. The former, which is a reminiscence of outlawry, lasted till the 17th century from the love of confiscation, by which it was generally accompanied. A trace of this is to be found in the provision, which the Imperial code retains, for expelling foreigners who have committed crimes. The latter became gradually more important, but the prisons were very inadequate, from the poverty of the persons to whom the privilege of holding courts of justice was granted. Three degrees of prisons came gradually into existence: the ordinary prison of the village or commune for simple imprisonment and the expiation of lighter offences; the prison of the province or state for those condemned for greater crimes and longer periods, in which several institutions were generally united; for instance, in Hamburg in the 17th century the same building contained paupers, vagrants, madmen, and criminals; lastly there were the fortresses set apart for those who were condemned to penal servitude. The object of these institutions was to put the criminal out of the way, and it was a matter of indifference how many persons were corrupted in the process.

In the 18th century the faults of the old system were for the first time seen, and a remedy attempted in two different directions by the system of enforced silence, known as that of Auburn, and the system of isolation, known as the Pennsylvanian. The first impulse to reform had come from the Englishman John Howard, who made proposals of reform in the House of Commons as early as 1774, and published in 1777 his remarkable work on the state of the prisons in England and Wales. The result of his efforts were the laws passed in Parliament between 1776 and 1794, and the erection of the prison of Millbank. The principle on which Howard based his system was that isolation and silence bring the criminal to reflect and repent. By means of Benjamin Franklin the idea was carried over to America and in 1785 the Quaker Society for the Reform of Prisons was founded in Philadelphia. The result of the activity of this body was the reform of the Pennsylvanian prisons, which was carried out between the years 1786 and 1792. Penn's prison was divided into thirty cells. Absolute isolation was enforced day and night, and no employment was given to the criminal till he asked for it. A certain freedom was allowed in isolation, and pride nourished as an element of improvement, the prisoner being conducted in silence to his cell and his name never mentioned.

The example of Pennsylvania was followed by New York, New Jersey, Maine, Virginia, and other states; but the principle of isolation was carried to an extremity which led to the madness of the prisoners. The result was the application of the second of Howard's principles, that of silence. In 1823 the prison at Auburn in the state of New York was built and this idea put into practice. The men worked together by day in absolute silence and were isolated at night. The weak point in this system is, that men soon invent a language of their own, and besides like its forerunner it leads to madness. It may be a success under persons with an extraordinary power over their fellow-men, but as a rule it has failed.

In France the Philadelphian system found many supporters, of whom the most able were Brissot and La Rochefoucauld-Liancourt; and also in Germany, where the subject produced as usual a complete literature. Koster translated Howard's work in 1780, and in 1791-2 appeared the work of Wagnitz on the prisons of Germany. In Prussia the ministry at first favoured the Auburn system but it was never carried out from want of funds. It was not till Frederick William IV. had convinced himself by a personal inspection of the advantages of the English system, that the institution at Moabit in Berlin was built, and with the prison at Brucksal in Baden became the model for all Germany.

Within the last three decades the so-called Irish system has found great favour. Imprisonment is divided into four stages. The first is solitary for nine months and can be diminished through good behaviour by one month. The second is labour in common with other prisoners, and of this there are several grades, each bringing the convict some new privilege, and here too the period may be shortened by good behaviour. Thirdly there are intermediate institutions, in which the convict has more freedom and work, partly of an industrial partly of an agricultural nature, and at this point the only punishment is degradation to a previous stage. Lastly comes the conditional release by ticket-of-leave. This system was first applied in Ireland in 1856, and hence its name. In 1864 it was adopted for the whole of Great Britain without the third stage. It was first made known in Germany through the works of Mittermaier in 1858, and later more completely by those of Holzendorff. Since 1846 the subject has been considered by international congresses, of which the first really to deserve the name was held in London in 1872.

On March 4th, 1870 a resolution of the Imperial Parliament empowered the Chancellor to lay before the Federal Council a proposal for the management of the prisons of the empire. The result has been after much deliberation a draft law, which was passed by the legal committee of the Federal Council. This so far departed from the original plan, that it could no longer be laid before the Imperial Parliament, but rather forms a suitable model for the local legislatures to follow. The draft lays down the necessity of a special education for the prison officials, and further deals with the question of the keep, instruction, and labour of the prisoners. In the first place, clothing and food must only be sufficient to sustain life; the criminal must not be better cared for than the free labourer. Order and cleanliness must be strictly enforced but without the aid of corporal punishment. Except in cases of confinement in a fortress and mere arrest, the prisoners must not be allowed to live at their own expense. Fortress prisoners, and others who have not been deprived of their civil privileges, may provide their own bedding and clothes. Air and light must be allowed in conformity with the legal standard prescribed for all prisoners alike. The teaching will only include what is taught in the national schools, and the instruction in a trade, where that is necessary. For the cure of souls special provision must be made by the choice of a clergyman of special talent. Attendance at divine service will be compulsory but not at the sacrament.

With regard to the labour done, there are two systems to be distinguished, private and public enterprise, of which the latter is undoubtedly to be preferred. The private master has only profit in view, and is a disturbing element to the discipline of a prison; these disadvantages are obviated, if the workmaster is an official of the prison. Besides, it is sometimes easier for a private person to sell the manufactures than for the state. The labour must be productive in spite of the outcry of the free labourer against competition. If it were limited to military works, the competition would still exist, and besides the state is bound to diminish the cost of the convict to the taxpayer as far as possible. At the same time the state ought not to under-sell the free labourer in the market. It was recognized in 1878 by the Commission of the German Commercial Union that the penal labour must in the first place keep punishment in view, and that fiscal and industrial objects must be only considered as secondary. The labour in the employment chosen must be proportioned to a man's power, and such as is best for the public and also for the criminal himself. It is generally agreed that the convict should be remunerated, but what the standard of remuneration should be is a moot point. It must not be the same for the strong as for the weak, nor the same for the man, who has a short time, as for him who has a long time to serve. For persons under simple arrest, or those confined in fortresses labour is voluntary, and the profits therefore fall to the prisoner. It would be right to give smaller remuneration to those who are undergoing penal servitude than to those who are under a sentence of imprisonment with labour, if the sentences of penal servitude were always longer than those of imprisonment.

Correction is to be administered by means of reprimand and withdrawal of all privileges for a space of three months; namely withdrawal of work for periods up to a week, of books for periods up to five months, of the wages of the last three months, of bed and bedding for a week, and diminution of diet for a week. Further resort may be had to solitary confinement, and this can be made more severe by the reduction of diet and darkening the cell. The prisoner may also be chained for periods up to four weeks; and lastly, if he has been deprived of his civil privileges, he may be subjected to corporal punishment. In the case of criminals confined in a fortress, the advantages of diet which they enjoy can alone be withdrawn. In the case of persons under arrest reprimand can be inflicted, work, books, and bed can be withdrawn, and diet diminished. An exception to this is made with regard to persons arrested under § 361, iii.—viii. In cases where the prisoners are violent the strait-jacket can be used.

It is now generally held that the prisoner should not be at once released, but should be gradually taught how to use his liberty, and the influence of this view is shown in the conditional release and police supervision, for which the Imperial code provides. In this respect societies for the assistance of released prisoners are of the greatest use and should be encouraged as far as possible.

Imprisonment under the Imperial code is divided into penal servitude, imprisonment with labour, arrest, and confinement in a fortress. The institutions, in which these penalties are carried out, are distinct. Penal servitude may be inflicted for life or for periods of from one to fifteen years. In the Prussian code the periods were from two to twenty years, but it was found that, when a man has been in prison for twenty years, he is no longer fit for society, and may as well be kept there for life. One year was fixed on as a minimum, because penal servitude is too serious a penalty to be imposed for smaller periods, and moreover it would be useless to teach a man a trade for a shorter time. The essential marks of this penalty are not so much that it disqualifies for the public service, as that it is undergone in a certain place, is of a certain duration, and involves compulsory labour of a certain kind. It is true that the labour may be performed outside the institution, but the convicts must be kept separate from the free labourers. Herein lies an inconsistency. The code assumes that the convict is degraded, it retains the name *Zuchthaus*, with all its degrading associations, it makes penal servitude disqualify a man for the public service, and enacts that when the choice lies between penal servitude and confinement in a fortress, the former shall be the sentence only, when it is proved that the offence arose from a dishonourable disposition; yet at the same time it assumes that penal servitude is not dishonourable in itself by making the loss of civil privileges a special sentence apart.

Imprisonment with labour may be inflicted for periods varying from one day to five years. In cases of the concurrence of offences it is possible that so much as ten years may be given, § 74. Youthful criminals may be sentenced to as much as fifteen years, when imprisonment with labour takes the place of the sentence of death or penal servitude for life. Imprisonment with labour differs from penal servitude in regard to the institution where it is carried out, in regard to its duration, and to the nature of the labour which it involves. The labour must be suited to the capacity and condition of the prisoner, but it need not be in the calling which he has exercised. It may be compulsory, but as it may be expensive in some cases, the officials are not obliged to provide it in every instance unless it be demanded. The prisoner can only be employed outside the prison with his consent.

Confinement in a fortress may be for life, or for periods varying from one day to five years. Labour is not compulsory here, but a supervision is exercised over the occupation and way of life of the prisoners. This sentence cannot involve the loss of civil privileges, it may only involve the loss of rights obtained by public election. This form of *custodia honesta* is especially intended for political offenders, duellists, and other persons whom the law does not wish to contaminate by bringing them into contact with the criminal classes.

Lastly simple arrest which consists merely in the deprivation of liberty, ranges from one day to six weeks, but can in cases of the concurrence of offences rise to as much as three months. The place of the execution of this sentence is not mentioned in the code, but its nature shows that it cannot be in prisons for penal servitude or for imprisonment with labour. Labour is not compulsory except under § 361, iii.—viii.

The length of a sentence of penal servitude is always to be reckoned in full months, except where it is converted from imprisonment with labour. In all other penalties of imprisonment the period is measured by days. The day is reckoned as twenty-four hours, the week as seven days, months and years according to the calendar.

The code has not succeeded in keeping clear the line of demarcation between penal servitude and imprisonment with labour. Many periods of imprisonment with labour are shorter than those of penal servitude; sometimes penal servitude leaves the offender in the possession of his civil rights, while imprisonment with labour sometimes deprives him of them; and lastly, both sentences are worked out in the same institution. The advantages of isolation in imprisonment for the improvement of the prisoner have been pointed out. It can, however, be carried too far; even the Belgian code does not inflict it for more than ten years. Under the Imperial code isolation cannot be continued for more than three years without the consent of the prisoner, and even this will be modified, if the draft code mentioned above becomes law. Under its provisions, after six months' penal servitude and three months' imprisonment with labour, the prison officials can determine whether the prisoner shall continue isolated. For youthful criminals a long period of isolation is not desirable, and the draft code proposes to limit it to three months in their case. Isolation is excluded, when it is dangerous to the mind of the prisoner; it certainly should be enforced at night.

The institution of a ticket-of-leave arose from the English convict colonies in New South Wales. In 1791 the governor received the power of pardoning convicts on condition that they should not return to England. In 1824 the governor received the power of letting out convicts to private employers of labour with a ticket-of-leave, either for a limited time or during good behaviour. This became the first step to the former conditional pardon. Later when the colonies refused to receive the English convicts, the system was transferred to England by Act of Parliament in 1853; the condition of not returning to England was omitted, and the conditional pardon united with the ticket-of-leave came a few years later to form the fourth stage in the Irish system. Under the Imperial code tickets-of-leave can only be granted to persons condemned to a period of penal servitude or imprisonment. The ticket-of-leave is only granted when three-quarters of the sentence has expired, and no sentence of less than one year's penal servitude is permitted; such remission, therefore, only takes place in sentences of more than twelve months. The convict must have behaved well during the term in prison and must further agree to be released. The ticket-of-leave can be recalled on misbehaviour or non-fulfilment of the conditions of the release, and when it is recalled the full period has to be completed without counting the time spent at liberty. The conditional release can never be demanded as a right, it is an act of mercy emanating from the ministry of justice after hearing the evidence of the prison officials. In case of misbehaviour the local police can arrest the convict, if the case is pressing, but cannot decide whether he shall be committed for the rest of his term. If the appointed time comes to an end before the release is cancelled the penalty has been paid and the sentence completed, although it has been contended that a period of probation should follow.

Supervision is the regular consequence of penal servitude but only in exceptional cases of imprisonment with labour, especially those of procuring and receiving stolen goods. Such supervision now requires the sentence of the judge and a decree of the superior police of the state, and under it a man may be forbidden certain places, may have his house searched whenever the police think fit, and if he be a foreigner may be expelled from the Imperial territory. In conclusion, the Imperial code provides that beggars, gamblers, drunkards, and others may be committed to the workhouse (*Arbeitshaus*) under § 362. Under most of the German codes the penal workhouse was a distinct grade of punishment between penal servitude and imprisonment with labour. This penalty was carried out in distinct institutions with compulsory labour and a severer discipline than penal servitude involved, but unlike the latter, it did not imply dishonour, and was on the whole a milder form of punishment. The Prussian code only adopted this additional penalty as correctional, in the case of vagrants and procuresses and its example is followed in the Imperial code.

The length of this additional imprisonment is left to the decision of the police of the several states, who are best able to judge what the public interest and security require. The judge has to decide the harder general question, whether the person be a poor man out of work or a lazy vagabond. The institution in itself is an undoubted advantage, as it is a terror to those idle members of society, who would have no objection to spending a winter under simple arrest, and to committing any small offence necessary thereto.

The last penalty, with which the criminal law threatens offenders, is loss of property. This takes the form either of a fine to the treasury, of confiscation of all or some of the offender's goods, or of compensation to the injured party. The fine payable to the treasury is, when inflicted, the chief penalty, and the amount will be stated in the sentence, and it has the advantage of being easily assessed. Fines only affect the guilty person, but where there are more offenders than one, the whole body is jointly liable. In felonies and misdemeanours the fine must not be less than three shillings, in minor offences not less than one shilling. No maximum is fixed but fines to the amount of £300, and in one case of £7500, have and therefore can be inflicted. According to many supplementary Imperial and local laws the fine consists in a multiplication or a fraction of the sum wrongfully obtained, for instance, of the tax or duty avoided. In many cases a particular minimum is laid down as for instance in the law respecting bank-notes of December 31st, 1874. The fine will be levied according to the code of civil procedure, and interest will not be demanded. The sum paid goes to the Imperial or local treasury failing a special provision. In assessing the fine the circumstances of the offender must be considered.

Under the Roman law confiscation was the tacit consequence of every instance of capital punishment and was besides often expressly enacted. The Carolina only permits confiscation where the law particularly enacts it, that is, in treason and other cases. Modern legislators content themselves with the confiscation of particular objects, although in Prussia, till 1848, deserters from the army lost the whole of their property. Confiscation may be for punishment, for security, or for compensation, either to the treasury or to private persons. It is chiefly as a means of security that the penalty commends itself to modern legislators especially in cancelling documents and such measures. In the Imperial code provision is made for the confiscation of the instruments and productions of the crime; for instance, in cases of poaching, coining, and the possession of false weights and measures. As a rule the provision is only enacted when the articles belong to the criminal, but an exception is made in the case of coiners' tools and productions and in the case of illegal weights and measures.

Lastly the property penalty may take the form of compensation to the injured party. This is only recognized by the code in the case of slander (*üble Nachrede*), of defamation (*Verleumdung*), and of bodily injury; but is it to be found in several supplementary laws, such as that of copyright (1874), that of trade-marks (1876), that of copyright of artistic productions (1876), that of protection of photographs (1876), that of the protection of models (1876), and the patent law (1877).

From the private nature of compensation it follows that it cannot be converted into a punishment and also that it cannot be remitted by an act of pardon. Further it can only be given on the demand of the injured person, and the liability of several persons will be assessed according to civil law. If the injured person requires a larger amount of compensation than that laid down in the criminal law, his remedy is at the civil law. The criminal judge has free power to decide how much compensation shall be given up to a certain maximum, which amounts as a rule to £300, but falls to £250 in the law as to trade-marks, and rises to £500 in the law for the protection of patents.

The question of the commensurability of the various forms of punishment has often been debated. In most cases it is obviously out of the question, but in order to put the rich on a level with the poor, it is necessary to make a certain fine equal to a certain period of imprisonment, and in order to meet cases of accumulated offences, it is necessary to resolve penal servitude, imprisonment with labour, and confinement in a fortress into one another. The code therefore enacts (§ 21) that eight months' penal servitude shall be counted as equal to twelve months' imprisonment with labour, and eight months' imprisonment with labour as equal to twelve months' confinement in a fortress. One day's arrest for a minor offence is to be considered equal to a fine of from one to fifteen shillings, and one day's imprisonment for a major offence as equal to a fine of from three to fifteen shillings.

The powers of the judge in the application of the penal law, which were very wide from the middle ages down to the beginning of the present century, are now strictly defined. Under the new codes the maxim *nullum crimen sine lege* is strictly applied. Law not custom bears rule, and even analogy, of which so great a use was formerly made, is now only permitted where the sense and object of the law points undoubtedly to its application, that is, analogy must only be used to interpret, not to extend the law. Further, the judge must not give a different penalty to that laid down by the law, *nulla pœna sine lege.* Lastly no crime must be allowed to pass unpunished, *nullum crimen sine pœnâ,* although an apparent exception is constituted by the principle of prescription.

The law comes into force by publication, and no law can be applied till it is published; but in cases where a new law has been passed reforming the old law and making its provisions less severe, the judge may even before the new law comes into force give a milder sentence than the old law would have allowed (cf. § 2). In publication there must be a period allowed in which the subject may become acquainted with the new law, after which ignorance cannot be pleaded. Knowledge is also assumed in the case of the most trivial police regulations but it is the duty of the local police authorities to make them as widely known as possible. A law must be abolished by a law; a provision can only fall into disuse when it is left absolutely to the discretion of the judge whether he will enforce it or not.

The question of the application of the criminal law in point of place brings several difficulties for solution. Within the German Empire there is now one criminal law, that of the Imperial code, which under the so-called territorial principle must be applied to all offences committed within the Imperial boundaries, whether the offender be a German or a foreigner. Exceptions are made to this principle by international law, under which, for instance, the ambassadors and their suites and dependants are treated as *extra territorium,* and hence no criminal proceedings are commenced when such persons commit an offence, but satisfaction is demanded of the state to which they belong.

With regard to crimes committed outside the German Empire several principles come into operation. A German who commits other minor offences abroad is liable to punishment in Germany by virtue of his personality. If the state only punished crimes committed outside the territory of the German Empire in virtue of the territorial principle, the other states must have transferred to Germany the right of punishment, and Germany must apply the foreign penal law. But such a transference has never taken place, and the idea of the application of a foreign criminal law is rejected by all the modern codes. Over crimes committed by foreigners abroad the state has no jurisdiction, in virtue either of the territorial or of the personal principle; at the same time, when a foreigner has committed a crime in a desert, or in another state which refuses to use its right of punishment, and thus deprives the Empire or its dependants of a legitimate satisfaction, the Empire acquires a natural right of punishing that foreigner. Lastly international contracts bind Germany in many cases to support other states in the maintenance of public law, for instance, when a foreigner commits a crime outside the territory of the German Empire and is arrested within that territory.

Acquittal, reprieve, prescription, and punishment suffered in another country for offences committed, constitute a release in Germany, where prosecution is also excluded in the case of an offence committed abroad, if the foreign law in that particular instance requires the injured person to propose the prosecution and he does not do so.

A man may be deprived of his civil privileges for crimes committed abroad, because such crimes show his unworthiness to possess them, and he may therefore be deprived of them after a fresh trial according to German law. Acquittals and so forth abroad do not prevent a man being tried within the empire in two cases, namely if he is a foreigner and has been guilty of a treasonable act against the Empire or one of the federal states, or of a crime under the mint act, and also if he is a German guilty of such an offence abroad.

Besides the members of foreign embassies the criminal law has in regard to persons no power over foreign sovereigns and foreign troops; when these have committed an offence within the Empire, the only course open is to demand satisfaction.

In the application of the criminal law by the judge, the crime may be viewed according to the nature of the will of the offender or the nature of the deed, which that will has produced. Malice merits a heavier punishment than negligence, and malice is the more criminal the clearer the intent has been. Inversely, anger and necessity extenuate an offence, but forgiveness cannot come from the injured but only from the law.

Further, too much weight should not be attached to the good character of the offender, for this proves also what a clear idea he must have had of the act he was committing. In cases where more persons than one have united in committing a crime, the instigator and the actual criminal must be punished alike according to the code, but this does not exclude the consideration of the quantity of malicious intention, and the same is true with regard to accomplices (*socii* or *Gehülfen*).

Objectively the more important the right injured, the greater is the criminality of the act. The criminality of the act is further increased according as more rights are injured and greater damage done. A completed act must be more heavily punished than an attempt, more immediate participation more severely than more remote. The fact that crime is committed in public or with unusual audacity and impudence, and therefore with greater influence for harm, raises the penalty. So too secrecy should increase the punishment where it is the mark of treachery.

In giving sentence the judge has no longer such wide powers as before the days of codification; he cannot make any change where a definite penalty is enacted, but where there is some latitude allowed him he should take his stand as it were in the middle, between the two limits, and inflict more or less punishment according to the merits of the case.

Under the old common law of Germany the judge could in extraordinary cases go below the legal minimum of punishment, especially if there was insufficient evidence, and he was convinced of the guilt of the prisoner. In the new codes youth and weakened intellect are recognized as grounds for a milder sentence. Further if through the fault of the court, the case takes an inordinately long time to decide, the period which the accused spends in prison may, if he be eventually condemned, be reckoned as part of the time he has to serve. The new code of criminal procedure has not made trials short enough to enable the criminal law to dispense with this provision, which is left by the Imperial code entirely to the discretion of the judge. The codes of Brunswick and Austria mention an extraordinary right of mitigation, where numerous grounds for this exist, which have no further *locus standi* than their general importance. This idea finds its strongest expression in the extenuating circumstances of French law. The Code Pénal was found to be too severe, and especially the minimum of punishment, which it provided to be too high. To meet this a law of June 25th, 1824, allowed a reduction of the minimum in certain cases, especially that of child-murder, if extenuating circumstances were shown to exist. A law of April 28th, 1832, extended this principle to all offences under the code and in the case of felonies (*crimes*) gave the jury the right to compel the judge to mitigate the sentence. A law of May

13th, 1863, fixed a limit to the judge's power of lowering the penalty in correctional cases, but this was rescinded by a decree of the Government of the National Defence on November 27th, 1870. The Prussian code accepted the principle in allowing the judge to recognize extenuating circumstances in certain cases, but limited the jury to its function of deciding the point of fact. The same spirit, which animated the Prussian code, prevailed in the Imperial code down to the Novella of 1876. Till 1876 the law directed the judge to give a milder sentence in the case of all felonies, if there were extenuating circumstances; the Novella further empowers him to do so in the case of nine misdemeanours as well. The judge is not ordered to give a milder penalty in the latter case, because there is no legal minimum of punishment for misdemeanours, and therefore in reality no need for this further provision.

Besides empowering the judge to give an extraordinarily mild penalty under certain circumstances, the common law further empowered him to give an excessively severe penalty in other cases. In the Code Pénal a heavier punishment was reserved for relapse, because it betokened, according to the French jurists, deep intensity of malice and the insufficiency of the first punishment. The Code Pénal was followed by, the Prussian code, which enacted that, when the crime is similar, the judge may inflict half as much again as the original penalty. The codes of Darmstadt, Baden, and Bavaria (1861) require that the offence be similar, and only allow an increase of punishment in certain distinct cases. The difficulty is to decide what constitutes similarity and, as this is the point on which the extra severity of the penalty turns, it has been defined by different codes, some laying down similarity of motive, others similarity in the right injured. The problem may however be given up as insoluble and such is the view of the Imperial code, which makes no mention of relapse in the general part, but retains a severer punishment for it in certain cases of robbery and theft.

It happens occasionally that the penalty must be converted and another substituted for that, which the law demands, owing to the state of the offender's health, or the concurrence of several crimes, for which different penalties are provided. Imprisonment of one kind may be substituted for imprisonment of another kind, a milder or a more severe, but arrest will never be converted at all, nor imprisonment with labour into confinement in a fortress. Imprisonment with labour can only be converted into a fine, where a fine has already been converted into imprisonment. Fines which cannot be paid will be converted into imprisonment, except in certain special cases—for instance, that of piracy in printing.

In case of felony and misdemeanour fines may be converted into imprisonment with labour, in minor offences into arrest. A fine inflicted for a misdemeanour can be converted into arrest only under the following circumstances: either the offence must be threatened only with a fine, that is, the legislator, so far from thinking a severe imprisonment requisite, does not even consider mere imprisonment necessary, or the penalty must be first a fine and only secondarily imprisonment, or arrest and fine must be at the judge's discretion. Further, the fine inflicted must not exceed £30, that is, arrest is only permitted in place of the smaller fines and the term of imprisonment, which takes the place of a fine, must not exceed six weeks.

If a fine be inflicted together with penal servitude, it will be converted into penal servitude. It will first be converted into imprisonment with labour, which must not exceed one year, and thence into penal servitude which cannot therefore on this ground exceed eight months.

To insure a separate consideration of each case the code has laid down, as we saw, a relative standard for the conversion of fines into imprisonment. Within these limits the judge can choose, according to the nature of the case inflicting naturally a heavier fine on a rich than on a poor man, and also with regard to the latter considering the effect of taking him a long time from his work. To prevent the substitution of imprisonment for a fine becoming merely a hardship for the poor, the maximum which may be converted is set at six weeks' arrest and a year's imprisonment with labour. But these maxima do not hold, where several offences concur. If a fine and imprisonment are left to the choice of the judge, the former is for the less, the latter for the greater offences. It would, therefore, be wrong if a converted fine exceeded the amount of imprisonment threatened as an alternative to the fine; but it is not unjust that the converted fine should sink below the minimum of equivalent punishment; the former is therefore forbidden and the latter tacitly permitted.

Several crimes are said to concur, when they have been committed by one person before he has been punished for any of them. In such cases the penalties must not be accumulated till they are too many for one man to bear, and at the same time it is desirable to inflict punishment in proportion to the offences, which have been committed. The concurrence of crime may be either ideal or real, either formal or material. An ideal or formal concurrence exists where several crimes are committed by one and the same act; real or material concurrence where several acts are committed which may either be different, or the same offence repeated. In the case of ideal concurrence the common law inflicted the penalty of the greater crime only but to its fullest extent. With regard to the material concurrence three views have been held. The penalties should, according to the first, be added together as far as possible on the accumulation principle of *quot delicta tot pœnæ.* This is unjust to the criminal, because the accumulation of the penalties changes the character of the punishment; besides the punishment would often be too great for one man to bear. Further public security only requires a proportional rise in the punishment according to the number of offences committed. The second principle is that the greater penalty absorbs the less, the man who commits several offences getting as it were some of the penalties into the bargain. This is neither just nor desirable. Justice requires that some penalty should be attached to each of the crimes, and it is undesirable that a man who commits one great crime should be licensed to commit smaller offences with impunity. The third and proper principle is that the penalty for the greatest offence should be inflicted and raised proportionately according to the quantity and quality of the other offences committed.

Ideal concurrence is met in almost all modern codes by the penalty for the chief offence. Real concurrence is punished by raising the penalty proportionately in the codes of Wurtemberg, Baden, and Saxony. The Bavarian code of 1861 on the other hand adopted the principle of absorption. Under the Prussian code of 1851 the penalty should be raised; according to the law of 1853 the judge was left to decide between the principles of accumulation and absorption. The Imperial code enacts that the *pœna major* shall be raised in proportion to the other offences; but as in fines addition does not alter the character of the punishment the principle of accumulation is put into force.

The question of the difference between continued and repeated crime is one of much difficulty; the distinctive point however seems to be the unity of malicious intention and not unity of plan alone, though the latter often accompanies the former. Continued crime then is committed where the offender is animated throughout by one and the same intention, and is punished as if for one act. As a rule, where several acts have been committed against several persons, we have more than one malicious intention; but it may be possible, as in the case of offences against the laws of property, to treat them as one. The Bavarian code of 1813 required one injured object or one injured person to constitute continued crime, but this definition has been abandoned by all later codes. The Prussian code left it to science and practice to define, and this example has been followed by the Imperial code.

The rights of the state against the criminal fall into abeyance from personal grounds, from grounds of procedure, and from grounds of equity. The criminal may die before the prosecution is begun or before the sentence is executed. The prosecution may be withdrawn or the sentence be declared null and void. Lastly the case may fall under the law of limitation or be met with a pardon. If the criminal die before the prosecution is begun or before the sentence is executed, he is beyond the pale of the law, which no longer permits such acts as insults to the dead in the hope of deterring others from similar offences. An exception to the general principle is made by the Imperial code in the case of fines, which were legally leviable in the lifetime of the deceased, an exception which is not regarded with favour either by theorists or by the practical legislation of other countries.

Further, no one is obliged to defend himself on the same charge twice, except when *dolus malus* can be brought home to the judge or the witnesses in the trial in which he was acquitted. There is no decisive provision to this effect in the new codes, but the supreme tribunal in Prussia has pronounced in favour of this view. Moreover, prosecution is not in every case obligatory; there are proceedings in which it is for the public good that a man should not be obliged to prosecute. These cases are limited to four under the Carolina: abduction, rape, adultery, and theft committed by a relation; but later they were by analogy extended further and further both in practice and in the modern codes. The smallest number was that contained in the Prussian code, but the Imperial code following that of Saxony contained at first a large number. A limit was however drawn by the Novella of 1876. Prosecution became obligatory in qualified immorality (§ 176) and rape, in cases of violence and threatening, and in cases of fish and crab poaching. The withdrawal of the proposal for prosecution is as a rule forbidden, but it is allowed in certain exceptional cases before a sentence has been passed.

The cases in which prosecution is not obligatory include four felonies, namely, hostile action against a friendly power, seduction under promise of marriage, forcible abduction, theft committed by a member of the family or of the household, a number of misdemeanours, and two minor offences (§ 61 *note*).

We must distinguish from the last-mentioned the similar case, in which a sovereign or regent of one of the federal states has been insulted. Here the police do not wait for the prosecutor to come forward, but go to him and obtain his permission to prosecute the offender.

Where the proposal to prosecute is not obligatory proceedings must be commenced within three calendar months. When once opened the prosecution includes all participators in the offence and is not cancelled by the death of the prosecutor. Once withdrawn it cannot be renewed, but since the Novella of 1876 it can only be withdrawn in the case of insult, of hostile action against friendly powers, and in certain misdemeanours against the life, body, or property of a relation or dependant, theft of food and fodder, and in certain cases of piracy where the law expressly allows it. When once judgment has been pronounced the prosecution can in no case be withdrawn (§ 64, *note*).

Prescription may also act in the favour of the offender on grounds which have long been debated. Briefly, these may be said to be the difficulty of proving what has taken place long ago, the presumption that improvement has taken place in the offender, and the effect of time in effacing the memory and effects of the deed, thus making punishment unnecessary. Criminal prescription is not, as Feuerbach would have us believe, a transfer from the civil law, for the real ground under the common law could not be the negligence of the private prosecutor, because prosecution was the duty of the judge.

Roman law recognizes three periods of prescription: the first of twenty years for criminal offences as a rule, except parricide, and later apostasy, and *suppositio partus;* the second of fifteen years, under the *lex Julia de adulteriis* of 17 or 18 B.C., for *stuprum, adulterium,* and *lenocinium;* the third of one year included almost all private *delicta.* After the sentence had once been pronounced Roman law recognized no prescription in bar of execution. The common law of Germany followed suit, but the Code Pénal and later the codes of Saxony (1858), Wurtemberg, Brunswick, Baden, Thuringia, and Bavaria (1861), extended the law of prescription to cases in which sentence had been pronounced. The Prussian code expressly refused to sanction this principle, which the Imperial code has as expressly approved.

Prosecution in criminal cases in Germany must now take place in the case of felonies within twenty, fifteen, or ten years; in the case of misdemeanours within five or three years, and in the case of minor offences within three months. The period of limitation is however broken by any commencement of proceedings and begins to run afresh as soon as these proceedings are broken off. Judgment falls under prescription in the case of felonies in thirty, twenty, or fifteen years; in the case of misdemeanours in ten or five years; in the case of minor offences in two years. The prescription is however broken by any act of execution. In both cases time begins to run not *a momento ad momentum* but *de die in diem*, and the *dies inceptus pro completo habetur*. The effect of prescription is to nullify the penalty but not a private claim for compensation.

Punishment may also be removed by pardon, a provision which is founded on the inability of human legislation to meet every possible case. Pardon is granted either on the ground that the offender is better than his act would seem to show, or for higher reasons of state or social policy. In the case of men who have served most of their time pardon is based on the improvement which the penalty has produced.

The power of pardoning falls to the supreme power in each of the federal states, whether that power be prince or a senate or, as in the case of Alsace-Lorraine, the Emperor. The Emperor has also a right of pardon with regard to the decisions of the Supreme Court of the Empire at Leipsic, and with regard to the decisions of a consul or a consular court of the first instance.

The exercise of this right can be transferred for certain purposes, as, for instance, to the Finance Minister for cases under the laws of taxation; and under a law of June 4th, 1879 the Emperor can make over the use of the prerogative of mercy to a vicegerent (*Statthalter*).

Pardon may take the form of cancelling the inquiry while it is in progress, and this form is recognized by the Prussian Constitution, but only when the King is supported by the Prussian Parliament. The Emperor has not the right in any case.

Pardon may further take the general form of amnesty,

that is, cancelling all inquiry on great occasions, such as the birth or succession of a prince.

The criminal may also be pardoned, when judgment has been passed, and this act of mercy may either be complete, in which case it restores the man to his civil rights, or incomplete, in which case another crime will be counted as a relapse.

The pardon of a minister is excluded, because the responsibility of the Ministry would be thereby nullified. Under the Prussian Constitution such a pardon can only be granted at the request of the accusing chamber and, according to a Bavarian law of July 4th, 1868, the rehabilitation of a condemned minister can only take place with the assent of the Estates of the realm.

Lastly, be it observed that, while pardon cannot be refused, no one can be compelled to resume an office by rehabilitation.

The first eight chapters of the particular division of the Imperial code deal with political offences, high treason, treason, insults to sovereigns, hostile acts against friendly states, and offences committed in the exercise of civil rights, resistance to the power of the state, offences against public order, and offences relating to the coinage.

The Roman law of earlier times punished most of the important offences, which are now included under the name of treason, as *perduellio,* or active hostility to the state. In the revolutionary period of Marius and Sulla the ruling classes required and sought protection against the tumults and riots in the streets, and for this object the Lex Cornelia was passed in the year 80 B.C. In this law the *crimen majestatis* for the first time finds a place side by side with the older *perduellio,* which was gradually absorbed in the new term. The new idea was more fully developed in the Lex Julia of Augustus, which defined the *crimen majestatis* as *illud quod adversus populum Romanum vel adversus securitatem ejus committitur.* Under this head were included all violent attacks on the existing government, and the act of declaring war on the state, or betraying its soldiers to the enemy. Further any one was guilty of treason, who as a provincial governor remained in office after the appointment of his successor, any one who slew a magistrate of the people, and later any one who slew senators and illustrious knights. Desertion from the army, forgery of state documents, and all proceedings which could be said to diminish the majesty of the Roman people completed the catalogue.

Tiberius allowed the law to be turned to the destruction of the richer citizens, and the love of confiscation induced later emperors to include all manner of offences under the head of *majestas;* for instance, Valentinian made all violence, adultery, and poisoning treasonable offences.

Under the emperors Arcadius and Honorius a further extension was made. The Lex Quisquis, issued in 397 A.D., punishes not only the guilty but the guiltless, not only the act but the intent to commit the act. It is an act of extraordinary mercy on the part of the Emperor that he does not deprive the sons of such offenders of their lives, but care is taken *ut his perpetua egestate sordentibus sit et mors solatium et vita supplicium.* For the daughters a somewhat milder provision is made, but this mildness is compensated for by a later section: "*id quod de prædictis eorumque filiis cavimus etiam de satellitibus, consciis ac ministris filiisque eorum simili severitate censemus.*"

Under the Carolingian constitution the Empire was held to be the sacred counterpart of the Popedom. Any assault on the Emperor was therefore punishable with death, in the same way that any attack or participation in an attack on a cardinal was also a capital offence. When the Empire fell to pieces the personal idea of fealty took the place of the notion of the sacredness of the state and the monarch as its representative.

Under Charles IV. the Golden Bull adopted the Lex Quisquis, but the Carolina avoids all reference to treason, dealing only with treachery, as was natural from the position of the Protestant princes towards the Emperor. Under the common law the Lex Quisquis was applied as far as it was understood to the subjects of the different princes of the Empire with reference to the princes, and not to the princes themselves with reference to the Empire. Treason included all offences against God, against the fatherland, and the prince as its head, treachery, fraud, and unnatural crimes.

The new codes distinguish the crimes which involve danger to the existence of the state—high treason, treason, and insults to the sovereign—from the *delicta sui generis*, such as desertion and forgery of state documents, which involve no such danger. The Imperial code includes at last the whole of the Empire and is a distinct improvement on the Prussian code, in that it introduces the alternative of confinement in a fortress with penal servitude, permitting in many of the political crimes, where extenuating circumstances are found, the former in the place of the latter punishment.

High treason has been defined to be a criminal attack on the position of the sovereign, on the constitution, or the territory of the state. It is a crime against the existence or essential institutions of the state. The severe penalties of the common law were little improved by the Prussian Landrecht (1757), and the milder regulations of the Austrian code of 1803 were too indefinite and vague. The first real reform of the law on this point was due to Feuerbach and the Bavarian code of 1813. The Imperial code goes further in mitigating the penalties of former times, but it includes, besides all Germans, foreigners under this section. Germans themselves may be guilty of high treason not only against their own, but also against foreign sovereigns, who are on friendly terms with the Empire. The feudal idea, which made fealty a personal matter, obtained even in the Prussian code, under which only Prussians could be accused of high treason.

To constitute this offence a malicious intent to destroy is required, and thus all constitutional attempts at reform are excluded. The distinctive feature is the violence used in the execution; thus, for instance, the incorporation of one federal state in another is only criminal, if force is used. From the fact that the very tendency of high treason is so dangerous to public security the preparation for such an offence is criminal. At the same time, this must not be extended to mean that preparation and attempt are the same thing, and must therefore be punished to the same extent in this particular offence. So far from countenancing this view, the Imperial code recognizes five stages in which such a design is criminal.

In the first place, in § 80, murder and attempted murder of the sovereign are met by the same penalty. In § 81 the code, without making any distinction between attempt and consummation, speaks simply of a highly treasonable undertaking. § 82 explains this by adding that every act, through which the purpose must be carried immediately into effect, is to be considered as an undertaking through which the felony of high treason is consummated. It would have been, as Professor Berner points out, simpler and better to have said that attempts will be met with the same punishment as the crime when consummated. Owing to the present state of the law doubts have arisen whether a man, who withdraws from the undertaking of his own free will, is liable to punishment or not, because undertaking is said to be consummation in this case and withdrawal is only allowed to go unpunished in attempt. Berner against most interpreters holds that the undertaking is not liable to punishment, if the offender withdraws therefrom, not only on grounds of policy and justice, but because otherwise the attempt to murder the Emperor or the sovereign of the federal state in which a man lives, or to which he belongs, would be made with impunity in the case of withdrawal (§ 80), while the undertaking to murder a federal prince would be punished. Manslaughter [1] is not included in the idea of undertaking, and the words 'purpose' and 'high treason' obviously exclude it, so that § 81 as well as § 80 is to be limited to murder and attempted murder.

In the second place, the code in § 83 deals with conspiracy to commit this offence.

The new codes either include conspiracy to commit high treason under that offence, as do those of France (1810), Wurtemberg, and Darmstadt, or, like the Prussian and Imperial codes, give it a place apart. § 83 requires an agreement for the execution of the highly treasonable undertaking, so that it is not a question merely of preparatory acts or parleys with a view to the undertaking.

The third stage distinguished consists of the serious preparatory acts, which are punished in the same way as conspiracy.

The fourth stage consists in the invitation to undertake a highly treasonable act, and this invitation must not be indirect agitation but must relate to a definite act. Lastly come all other acts preparatory to the undertaking of a highly treasonable act.

In punishing this most serious offence the new codes have left out most of the barbarous punishments of former times, such as penalties inflicted on the guiltless children. The codes become milder and milder and those of Thuringia, Nassau, Anhalt, and Oldenburg even exclude the penalty of death for attempted high treason and inflict instead penal servitude for life. The Prussian code on the other hand in the case of treasonable

[1] Cf. *infra*, p. 143.

attempt against the King's person withdraws the offender's civil privileges, and in cases where a man has been condemned to death for high treason withdraws his right to deal with his property.

No new code punishes the man, who refrains to hinder the high treason which he knows to be in progress with the full penalty appointed for the offence itself (§ 139), and all of them allow the participator who turns informer a milder punishment, some even offering a reward, an example which the Imperial code does not follow.

The Roman law included under the *crimina majestatis* the incitement of a war against the Roman people, the betrayal of part of the Roman territory to the enemy, the support of the enemy, and leading a Roman army into an ambush of the enemy. Ancient German law treated the invitation of a foreigner to invade, the support of the enemy, and desertion as aggravated breaches of the peace. The common law placed all these cases under high treason. The Universal Prussian Landrecht distinguished as treason (*Landesverrath*) all acts, which involved an offence against the external security of the state, and included thereunder not only the incitement of a war and the support of an enemy, but also favouring foreign powers to the prejudice of the state and the separation of part of the states territory. The Bavarian code of 1813 recognizes jointly with insults to the sovereign, state treason, a comprehensive term, which includes high treason, and three kinds of treason, and under the latter, as in the Prussian Landrecht, the offence of separating one part of the states territory from the rest.

The Austrian codes have not attempted any division of high treason; the rest of the new codes have followed the Prussian Landrecht, except that they have placed the alienation of the states territory under high treason. The codes of Saxony and Thuringia alone name treason (*Landesverrath*), state treason (*Staatsverrath*), a term which it would have been better to apply to the whole class of treason, as have done the codes of Hanover and Bavaria. Under the Imperial code treason is divided into military and diplomatic, the former including incitement of an enemy to make war, and treachery during war, the latter including the betrayal of state secrets and state business, and the forgery or destruction of state documents.

Insults against the sovereign were included in Roman law under the *crimina majestatis*, but it was not till the time of Augustus that any notice was taken of mere words whether written or spoken. The example set by the first emperor was followed by his successors, the chief motive for prosecution generally being the desire to confiscate the property of rich citizens.

German law followed the law of Rome till the 18th century, when Böhmer and his contemporaries introduced the distinction between treason and insults to the sovereign. The attempt to divide the latter class into insults to the sovereign as ruler and as a private man has met with no favour in later legislation. With the sovereign of the state, to which the offender belongs, or in which he is staying, other sovereigns can only be included in so far as they pass similar laws for the protection of German princes.

The code includes under insults to the sovereign, not only insults but acts of violence not included under § 81, i., a provision which does not hold good of insults to private persons. In so far as such an act would be criminal if committed on another person, as it would be in the case of robbery, we have an ideal concurrence of offences. The offence of insulting the sovereign must be malicious, that is, committed with intent, and on the reigning, not on any deceased sovereign. The members of the royal houses are also protected, but in Prussia the Hohenzollern princes, who belong to a distant branch of the reigning family, are not included in this category. With regard to the prosecution of such offenders, the code has consulted the dignity of the personage insulted by making the prosecution of the offender depend on his permission, a measure which prevents prosecution being made by some zealous or servile official in a case beneath the notice of the prince.

The introduction of constitutional government into Germany led to the necessity of regulations with regard to the use of civil rights on the part of the citizens. The most practical directions in modern legislation were those of the Code Pénal, which has been closely followed by the Prussian and the Imperial codes. The latter lays down regulations with regard to acts committed against the Chambers or their members, offences in connection with public elections and voting, including therein the senates and freemen of the free towns, as well as the legislative bodies of the empire and the other federal states. It is forbidden to undertake,[1] or in other words to attempt and effect, the dissolution of the different legislative bodies; to compel them to pass or forbear to pass resolutions; to remove members from among them by force. Further, it is criminal to hinder a member from betaking himself to the place of assembly, and from voting. The code further punishes the hindrance of voting at the public elections for representatives of the parish, hundred, province, and state. Heavy penalties are also provided for the falsification of the returns, a distinction being drawn between the officials intrusted with the management of the elections and other persons. Lastly, traffic in votes at public elections for money or other advantages may involve, besides imprisonment with labour for from one month to two years, the loss of civil privileges. For the consummation of this offence unanimity of intent alone is necessary. Thus on the one hand the promise or even the transfer of the advantage, and on the other hand the recording the vote, do not alone constitute criminality (Leipsic, April 3rd, 1882). This

[1] Cf. §§ 81, 82, 102, 105, 114, 122, 159, 160; but *per contra* § 357.

limitation of corruption to buying and selling is unsuitable, as Berner points out. The Bavarian code of 1861 contains directions far more complete with regard to the use of influence at elections.

From the constitutional offences we pass to those which are directed against the power of the state. In the first place the state must assert its authority and enforce obedience to its commands. Invitations to disobey the laws are to be punished, and here the Imperial Parliament modified the Prussian code. Under the latter obedience was demanded "to the laws and ordinances of the state." Lasker introduced the qualification "valid" in front of "ordinances," and Planck added the clause, "and to the regulations made by the magistrates acting within their competence." Lasker introduced his alteration to meet the fact that in German public law many public ordinances exist, which are formally correct but are not legally valid. The clause introduced by Planck implies according to him that it is the duty of the judge to examine not whether the magistrate had the authority to make the regulation at all, but whether the conditions are present, the examination of which the law left to the magistrate, which seems an obscure manner of putting the same fact. The code then punishes public invitations to disobey lawful regulations, and further invitations to commit criminal acts, and lastly any encouragement to soldiers to disobey, especially in the case of those on furlough.

In the same chapter the code treats of the compulsion of officials, resistance to officials in general, and those connected with the forest administration in particular. All officials are guaranteed freedom of action, whether immediately or only mediately in the service of the state. The protection naturally only refers to acts which are to be committed or omitted in the exercise of the duties of their office. It must be proved that the force or threat used was intended to serve, and has indeed served, as a means to divert the official from a lawful course of action. The lawful exercise of his office is not required in § 114, because the unlawfulness of an official act cannot give a private man the right to compel the official to perform another act. The resistance offered to the official under § 113 requires either bodily force or real opposition by threat combined with force to make it criminal. If the opposition be effectual, it does not matter whether it was meant to be in earnest or not. The violent assault mentioned in the same section must be committed on the person of the official while he is exercising his office. The Supreme Court holds that to pull an official out from a room by force, with the intent to beat him, is not an attempt, but the consummation of the offence. The section requires that the official should be one of the executive, and the act resisted a lawful one.

Resistance to and compulsion of official inspectors of woods and forests, and the possessors of the same, are treated as aggravated cases of the resistance to and compulsion of officials in general, and punished accordingly. It was not till the Novella of 1876 that extenuating circumstances were admitted in mitigation and that minima of punishment were laid down.

Violence used to officials becomes far more serious when it is attempted by a number of persons tumultuously assembled together in the public roads or places. The common law distinguished such acts according as they were intended to compel or prevent an official act. The former was termed riot (*Aufruhr*), the latter tumult. The common law further was at pains to lay down that such an assembly could be constituted by ten persons, in which women were counted, but not children and persons attracted by curiosity. The Imperial code has avoided any such hard and fast definition, but rather takes for granted that the number must be such as to constitute a danger of a breach of the peace; such a number would vary according as the assembly took place in the town or the country. From a peaceful to a tumultuous assembly there is often but one step, and the code provides that, when the local authorities think that such a transition is about to take place, they shall thrice summon the persons present to withdraw. Those who refuse may be punished for tumult (*Auflauf*). It is assumed that the demand is made by some competent official, and it has been decided (Leipsic, March 15th, 1882) that a police sergeant is competent. The summons only counts as such when made in the pauses of the uproar, so that it can be heard.[1] If in such a tumult the officials or armed authority are violently resisted by the persons assembled with combined force, the penalty for tumult may be inflicted. To constitute riot (*Aufruhr*) itself a public tumultuous assembly is required, in which officials are resisted or put under compulsion by the combined force of the assembly. The persons assembled must be gathered together with a common malicious purpose, and it is sufficient if this common malicious purpose is only formed after they have come together. Thus, to constitute criminal participation in a riot, it has been decided that it is enough if the accused had knowledge of the criminal object of the tumultuous assembly. In this case the term 'public' is not confined to public roads, streets, and places, but includes all buildings to which access may be had. Further there must be resistance or violent assault or compulsion of an executive officer, and in the commission of the offence the combined force of two or more of the assembly must be used. As soon as such two or more persons have so acted, the whole assembly are parties to the offence of rioting, although they may not have actually taken part in the commission of the act in question. Those who have actually taken part in the act, are however guilty of a far graver

[1] Prussian Obertribunal, June 11th, 1876.

offence, and share with the ringleaders the severer punishment, which may amount to ten years' penal servitude with police supervision. The liberation of prisoners and aiding such liberation is generally speaking only to be punished where the intent exists. But such acts are also criminal, when committed through negligence by officials employed in the management of the prisoner. Self-liberation in itself is only an offence against the prison rules, but where violence is used, the prisoner is punished as he would be for such acts outside the institution. A mutiny however involves a tumultuous assembly of the prisoners and action with combined force. Here a distinction is made. In the first place the mutineers may either attack the officials with a view to compelling them to do or forbear certain acts, or may resist them, or may undertake, that is, attempt and consummate, either of the above offences. In the second place the prisoners may undertake a violent outbreak from the prison inclosure. These two offences are met with imprisonment with labour for not less than six months. The third case of aggravated assault on the officials may be punished with penal servitude for ten years together with police supervision.

The seventh chapter deals with a somewhat motley group of offences, which have more or less the distinctive feature of being directed against the public order.

The first of these is the breach of the peace of the house or forcible entry. The *Lex Cornelia de injuriis* of Sulla allowed a criminal action *quod quis pulsatus verberatusve domusve ejus vi introita sit.* In ancient German law such forcible entry constituted not only a criminal but a religious offence against the household gods. Further under forcible entry was included the offence of remaining unwarrantably in another's house. The punishments inflicted were fines, imprisonment, and penal servitude, and these punishments were increased if the house in question were a palace or castle belonging to the sovereign.

The Imperial code[1] distinguishes breaches of the peace of the house properly so called from the forcible entry of a mob. The former offence is committed by any one who enters the dwelling, business rooms, or enclosed property of another, or closed rooms appointed for public service, either breaking in with illegal force or remaining unwarrantably after being requested to retire. The fenced property must be visibly marked off and joined to the house in such a way, as to serve the purposes of domestic life.[2] The fence need not be without gaps. Except in cases where arms have been used or several persons have joined in the act of house-breaking, prosecution is not taken up by the state. Severe penalties are reserved for house-breaking on the part of a mob with the intent to commit acts of violence on persons or property.

The second offence against public order is a breach of the public peace on the part of a mob (§ 125). The nature of the offence is best explained by a comparison with §§ 116 and 124, which deal with riot and house-breaking by a mob. In §§ 124, 125 we are concerned with acts of violence directed against persons or property. In the former the acts of violence are only intended, so that the offence consists in the forcible entry; the actual commission of the acts of violence constitutes a breach of the public peace. The forcible entry of the mob is limited to enclosed spaces, while on the other hand a breach of the public peace can be committed by the mob in spaces of every kind. Further while the breach of the public peace is directed against the peace, a riot is an offence against the public power; and as the forcible entry of a mob easily degenerates into a breach of the peace, so

[1] §§ 123, 124.
[2] Decision Leipsic, March 16th, 1881.

from a breach of the public peace the transition is easily made to riot, if the authorities interfere to protect persons and property and are met with resistance. In this, as in the analogous cases, the ringleaders and those who actually commit the acts of violence are liable to a severer punishment than those who were merely parties to it.

§ 126 deals with threats to commit an offence involving danger to the public. Under the common law any one was guilty of a capital offence, who, after the public announcement of intended feud, robbery, arson, and so forth, betook himself to the place, from which persons were to set out to commit the offence. Modern codes enact punishment for those who threaten to commit such act, and the Imperial code follows their example. The criminality of the act consists solely in the threat, not in the execution, or even the intention to commit the act. It is the disturbance of the peace resulting from such a threat that is to be prevented. In contradistinction to threats of crime in general, the threat here in view is one, which menaces a circle of persons with danger. Where this special feature is wanting, where the threat does not disturb the community, it can only be punished as the threat to commit the offence specified, for the code does not punish the mere attempt to threaten an offence involving danger to the public.

The code goes on to deal with armed bands and forbidden societies in §§ 127—129. Under the Roman law the foundation of all societies without express permission was forbidden. At the time of the adoption of the foreign law in Germany this regulation seemed unnecessary. Societies for treasonable, riotous, and other criminal purposes were treated as attempts to commit such offences. Other societies were considered as lawful, but the police had the right to be informed of their objects; but special Imperial laws were passed to regulate the associations of the princes and Estates of the Empire. With the French Revolution such societies took a fresh departure, and hence in 1819 the German Confederation passed a resolution against secret societies of students.

On July 5th, 1832 followed a general prohibition of the foundation of, or participation in, any society for political objects. Together with the legislation of the Empire and Confederation, the several kingdoms, electorates, &c. from 1788 onwards issued laws and ordinances on the subject. The most remarkable perhaps is a Prussian edict of October 20th, 1798, which practically silenced the people on all political subjects. The evil influence of this edict was visible even in the draft code of 1845, which, while permitting lectures and learned discussions, prohibited all societies with practical objects. The right of forming political societies with practical objects has latterly been recognized. The Imperial code requires that the existence, constitution, and object of societies should not be concealed, that unconditional obedience must not be promised to a known or unknown commander, and that the object of such societies must not be the hindrance of administrative regulations or the execution of laws.

The Prussian code contained a prohibition of public acts, which tended to incite the subjects of the state to hate or despise each other. The Imperial code in § 130 confines such punishment to those, who endanger the public peace by publicly inciting one class of the population to commit acts of violence on another. By a class of the population is meant a number of persons who can be treated as a whole, and included under a common name on the ground of similar position in life of agreement of opinion, objects, or interests; it being always assumed that such number of persons can be definitely recognized and marked off from their fellow-countrymen. Vague abstractions, such as the 'illiterate,' do not form a class. The Imperial Parliament inserted "acts of violence" in place of "enmities," to show that the incitement must have a practical end in view. The incitement must be public, but actual violence is not necessary to constitute the offence, according to a decision at Leipsic, October 21st, 1881. Such regulations are justified by the social and political circumstances of Germany, and have been issued in far stricter form in the law against socialism which was passed October 21st, 1878, and renewed again in 1880 and 1884, of which a translation is appended. The punishment under the Imperial code has no minimum attached to it, and cannot be said to have too high a maximum.

§ 130 *a* is due to the encroachment of the Ultramontanes and places a limit on clerical criticism. §§ 132—138 call for no special comment but § 139 is interesting. As a rule the neglect to inform against projected crime is not criminal in German law, and was only punished under the common law in high treason, coining, blasphemy, and *Handwerkschelten*. The Imperial code makes such neglect criminal in three cases: felonies which involve danger to the state, high treason, and treason; felonies which involve danger to the public, and felonies relating to the coinage; and lastly in the gravest offences against private persons, murder, robbery, and kidnapping. Three conditions constitute criminality—credible knowledge of the purpose, the possibility of informing in time, and the commencement or consummation of the offence of which information might have been given. The information must be given to the authorities or the person threatened with the crime. All persons will be punished alike for not giving such information, because the object of this section is not the punishment, but the hindrance, of the offence.

The regulations with regard to military service fall under the different military codes. Under an ordinance of the President of the Federation issued on December 29th, 1867, the Prussian military code of 1845 was introduced throughout the territory of the North German Confederation. Saxony, however, retained her code of November 1867, and tried to bring it into harmony with the Prussian code by the Novellæ of 1869. After the establishment of the Empire, the Prussian code was adopted at once by Baden and South Hesse; Bavaria and Wurtemberg however retained their own military code till the passing of the universal code for the Empire, which came into force on October 1st, 1872. The Imperial criminal code contains however in addition to this local legislation four paragraphs directed against those, who withdraw themselves from military service, or induce others to do so. The duty to serve in the militia lasts from the end of the seventeenth to the end of the forty-second year. Under § 140, which was enlarged by the Novella of 1876, not only is the attempt to evade this duty criminal, but the offender's property may be sequestrated to cover the fine. The duty to serve in the regular army begins with the 1st of January of the year, in which the twentieth year has been completed, and lasts seven years. On February 22nd, 1868, a treaty was concluded with the United States, which removed a real hardship. Under this agreement a German, who has become naturalized in America, can only be prosecuted on his return for offences committed before he emigrated; that is, he cannot be punished, if by emigration he withdrew himself from his duty to serve. According to a decision of the Supreme Court (Leipsic, November 20th, 1880), attempt to evade this duty is constituted by the offender's leaving his place of residence and entering on a journey to be made outside the boundaries of the federal territory, with the intent to withdraw himself from entering the service of the standing army. It has also been decided that deserting the colours is not a lasting offence, but is completed on leaving the colours without permission, so that assistance to desertion does not now seem possible (Leipsic, February 1st, 1882). The connection of the criminal regulations with regard to collisions at sea (§145) with the military offences which precede, or the offences relating to the coin which follow, is hard to see.

The law relating to the coin is almost entirely modern, for the common law assumes only the existence of metallic money, and lays down directions and calculations suited to the very different political relations, and entirely unfitted for the present time. In the codes which appear after 1813, and also in the Prussian draft codes of 1827 and 1830, the offences relating to the coin were placed under the offences against public credit. However, in the draft code of 1850 the universal Prussian Landrecht was followed, and these offences were placed under the crimes committed against the state. The Prussian and Imperial codes have both pursued the same method, although they place foreign money in this respect on the same footing with that of Germany, and the paper money issued by the Empire on the same footing with that issued by private persons. To constitute an offence relating to the coin, it was formerly said that two conditions were necessary—the *animus lucri faciendi*, i. e. the desire for gain, and either the creation of new or the debasing of old coins. This would not take in all the offences under modern laws. Money is the means of exchange, which the state authorizes. Coins which no longer serve the purpose of exchange are no more money, than imitation coins made as playthings or sweetmeats for children. Paper money, which is issued by the state, and bills payable to the bearer and recognized by the state are placed on the same footing as money. On the other hand notes running in the name of persons are only protected under the sections against the forgery of documents. The confiscation of all implements connected with offences relating to the coin is not only permitted to, but required of, the judge. All three classes of offences are represented here—felonies (§§ 146, 147), misdemeanours (§§ 146-52), minor offences (§ 360).

With regard to coining, the distinction must be drawn between genuineness and full weight. The former consists in the authority given by the issue of the state, the latter in the harmony of the real with the nominal value. A coin under weight is often genuine, as is the case with the small coins in most countries. Indeed it would be possible for a coiner at present in Germany to issue silver coins of full weight, and yet make a profit of twenty-five per cent., but the fact that such false coins are of full weight does not diminish the danger to the public credit.

The code further punishes here the increase of the value of the paper money by adding a figure, or the decrease of the value of the coin by cutting off the outside and filling up the centre with inferior metal. On the other hand gilding or silvering coins of inferior metal is not a coining offence. It is also criminal to alter and bring into circulation money that has been called in. To prepare such coins constitutes the offence, it being indifferent whether the offender means to put them in circulation himself or by means of another. It would however, according to Professor Berner, be no coining offence to use for a purpose other than circulation coins or paper money that have been called in; for instance, to show a tradesman a handful of such coins or a piece of such paper money with a view to obtaining credit. But one who has made coins so unlike the real article that they are useless is guilty of attempted imitation. § 147 punishes just as severely the bringing into circulation money which was made by the offender himself without such intent or procured from elsewhere.

§ 148 sets too light a punishment on those who

pass on the money which they have received as genuine and recognized to be false. The penalty provided is inadequate to meet cases, in which the sum in question is very large, and also cases, in which the offender has stolen the money or obtained it in some unlawful way, thinking it to be genuine.

The depreciation of money without bringing it into circulation is not criminal, and the perfection of modern minting makes the recognition of light coin, when it is brought into circulation, so easy that the code has imposed small penalties for the offence. No punishment is inflicted on the person, who tenders the depreciated coin at its right value.

The possession of implements necessary for coining is punished as a *delictum sui generis.* The offence is such a serious one when consummated, that the legislator is justified in departing from the general rule and punishing it in the preparatory stage.

The ninth and tenth chapters are occupied with perjury and false accusation, which are at the same time offences against the state and against religion and morality. Under the Roman law perjury was visited by censure as a religious offence and only punished when a legal injury resulted therefrom. The Carolina followed the canon law in laying stress on the profanation of the name of God, but limited criminal perjury to that committed before the courts of law. According to the modern point of view the criminality of perjury lies in the blow thereby inflicted on public credit, and only secondarily in the religious side of the offence. The Carolina distinguishes perjury in criminal from perjury in civil cases. In the first case the punishment of the innocent person, who has been condemned, falls on the perjurer, in the second the perjurer must pay compensation and forfeit his political and social privileges. Modern legislation distinguishes perjury properly so called, and the breach of an oath, and further lays down enactments with regard to subornation and negligent oaths. Perjury properly so called is the violation of a declaratory oath; the breach of an oath is the violation of a promissory oath. In the former case the offence is consummated as soon as the formula of the oath has been uttered, in the latter where the promise is broken; in the case of the witness's oath which has preceded the evidence, as soon as such evidence is complete. Private perjury is impossible, because perjury itself is only criminal in so far as it is publicly committed, that is, under some public obligation.

But responsibility is not cancelled by the fact that the perjured person has not been previously warned, nor by the fact of such person having deceived the magistrate as to his religion, and hence made the oath according to a wrong formula. Under the codes for civil and criminal procedure, the formula is at present the same for all creeds.

With regard to false evidence it is to be noted that unimportant irregularities in answering immaterial questions, such as those with regard to age, do not constitute perjury. A charge of perjury can be founded against experts not only on the observations that they communicate, but also on the opinions they express. It would however be almost impossible to prove malice in the latter case.

Subornation to perjury was threatened with punishment under the Carolina. Since then however the punishment, if the person suborned actually committed the offence, was the same as that of perjury. But if the perjury was not committed, the suborner was left unpunished under the general rule. Here the Imperial code makes an exception in the case of unsuccessful subornation to perjury, or the asseveration which takes the place of an oath, but this does not apply to a breach of an oath.

Suborning another successfully to swear a false oath

will be punished, but not the attempt, and so too in the case of a false asseveration; in both cases the person who swears the false oath does so in negligence or innocence.

The Carolina only punished the breach of an oath in the case of the solemn vow not to take vengeance, the Imperial code punishes the breach of all legal oaths.

While the breach of an oath is only punished in certain exceptional cases, an oath untruly sworn from negligence can be punished in all cases, which are punished as perjury where malice is assumed, but punishment is precluded, if the oath is withdrawn in time.

The Bavarian code (1861) excludes prosecution for perjury in a series of cases, especially where the declaration does not make facts known, but rests on an activity of the mind which is incontrollable, or where the offender is under moral compulsion; for instance, where perjury is committed to cover a relation. The Imperial code has under this influence mitigated the punishment to be inflicted where the truth would have laid the perjurer open to prosecution, or where he could have refused to make a statement at all about the person in whose favour he forswore himself, but did not know of his right to do so. The same mitigation is permitted under § 158, if the perjured oath or false asseveration is withdrawn in time.

The forfeiture of civil privileges and of the capacity to act as witness attach to all convicted of perjury, except in the cases of §§ 157-8. The latter is just, but the former is unjust in the case of a large class of persons, who have no idea of the gravity of the offence, and perjure themselves from frivolity or want of understanding.

False accusation (§§ 164-5) must be distinguished from false arraignment (§ 344). False accusation, like defamation, is the false imputation of a fact which would, if true, bring the person defamed into contempt, or lower him in public estimation; but it differs from defamation, in that the act falsely imputed is a criminal act or an offence against official duties, and lastly in that the false imputation is intended to mislead a magistrate. When once the proceedings against the person falsely accused are commenced, the proceedings against the accuser are suspended till the end of the main trial. As in the case of offences against honour, the person who has made the false accusation has to bear the cost of making the judgment known, and of sending a copy of the same to the accused.

The eleventh chapter deals with misdemeanours relating to religion. In the middle ages the Church had in such matters usurped the power of the state. The state really pretended to do but little more than keep the peace, all the other duties of government with regard to the welfare and education of the subject were performed, if at all, by the Church, and hence the power she obtained of enforcing her system of law. This state of affairs lasted till the Reformation, and traces thereof remain in the common law. The growth of the idea of freedom of conscience prevented the adoption in the Carolina of the articles adopted in the Bambergensis against heresy. Prosecution for heresy did nevertheless continue even in Protestant countries, and here Saxony under Carpzow took a prominent part. The punishment was however comparatively light, namely, banishment, in the case of repeated relapse. Under the universal Landrecht the foundation of new sects is only criminal when directed against God and the king, and modern legislation leaves the regulation of such matters to the laws relating to associations, and treats them purely from a political not from a religious point of view. The second great offence under the common law was sorcery, which has gradually disappeared, and now is only punished, where it is sought to defraud the ignorant.

Under the common law blasphemy was punished, alike in Protestant and Catholic lands, under the following heads—ascribing or denying to the Trinity attributes which the Church holds it to possess, and blasphemy of the sacraments, the Virgin, the saints, and the Bible. Under the canon law this was a capital offence, and there are instances of the execution of persons for this crime in Baden and Wurtemberg as late as the 18th century. Blasphemy was so punished under the idea that God is "a jealous God," and that, in the words of the Novella 77 of Justinian "*Propter ejusmodi delicta et fames et terræ motus et pestes oriuntur.*" The punishment of such acts, although untenable from the point of view of the jurist, or even of the moralist, is retained on two grounds: such acts are an injury to the religious societies, who are insulted in the object of their veneration, and an attack on the religious basis of the state.

In § 166 three acts are distinguished—the creation of a scandal by public blasphemy of God, the public insult of one of the Christian Churches or any religious society existing with corporate rights in the federal territory, and insulting misconduct in a church or any place appointed for religious assemblies. It was a mistake to make the scandal or offence caused to private persons constitute the criminality of the offence, rather than the offence to public order. The offence given is at best a fluctuating idea and hard to prove, and further public blasphemy has no claim to impunity on the ground that the accidental effect of giving offence did not take place. It would have been better to have dropped the condition of giving offence, and adhered only to the requisite of publicity, as was done in the Prussian code of 1851.[1] It has been decided that it is wrong to try and remedy this defect, as Oppenhoff and Rudorff have done, by explaining that any expression is sufficient which is calculated to give offence,

[1] Leipsic, June 12th, 1880.

because the law as well as the report which accompanied the draft code expressly require injury done to the feelings of another, and offence actually given.

The words "opprobrious language" were inserted by the Imperial Parliament to exclude thoughtless expressions, which are well understood neither to mean nor to give offence.

The code also prohibits insults to any of the Christian Churches; that is, the old Catholic, the Catholic, the Lutheran, the Reformed, the United Evangelical, and the Greek Churches, and to any other religious body with corporate rights in the federal territory. Further, all insults to the institutions of such bodies, such as the popedom, celibacy, or confession, and all usages such as the tonsure, processions, and so forth. But expression of opinion and criticism of the basis of such institutions and doctrines is allowed.

The offence of hindering or disturbing the service of God, which is forbidden in § 167, was punished under the Roman law with death, and under the common law with arbitrary sentences of imprisonment. At first only the Christian services were protected, but this protection was later on extended to those of the Jews as well. The Imperial code distinguishes the hindrances directed against individuals, and herein requires violence or threats, and the hindrance of the service itself by creating a disturbance. Under a later section it is provided that, if such offences are committed by an official, it is sufficient, if there be misuse of his official power, or a threat of such misuse, to constitute the offence. The Prussian code also threatens any one, who should compel the performance of divine service, but this the Imperial code allows to be dealt with under the section with regard to compulsion (§ 240). The services which are chiefly referred to are baptism, confirmation, marriage, and burial.

§ 168 threatens the desecration of dead bodies and

graves, offences which have been punished under all codes, because of the outrage thereby inflicted on the feelings of the community, no less than on those of the family. The Roman law punished the *violatio sepulcri* with death, and included thereunder all insults whatsoever offered to the dead body or the grave. The common law substituted an arbitrary punishment of imprisonment. Under the new codes generally distinction is made between the stealing of the body and of objects belonging to the grave. The crime is aggravated, if it is committed by the gravedigger or superintendent of the churchyard, and it is not excused by scientific aims, although in such cases a lighter penalty may be inflicted.

The Prussian code, which is followed by § 168 of the Imperial code, gathers three offences under the *violatio sepulcri*, to wit, the unauthorized removal of a dead body from the custody of the person entitled thereto, unauthorized disturbance of, and insult to, a grave. The removal of part of the body is made a minor offence under § 367, to avoid condemning medical men and students to imprisonment with labour. A grave is constituted by the presence of the dead body. Damage done to a monument is placed under damage to property (§ 304), but is often concurrent with damage done to a grave. The removal of objects from graves is theft. If such objects are removed with the dead body, the offence is theft concurrent with body-stealing.

Of the felonies and misdemeanours in relation to personal rank contained in §§ 169, 170, the only one, of which the common law took proper note, was *suppositio partus*, or changing children. Under the common law, to constitute this offence, the exchange must be made at a time when the child is of so tender an age, that there is no means of discovering his family, and this condition, failing any special provision, is to be assumed to hold good in the Imperial code.

§ 169 further punishes all change or suppression of personal rank, not so much on the ground of the disadvantage which may occur to the individual, as on the ground of the interest the public has that personal rank should be secured by means of the public register. If the offence has been committed from motives of lucre the punishment is increased. The said offence with regard to a child includes not only giving the name of a false mother or father, but also describing a bastard as born in wedlock, although the punishment merited in the last case would often be very slight.[1] § 169 speaks only of the change of the rank of another, and does not therefore include the case of a man, who may be led by vanity to claim a rank higher than his own.

§ 170 is the first satisfactory enactment with regard to marriage under false pretences that has been made since the Bavarian code of 1813. The codes of Saxony (1838 and 1855), of Wurtemberg, Brunswick, Darmstadt, Baden, and Bavaria (1861) all attempt to legislate on this point, with regard to which the Prussian code is silent.

The fraudulent concealment of a legal obstacle to marriage, and the fraudulent misleading of another to marriage, is punished by imprisonment with labour for not less than three months, always under the condition that the marriage has been dissolved for one of the reasons given. Prosecution is only commenced on the proposal of the injured party.

Fraud is defined as deceit to the prejudice of another. Under obstacles to marriage are included not those which postpone, but only those which disturb marriage, and it is through mere carelessness, according to Professor Berner, that the question is that of the dissolution of the marriage, because punishment is never more just than when the marriage is declared null.

[1] Leipsic, Nov. 10th, 1879; May 8th, 1880.

Sexual morality, which is dealt with in chapter thirteen, only concerns the state in so far as it relates to the maintenance of public order and decency. The state punishes offenders for acts, which are in themselves immoral, only so far as such offenders injure the rights of the family by bigamy and adultery, or of the individual by procuring and committing obscene acts in private, or, lastly, the rights of society by committing obscene acts in public and exhibiting obscene prints and pictures. The Roman law makes provision for an official prosecution of bigamy. L. 2: *Cod. de incest. nupt.* "*Neminem qui sub ditione sit nominis Romani, binas uxores habere posse vulgo patet cum etiam edicto prætoris hujusmodi viri infamiâ notati sint. Quam rem competens judex inultam esse non patiatur.*" The Carolina and the common law required besides the existence of the old valid marriage and the consummation of the new marriage, that the offender should know of the existence of the old marriage at the time he contracted the new. In modern times more weight is laid on the formal side of the offence. The offence is complete when the second marriage has been formally concluded, and prescription begins to run on the day, on which one of the two marriages is dissolved or declared null or invalid; bigamy is therefore placed by the lawgiver out of the range of prescription.

A marriage is dissolved by death, or by a declaration that one of the two persons is dead or has disappeared, or by a lawful divorce. A marriage is null, if there is an impediment in its way, such as near relationship, of which the law takes cognizance by an official prosecution. A marriage is invalid, if there is an impediment in the way, of which cognizance can only be taken on proposal. It is not, however, sufficient that the marriage should be null or invalid in point of fact; it must have been so declared by a court of law.[1] The Imperial code requires malicious intent on both sides; but while it requires proof that an unmarried party to such an offence had knowledge of the other's marriage, it presumes the knowledge on the part of a married party. All that precedes the formal marriage is merely preparation, but the commencement of the marriage ceremony constitutes attempt. The offence is completed at the end of the marriage ceremony, and hence, according to Professor Berner, such offence is finished and done with, and a party thereto, who only has knowledge thereof after the ceremony, is not made a party thereto by remaining in the married state with the offender. It does not however appear that the court at Leipsic has yet approved the doctrine that bigamy is not, as the enactment with regard to prescription would tend to show, a perpetual offence in the intent of the code.

The ancient world treated adultery from a one-sided point of view. Roman law punished this offence only in the woman and the co-respondent. The canon law first gave the woman the right of prosecuting her husband on the ground that "*eadem a viro, quæ ab uxore, debetur castitas.*"[2] The Carolina punished the adulterer with death, and the adulteress with imprisonment in a nunnery; for which the common law substituted as usual arbitrary terms of imprisonment. As a rule, the prosecution took place on the proposal of the injured person, but in cases where a public scandal was caused the prosecution was official. The former principle is the one adopted by most modern codes, though the latter has found a place in those of Hanover and Brunswick. The codes of Bavaria (1813), Hanover, and Wurtemberg, punish the woman more severely than the man, but this is now generally recognized as

[1] Hinschius, 'Commentary on the Marriage Law of February 6th, 1875.'

[2] Causs. 32, qu. 4. Can. 4.

unjust. The Imperial code punishes adultery only when it has caused a separation of husband and wife. Hence the question has arisen, is such separation only a condition of prosecution, or a constituent element of the crime? The former view was approved by the Supreme Court at Leipsic, November 6th, 1882. To constitute the offence of adultery, the Imperial code requires besides intent carnal connection between two persons of whom at least one is married, and the consequent separation of the married pair. The period, in which the proposal to prosecute can be made, begins when the decree of a judicial separation comes into force, and prescription begins to run at the same time, because the offence is not till then complete.

Incest must be punished alike on grounds of health and on grounds of morality, but it is doubtful whether it should be made coextensive with the forbidden degrees of marriage, as in the Roman and the canon law. The Carolina in prohibiting incest mentions the step-daughter and step-mother as instances, and hence in practice this clause was extended to all near relations. The French code does not recognize incest at all; the other modern codes have not as a rule made incest coextensive with the degrees in which marriage is forbidden. The marriage law of 1875 was drawn from the standpoint, that it is not advisable to forbid at civil law, marriage between persons between whom the criminal law does not prohibit carnal connection out of wedlock. To constitute the crime, carnal connection must have taken place, and there must have been knowledge of the relationship, it being indifferent whether such relationship rests on illegitimate or legitimate birth. Unnatural offences and obscene acts are thus excluded, and further the code provides heavier punishment for the ascendants, and lighter punishment for the descendants, leaving to the discretion of the judge cases in which, as with step-parents, the elder person is not necessarily the ascendant.

§ 174 punishes obscene acts committed by certain persons of either sex, who occupy positions of trust on those under their care. Obscene acts have been defined by the Supreme Court to be all acts which are grossly offensive to morality and decency in relation to sex; but it is not necessary that such act should aim directly or indirectly at the satisfaction of sexual desire, nor does the fact that an act, though objectively obscene, is not in certain districts generally treated as such, have any influence in the consideration of the acts which constitute the crime.[1]

Unnatural offences were punished under the Roman law, only if committed between man and man, but under the Carolina also if committed between man and beast, and between woman and woman. Modern legislation has retained the first two of these offences in the criminal law.[2]

§§ 176—178 deal with *stuprum violentum*, and *stuprum nec violentum nec voluntarium;* the latter consisted of carnal connection with a person who is in a state of unconsciousness or to whom volition is wanting. If this condition was brought about by the offender with a view to committing such offence, the offence falls under the former category.

The Roman law, like the present Imperial code, punished the rape of boys as well as of women. The earlier German laws, such as those of the Alamanni, the Burgundi, the Frisii, and the Langobardi, punished rape with a heavy fine; the later punished it with death by beheading (Sachsenspiegel), or by beheading in the case of rape of a married woman, and burying alive in the case of a virgin (Schwabenspiegel). The Carolina was equally severe. The common law confined rape to a man as the subject, and an irreproachable woman as object, that is, a woman who, whether maid, wife, or widow, was still in possession of her honour. The crime

[1] Leipsic, February 28th, 1880. [2] § 175.

in this view lay in the injury to the woman's honour, but modern legislators have laid stress on the other side of the crime, the encroachment on the woman's freedom, and some codes have gone so far as to class rape among the offences against personal freedom. The Prussian code was the first to extend rape to offences committed by women on men, excluding however, like all other modern codes, unnatural offences from the category. The new codes, further, may be distinguished from the common law with regard to rape, by the fact that they do not require the woman to have an irreproachable character. The Imperial code does not include women as subjects to this offence, and returns to the common law view of rape as a crime by itself. The offence is constituted by carnal connection with violence. Most modern codes allow prosecution only on proposal, with a view to sparing the woman, except when public scandal has been given. The Imperial code till 1876 permitted prosecution only on proposal, but it did not allow such proposal to be withdrawn when once made. On the other hand no proposal was necessary when the offence caused death. The Novella of 1876 removed the necessity of a proposal once and for all.

In §§ 179—182 the Imperial code further punishes persons, who either induce women to carnal connection by exciting or taking advantage of erroneous ideas, or who seduce irreproachable girls under the age of sixteen under any pretence whatever. The term 'irreproachable' is not, according to a decision of the Supreme Court, identical with the term 'virgin' in the physical sense. To constitute reproach in the sense of the code, some obscene act must have been committed by the girl, which obviously arises from an immoral disposition. The law wishes to protect girls at an age in which physical development exposes them to peculiar dangers.

Procuring[1] is an offence punishable as such apart from

[1] §§ 180, 181.

the fact that it is participation in crime. Personal relationship to the woman concerned, as well as the manner and object of the offence, aggravate its criminality. The code punishes any one who assists obscenity by his presence or by affording or causing an opportunity for it. To constitute the offence it is unneccessary that the obscene act should itself be criminal, but there must be a positive act and not merely an omission, and hence the difference of the two kinds of procuring. Simple procuring is the offence committed either habitually or from motives of lucre; aggravated procuring is the offence committed with the help of fraudulent misrepresentations, or by persons occupying a position of trust on those committed to their care. To constitute habitual procuring it is not necessary that more than one person should have been abetted, it is enough that the act has been committed more than once. If the offender has once acted from motives of lucre, he is liable under this section (180).

The fraudulent representations need not absolutely deceive under § 181, but the obscene act must be committed with a human being, and be completed, to bring the offender within the power of the law. The result of these sections is the prohibition of brothels by the local governments, while at the same time the profession of a harlot is recognized by the police (§ 361, vi.). The wisdom of this measure is at least open to question, for although the state should undoubtedly discourage immorality in every way as the fountain of all crime, some such establishments are certain to be found in large towns as long as human nature remains the same, and it is probably better to place them under the control of the police, than to shut one's eyes to an unpleasant fact in the hope that the evil will cure itself.

§ 183 punishes obscene acts which create a public scandal, and § 184 obscene writings, pictures, and representations.

Under the last head it is to be noticed that no work whatsoever that is produced with a purely practical object renders its author liable to punishment. It is left to the judge to decide whether immoral purposes do or do not lie behind a work which has professedly a scientific object. The Supreme Court has decided that even a scientific work can, in a peculiar edition, be rendered obscene by the way in which certain passages are printed. The publishers of such works and any one who makes them accessible to the public are liable to punishment but not necessarily the composer. To constitute the offence the law requires intent to be proved and the nature of the offence requires the confiscation of all copies and materials even without an order of the judge.

The next thirteen chapters deal with offences against the honour, the life, the person, the freedom, and the property of the individual citizen.

In all matters connected with honour the Germans still hold a mediæval point of view; in fact the generic term employed by the code to denote insult (*Beleidigung*) is a translation of the *injuria* of the common law. In Roman law *injuria* included a number of offences, which are now considered outside the idea of insult, such as bodily injury, imprisonment by a private citizen, hindrances placed on the use of property, forcible entry, and even breaches of confidence with regard to wills, which had been intrusted to the offender's care. These and other such offences were gradually excluded by the common law from this division, but not without a struggle, and never with complete success. The doubtful state of the law led to the permanence of an institution on which it will be necessary to speak later—the duel.

Under the Imperial code insult may be defined as contempt deliberately shown by word or deed of the honour of another by one who has no right to show such contempt. Under honour is included the honour to which each is entitled as a man, as a citizen, and as a member of the class to which he belongs. The extension of honour to credit in § 187 is in this view a mistake, for protection is elsewhere afforded to this right, whether it refers to science, art, industry, or trade. The honour assailed must be that of an individual person, whether such person be named or indicated. A collective unity, as Christians, Jews, cannot be insulted as such, but only those members of it who are distinctly designated by the terms applied. Insults inflicted on a corporate body cannot be prosecuted, except in so far as they are insults to individual members. Hence a commercial society cannot be insulted as such under §§ 185-6, but the individual members can demand prosecution, in so far as their personal honour is affected. On the other hand, once the credit of a society is attacked, it has a right to demand and obtain satisfaction in its corporate capacity. Officials and political bodies are protected from insult under §§ 196-7, but punishment for affronts to religious societies has already been provided from another point of view in § 166.

Indirect insults, *i. e.* insults directed against others than close connections of the person offended, are not recognized in the code. An insult directed against a number of persons only incurs one penalty, and any one who does not join in the proceedings brought by those who were insulted with him, cannot institute fresh proceedings later for his own satisfaction. Affronts put upon the memory of deceased persons are punished when they amount to defamation, and, as is natural, with a lighter penalty than defamation of the living. The right of proposing punishment cannot be inherited, so that if a person who has been defamed dies before obtaining satisfaction, no one can make the proposal in his stead.

Insults may arise from verbal or real affronts or from written or printed lampoons. A real insult in the view of the common law was one which injured some other right as well as the honour of the injured person. Thus, an act of violence against the person was considered a real insult up to the point, at which the violence was more prominent than the insult, when the offence was viewed as a bodily injury. In the Prussian code real injuries were no longer recognized, but in practice the advantage of the distinction became evident, and was made use of in spite of the law, and the Imperial code in readmitting real injuries has merely recognized a *fait accompli*.

The real injury is however limited in the Imperial code to acts of violence: as soon as damage of a serious kind is thereby done to property, it is no longer a simple offence, but a *concursus delictorum* with which the law has to deal.

Verbal insults are those, which arise from word of mouth and, like the symbolical insults recognized by the common law, are often hard to distinguish from an unpleasant joke. The further distinction of insults into *atrox* and *levis*, and the subdivisions *loco, tempore, persona, facto*, are only useful as points of view from which to assess the punishment.

Besides insults properly so called, the code punishes in the same manner under § 186 the assertion or publication in relation to another of a fact likely to bring that other into contempt, such fact not being demonstrably true. To constitute the offence, the words complained of may be spoken in the presence of the person insulted, so long as a third person is present. Under § 187 the code punishes as defamation the same offence as in § 186, if the fact asserted or published is false and known to the offender to be so. It is left to the judge to decide how far confidential communications made in good faith fall under § 186.

To constitute the offences in this chapter intent is necessary throughout, and not, as in the Prussian code, only in cases of the expression of a contemptuous opinion and of the proof of the truth. Besides, the offence must be committed by a person who is not privileged.

Criminality is excluded by the permission of the injured person, by the duties of office, *e. g.* when the judge calls a man a thief, and the rights of masters to reprove servants, and of fathers and teachers to correct children up to a certain age. Further all statements made in a defence in a court of law are protected, if they bear directly on the point at issue, and all statements, which are fair comment on any matter of public interest.

Under the common law official prosecutions for insult were rare; actions were brought by private persons either with a view to private compensation, to a public punishment or fine, or to a withdrawal of the expression used. Under the new codes actions with a view to private compensation, or withdrawal, alone have disappeared. (Cf. §§ 188, 200.) Until the Novella of 1876 proposals to prosecute in private actions could be withdrawn till the commencement of the execution of the punishment. Women and children if insulted have the right of proposing prosecution, and the same right is also enjoyed by their husbands and parents. In the same way, if an official has been insulted in some matter relating to his official duties, not only he, but his superior also has a right to prosecute the offender. When political bodies have been insulted there is no need of a proposal, but prosecution takes place officially, when the sanction of the body insulted has been obtained.

In some instances also the proof of the truth of the insult precludes punishment. The Roman law lays down the limits within which such a plea should be admitted: L. 5, Cod. "*Si non convicii consilio te aliquid injuriosum dixisse probare potes, fides veri a calumniâ te defendit.*" To take the common instance, one has a right to speak of a man as a thief after he has committed the offence, and while he is undergoing punishment, but one has no right to run after him in the streets and call out 'thief' when he has been released. If one has not the right to use a fact, for which the person spoken of is responsible, in this manner, still less has one the right to reproach him with a defect of body or mind, for which he is not responsible. The proof of the truth does not preclude punishment when the form of the assertion or publication, or the circumstances under which it was made, show that an insult was intended. If the fact asserted or published is a criminal act, it shall be considered proven if the person insulted has been condemned in a valid decision for it. But the proof of the truth is excluded, if the person insulted had been acquitted in a valid decision before the insult was uttered. If the proceedings with regard to the crime imputed are in progress, the action of insult must stand over till such proceedings are completed.

In the case of mutual insults, that is, according to the view of the courts, insults interchanged possibly at different times and without any connection, the code makes provision in § 198 that only one trial shall take place, and that if one side proposes prosecution, the other must either make a cross proposal before the matter has been concluded in the first instance, or forfeit his right thereto. Punishment for insult is precluded, if three months have elapsed without a proposal to prosecute being made, if the insult is forgiven, which is possible till judgment is pronounced, and if the person insulted die, except in the case of offences against officials, when the superior retains his right. Further, the insult is considered by the law to have been wiped out if it is retorted "on the spot." The words "on the spot" refer to the justification of the person insulted; for, as Professor Berner points out, they can have nothing to do with the person who is guilty of the insult. This impunity refers to all kinds of insult except those put on sovereigns and cognate cases (§§ 94—104). The Court at Leipsic has decided that a retort to an insult made by a deputy in a debate cannot count as such in a court of law, because the courts have under § 11 of the Imperial code no competence to take cognizance of expressions used in debate.

In the punishment of this offence the common law penalties of the *actio injuriarum æstimatoria* only remain under § 188, and the other kind of private satisfaction, which consisted in withdrawal of the insult, and took the different forms of *declaratio honoris, deprecatio honoris,* and *recantatio,* has disappeared. The public fine and imprisonment have been retained, on the ground that for some insults the former is too light, and for some the latter is too severe a penalty. The former wounds the feelings of the person insulted, and the latter, even in the form of arrest, is degrading to the insulter. Hence the combination which the code enacts. Fines and imprisonment are the alternative, under §§ 185-6, for simple insult and slander, and also in cases of defamation if extenuating circumstances exist; but imprisonment in cases of simple insult and slander may take the form of arrest, in cases of defamation it cannot. Further in the place of the different forms of withdrawal, the Imperial code directs that copies of the decision should be sent to the person who has been insulted, the decision itself made public, and inserted in the public papers at the expense of the guilty person.

A duel[1] is a form of criminal self-help entirely unknown to the ancient world, which was content with actions for injury in cases of insult. The duel arose under the system of club or feud law, which prevailed in the middle ages, and although of German origin, is at present French in form. The right of feud gradually died out, and was finally cancelled by the universal *Landfriede* of 1495. But side by side with this existed the judicial duel, which arose from the difficulty of proof, and under the idea that God will not permit the wrong to triumph.

[1] Cf. Gneist, Zweikampf, Berlin, 1848.

In France this institution became a means of oppressing the poorer classes; in Germany it was employed on the whole with moderation. Under the Sachsenspiegel the duel was only allowed to be used as a means of proof in civil procedure when the lay assessors (*Schöffen*) were in perplexity. In criminal cases it was the ordinary mode of proof, but was kept under the close supervision of the court. When the accused absented himself a mock performance was gone through, and he was condemned as if he had confessed his guilt.

In the 15th century the introduction of the procedure of the canon law furnished a practical mode of proof, and the judicial duel disappeared, and is passed over in silence by the Carolina. There remain however traces after the Carolina of the judicial duel. In cases of insult an accusation was made before the court, a duel was fought, and then judgment was given. This was the *raison d'être* of the battle-courts (*Kampfgerichte*) at Nuremberg and other similar institutions. In this form the duel lasted till the 17th century, when under the influence of French fashion it took its present form. Traces of its historical origin still remain in the weapons used, the challenge and the seconds, and the witnesses. Further the right is confined to certain classes who have the right of bearing arms. The duel continued because of the inadequacy of the law. The *actio injuriarum*, with its compensation of five thalers, was hardly sufficient satisfaction to a man whose honour had been wounded. To remedy this Imperial laws were passed, which gave the additional right to the insulted person of having an apology made to him.

This was hard to carry into effect, and often involved a fresh challenge. The result was that the private duel continued to exist. The Empire had no longer the power or the inclination to enforce its laws, but the sovereigns of the different states issued edicts on the subject. Austria set the example, and was followed by the Electors and other states down to the smallest. These edicts were, however, hard to carry out, because the princes themselves fought duels, and duels were obligatory on persons at court. The sovereign, in fact, as head of the state took a different view to that, which he held as head of society. The result of this contradiction was the multiplication of laws, and this led to such perplexity that soon after the Thirty Years' War the Estates of the Empire took up the question, and passed a stringent law which prohibited duelling peremptorily. Challenge and duel were forbidden on pain of loss of honour and banishment, and heavy penalties were provided for seconds and witnesses. If the duel ended in the death of one party the offence was threatened with death. Duel was defined to be a fight between two persons for the satisfaction of injured honour under mutual consent with deadly weapons. Such a meeting might, however, be unpremeditated, in which case it was threatened with punishment as a rencontre. A one-sided attack was to be punished as such. Challenge was treated as attempt, and the offence was complete when the fight commenced. Seconds were liable as *socii criminis.* This was the state of the common law, but the Imperial ordinance, which should have embodied it, was never actually published, because the officials intrusted with the duty were only too glad to leave a loophole for the old practice. The law was, however, adopted under edicts of the different states with absurdly severe penalties. The Prussian Landrecht is the last embodiment of such regulations. Except in the case of the higher officers of state, the nobility, and officers of the army, the duel was threatened with ten years' penal servitude. The upper classes were threatened with the penalties of attempted murder, and if the duel ended in the death of one of the parties, the other could be sentenced to confinement in a fortress for ten years. The Austrian code of 1803 led the way to reform, and in 1810 an exceptional law was passed in Prussia in favour of students. Since then legislators have treated the duel from the right point of view, with the exception of the Bavarian code of 1813, which does not mention it at all.

It is not an attempt at murder, in most cases there is no intent to kill, but it is a breach of the peace. As an institution it is based on the mediæval idea of classes, and the self-help to which persons then resorted. Professor Gneist calls the duel a relic of barbarism, and is confident that its abolition is merely a matter of time and the progress of civilization. If the English army and English universities can exist without it, there can be no reason why those of other countries should not do the same.

The passage from the work of Liszt in favour of duelling which Sir James Stephen[1] quotes, represents the view of a very large class of persons, and among them, I believe, the view of Prince Bismarck and the compilers of the present code; but I venture to think that it is a view which has had its day. The penalties of the Imperial code are not calculated to extinguish the evil. A challenge and its acceptance is punished with *custodia honesta* in a fortress up to six months, and a higher penalty is threatened in cases of duels *à l'outrance.* The offence when complete is to be punished with from three months' to five years' imprisonment in a fortress. Breaches of the rules of the duel will be punished under the sections with regard to murder and bodily injury. Bearers of challenges may be confined in a fortress for as much as six months; but they are free from punishment if they have really tried to prevent the duel taking place. Seconds, witnesses, doctors, and others who have been attracted to the scene are allowed to go unpunished.

[1] Vol. iii. 104.

The sixteenth chapter, which deals with homicide, presents considerable difficulties to the translator and commentator. Culpable homicide is, as in the Code Pénal, divided into two classes, murder and manslaughter, of which the latter forms a genus, and the former a species under it. Manslaughter is killing with intent to kill. Murder is manslaughter committed with deliberation. Homicide in cases where the offender only meant to inflict grievous bodily injury, or where he is reckless as to the effect of his acts, falls under aggravated bodily injury. But such homicide involves if possible greater moral guilt, greater danger, and a greater shock to the public than the murder which is committed with intent to kill, and carried out with deliberation. Further, premeditation does not always involve greater criminality than *impetus.* It is interesting to note the rise of the distinction between premeditation and *impetus.* The German criminal law of the early middle ages made no difference between murder and manslaughter; the same penalty of death was imposed for homicide under the Leges Bavarorum, the Sachsen, and the Schwabenspiegel, whether the homicide was committed through malice or negligence. The Roman law brought the inverse principle to bear; under the Lex Cornelia de sicariis all acts committed with intent to kill were punished as if they had taken full effect. The canon law combined the two points. Homicide *dolo premeditato* was punished as murder. Homicide committed under the influence of passion was punished as manslaughter. The Carolina adopted the view of the canon law, punishing the one offence with the wheel, and the other with decapitation. The common law treated the offence as aggravated, if committed with the help of poison, and if the object was a master, a relation, or a husband, or wife. The jurists further distinguished murder for money or assassination, murder by treachery, and murder to commit robbery. To constitute the crime of culpable homicide, a human being must have been killed in an unlawful manner by another human being acting with intent.

The basis of manslaughter and its species murder is malice, for both involve wilful killing. The difference between them lies, subjectively speaking, in the manner of the execution. The legislator would seem to have defined murder as a species of manslaughter, and not manslaughter as a species of murder, with a view to avoid the larger number of sentences of death, which would have been passed, if proof of passion was required to constitute manslaughter. With this object of excessive mildness the code requires deliberation to be proved, but that is only another way of saying that deeper *dolus* or malice must be proved. How can this be brought home? Will it be enough to show that a considerable time took place between the formation of the intention and its execution? or that the execution itself took a considerable time, and that only at the end were passions aroused? or that the consequences of the act were carefully weighed, and every provision made to obliterate the traces of the crime. All these are questions of temperament, and the judge must decide in each case *in concreto*. The punishment under the code is raised in the case of the slaughter of an ascendant, the only relic of the old punishment of parricide, and also if the offence is committed together with another criminal act.

Homicide due to negligence is punished as a *delictum sui generis*, if the offender could have thought the result possible.[1] It is a moot point whether such negligence is criminal when the offender could not have thought it possible, but practically a jury would not convict. The important case is that of medical men, who can only be punished for gross carelessness and neglect, but

[1] The fact that the act (*e. g.* leaving a well uncovered) is an offence against a police regulation does not always constitute negligence (Leipsic, Dec. 2nd, 1880).

not so long as they act *bonâ fide* according to their knowledge.

In the same chapter the code deals with child murder, that is, the wilful killing of a new-born illegitimate child by the mother. This offence was distinguished from that of ordinary murder by the Lex Cornelia de sicariis in Roman law. The German law in the early middle ages punished the mother murderess by burying her alive. The Carolina continued the penalty, and the commentators, while they considered it too severe, were far from giving such an act a privileged position. In the "period of enlightenment" in the last century Leyser took up the question, and pointed out the helpless and lonely position of most women under such circumstances, and the combination of mental and physical agitation. The result has been that all modern codes except the Code Pénal have treated the offence as less serious than murder properly so called.

The offence can only be committed by the mother, any one who assists her assists in a common murder. The object of the crime can only be a living illegitimate child at or immediately after birth. The codes of Austria, Brunswick, and Bavaria (1861) do not require the child to be illegitimate; the legislator laying stress rather on the agitation of the body and mind than on the wish to conceal shame, which has otherwise been considered the chief factor in the crime. The Imperial code adheres to the general standpoint, excluding from the term illegitimate children conceived before the marriage though born in wedlock.

"At birth" means during the act of birth, and thus excludes this offence from the class of procuring abortion. "Immediately after birth" includes such space as the judge shall think fit; the code of Bavaria (1813) limited the period to three days, and other codes to twenty-four hours, but it is better to lay down no hard and fast rule in such cases.

The offence deserves least punishment when committed at the moment of birth, but where the condition of the mother was notorious beforehand the punishment must be increased. If, however, the child has never breathed the penalty is lessened; in some of the codes the penalty was that of attempt, in that of Saxony it was diminished to one-half of that appointed for the offence when consummated.

Procuring abortion, which is dealt with in §§ 218—220, differs from child murder, in that the child has not yet a separate existence. In Roman law the offence was only criminal if committed without the consent of the parents; in the canon law and the Carolina it was punished as homicide if the embryo had begun to live: motion was the evidence of life. This distinction has long been given up, since the fact was established that there is no point at which life can be said to begin in the womb. To constitute the crime the fruit of the womb must have been alive, the act intentional and unlawful, *i. e.* not to save the mother's life. It is indifferent how the result is brought about, and the offence is complete when the fœtus is killed. If the child is born the offence is punishable as an attempt. It makes a great difference to the criminality of the act, whether the mother consents or not, and whether the act is done for money and as a trade or not; the Imperial code keeps these facts in view in estimating the punishment to be awarded.

Exposing children was no offence in antiquity, when the parents had the right to dispose of their children. The Christian emperors were the first to make this practice a crime. In the middle ages a distinction was drawn between exposure with intent to kill, and exposure when no such intent could be proved. In the latter case a lighter penalty was awarded for the danger to which a human life had been exposed.

Under the Carolina the only subject of the offence

was the mother, but under the canon and the common law all persons in a responsible position were included, and under the modern codes all persons whatsoever. The Carolina also excluded all but new-born children as objects, a restriction which was afterwards removed in practice, and the law extended its protection to all helpless persons. The punishment under the code varies according to the position of the offender and the result to the person injured; the place chosen for the exposure is also considered in giving sentence.

Bodily injuries, with which the seventeenth chapter deals, were for the most part punished by the Roman law as *delicta privata* under the Actio Legis Aquiliæ and the *actio injuriarum*. A public penalty was, however, imposed by the Lex Cornelia de injuriis and the Leges de vi. The Carolina only enacted a public penalty for the worst cases, such as castration and rendering women barren, and that penalty was death. The practice of the common law filled up the gap thus left with arbitrary penalties, ranging from a small fine to capital punishment. The Code Pénal punishes bodily injuries according to the result, not according to the intention. If twenty days' illness has been caused, the injurer will be imprisoned for from two to five years, and a fine of not less than 1600 and not more than 2000 francs will be imposed. If the injured person has been mutilated or sustained the loss of an eye or other such permanent injury, the offender will be imprisoned with labour for from five to ten years; or, if the person injured has died of his injuries, will be condemned to penal servitude for from five to twenty years.

The Prussian code divided bodily injuries after the French model, according to their consequences. On this principle, at first, two classes were formed of trivial and severe bodily injuries, to which a third of serious injuries was afterwards added. The uncertainty of the test of seriousness for offences induced the authors of the

Imperial code to return to the division into two classes. Serious injuries fell for the most part under trivial offences, and could therefore only receive a small punishment, and could only be prosecuted on proposal, provisions which endangered personal security and the authority of the magistrate. The Novella of 1876 tries to obviate this by abandoning the test of the consequence for that of the danger of the implements used, and of the manner in which the injury was committed.

Under § 232 trivial offences due to malice, and both trivial and serious offences due to negligence, will only be prosecuted on proposal unless the offender was at the same time transgressing duties peculiar to office, calling, or trade. The presence of malice, with or without deliberation, is in many codes a means of graduating punishment, but the Imperial code leaves the question to the discretion of the judge. Provocation is included under extenuating circumstances except in cases where death has been caused.

In cases where the code requires a malicious injury and a definite result therefrom, which was not intended (§ 224), attempt is inconceivable. But a trivial injury must, according to the Supreme Court, be punished with a heavy penalty if a severe injury has resulted therefrom, even though in a manner which no one could foresee. Further, where several persons have taken part in inflicting a trivial injury which results in a severe injury, all of them must be punished not as parties to the trivial injury, but as parties to the offence which has actually been committed. § 225 is inserted to make the law of attempt applicable in cases of severe bodily injuries.

It was formerly a matter of controversy who should be punished for a death which took place in an affray; whether it should be the man who began the quarrel, or the man who struck the last blow, or the man who struck the blow which actually caused death. The

Imperial code has settled the point by making the participation in an affray criminal as such, if death or a severe bodily injury is the result. The Supreme Court at Leipsic has defined a participator as one who co-operates in the struggle physically or intellectually (October 17th, 1881).

Under poison the code is careful to include all substances which destroy health. It is noticeable that a man who administers poison without the intent of killing is, if the poison kills his victim, liable to a heavier punishment than a man who kills intentionally without premeditation (§§ 212, 229). In the same way it is strange that if a man maliciously inflicts on another bodily injuries which cause death, he cannot be punished with more than fifteen years' penal servitude.

The eighteenth chapter deals with felonies and misdemeanours against personal freedom. The Roman law dealt with the offences here mentioned under four heads. Lex Fabia de plagiariis was directed against those who should enslave free men or appropriate the slaves of others, and was extended in the middle ages to include under kidnapping all cases in which men were reduced to a helpless condition with a view to making them serfs or carrying them off for foreign service.

Lex Julia de vi publica punished any man *qui hominem dolo malo incluserit aut obsederit*, and was interpreted as embracing all cases of wrongful restraint and unlawful imprisonment. The Constitutiones of the emperors further prohibited the abduction of girls, and in the middle ages the law was on this point almost identical with that of §§ 236—238, but it was a requisite under the common law that the girl should be a virgin, a provision which the Imperial code does not recognize.

Lastly, the offences contained in §§ 240, 241, were treated in Roman law as part of the extensive category of the *crimen vis privata.*

Compulsion, under § 240, is a misdemeanour against

the personal freedom, but it can be applied by means of force used on things, as, for instance, taking out a window to compel a lodger to leave the house. The force here mentioned is such as to subject the will, and the threat need not be meant in earnest to constitute the offence. The compulsion must be unlawful, and must be known to be so; the offence is complete when the act has been committed, suffered, or omitted. Prosecution under §§ 240 and 241 is now instituted officially. Under § 241 the threat must be of unlawful harm, and the person using the threat must be aware that the act is unlawful. The offence is complete as soon as the person to whom the threat is used knows of it, the object of the law being to protect the peace of private individuals.

Kidnapping of men with a view to exposing them in a helpless condition, or reducing them to servitude, is punished in § 234. The offence is complete as soon as the offender has got the victim into his power. Kidnapping of children (§ 235) consists in taking a minor away from his parents or guardian, the offence consisting not, as in § 234, in the infringement of the victim's personal freedom, but in the infringement of the rights of the parents or guardian. § 235 therefore applies if the minor, but not if the parents or guardian, consent.

Abduction is the withdrawal of a girl from the power of her parents or guardian with a view either to marriage or immorality, and is punished by penal servitude up to ten years in its most serious form, that is, when committed against the girl's will and for immoral purposes.

Withdrawal of freedom (§ 239) consists in unlawfully and maliciously depriving another of his right to choose his place of residence, whether by force or artifice. The offence can be committed mediately or immediately, is complete when the victim has been deprived of his liberty, and is aggravated by the duration and circumstances of the withdrawal.

Under the Imperial code offences against property generally may be divided under three heads: the first, contained in chapters 19—21, embraces six kinds of criminal appropriation; the second, in chapters 21—25, embraces also four kinds of fraud; and the last, in chapter 26, damage to property.

The first of these divisions deals with theft and embezzlement, robbery and extortion, favoring and receiving.

In Roman law, *furtum est cum quis rem alienam invito domino contrectat* (Gaius). Justinian defines theft as *contrectatio rei fraudulosa vel ipsius rei vel etiam usus ejus possessionisve.* The digest adds *lucri faciendi causa.* Thus, under Justinian's definition, a man may steal his own property, if he takes it when in pawn, or if he takes it from the usufructuary. The essential mark of theft in Roman law was handling the property unlawfully; the essential mark of theft in old German law was secrecy (*clandestina apprehensio*). Further, in German law, not only handling but taking possession of the property was required; the wide idea of *furtum* was thus considerably narrowed. Under the Imperial code theft is constituted by taking away any movable property belonging to another with the intent of unlawfully appropriating such property. The definition excludes immovables, incorporeal things like rights, the property of the man himself, and the fraudulent use of property lent or deposited, and requires that the act should be done contrary to the will of the owner, and the thing stolen taken from the custody of the person in whose possession it is, whether that person is the lawful possessor or not. Theft is consummated not by handling or merely carrying away the property, for in the latter case the difficulty would arise how far must it be carried, but by taking it into possession. This would include hiding the property in such a manner on the premises of the possessor that the thief had only to fetch it away; but it would not include hiding it in a place where the possessor could find it, which would only constitute a *preparatio delicti*. Custody is, however, a very wide term, and does not require the knowledge where the thing is or even of its existence, as, for instance, in the case of the animals belonging to the owner of a very large estate. Things which are lost are no longer in custody, and if found can be stolen from the finder. But such things are not lost which are put away, even if the proprietor does not for the moment know where he has put them. In the case, however, of fish and game, the property is out of custody, and appropriation is an injury to the right of fishing or hunting rather than theft. The term 'unlawfully' means without the consent of the owner, and the consent of the owner does not include cases in which such consent has been obtained under false pretences.

The intent of the thief is malicious, the malice consisting in his taking possession of property which is not his own, knowing it not to be his, and knowing further that the possessor has not given his consent to the act. Thus it is no theft, as we said, for a man to take his own property, nor is it theft if he handles that of others merely with a view to damage it, or to reinstate himself in his own rights, though all such acts are offences from other points of view. The *animus lucri faciendi* is not necessary in any sense of the word, it is rather the *animus furandi*, somewhat inadequately expressed in the French code by *frauduleusement*.

Theft under the Prussian code was divided into three classes: simple theft, serious theft, and theft under aggravating circumstances. Under the last head it included objects, over which no careful watch could be kept, in five classes: namely, thefts of beasts from the pasture, beasts of draught from the field, game from an enclosure, thefts of harvested crops from the fields, thefts of wood cut from the forest, thefts by one member of the household from another, and thefts committed in inns by landlords, servants, or guests. The Imperial code makes a great improvement in dividing theft into two great classes, simple theft which constitutes a misdemeanour, and serious theft which constitutes a felony. The latter is punished with penal servitude up to ten years, and may also involve the forfeiture of civil privileges and police supervision. If however extenuating circumstances are found, imprisonment with labour for not less than three months is substituted.

Simple theft under the code may be placed under four heads: the offence may be committed on members of the offender's household or family, or the thing stolen may be wood, or food of small value.

Simple theft is threatened in § 242 with imprisonment with labour, and the sentence may include the loss of civil privileges (§ 248). Under the Carolina simple theft was divided into great and small, according as the object stolen exceeded five gulden in value or not, an enactment which caused no little dispute owing to the variations of the value of the gold ducat. Modern legislation only considers the worth of the property stolen as of moment in assessing the penalty.

Under the common law, theft committed by servants, apprentices, &c. was punished more severely than ordinary theft in most countries, and prosecuted officially. The Carolina punished theft committed by one member of a married pair on the other with the same penalty as ordinary theft. The Imperial code recognizes no theft between husband and wife, and no theft committed by ascendants on descendants. Further, it embraces theft and embezzlement committed by one member of the family or household on another in one section (247). Relatives, guardians, and teachers are placed on the same footing. If the property stolen is in the possession or custody of different persons, or if the property belongs to several persons, and these persons are not all relations to the thief, the offence loses its trivial character and becomes simple theft. The so-called household theft assumes that the servants have free access to the objects stolen. Both household and family theft are only prosecuted on proposal unless a third person, not a member of the household or family, has been a party to the act, or unless the article stolen by a servant or apprentice is of considerable value, and the proposal may be withdrawn.

Theft of fallen wood was, under the common law, punished at one time as simple theft, at another time with a severer penalty. The Imperial code leaves legislation on this question to the several governments, making, however, provision in § 361, ix. for the frequent repetition of this offence by children. The importance of the question may be judged from the fact that there are said to be 500,000 cases of theft of wood annually.

A later section (370, v.) punishes the unlawful appropriation of food in small quantities or of small value as a minor offence, providing a special name (*Mundraub*) to avoid using the term 'theft.'

Relapse was punished by the Carolina with death after the third offence. To avoid inflicting this penalty the courts had recourse to several shifts, among others, not reckoning small thefts at all, and only reckoning serious thefts when the offender had completed his term of punishment. The universal Prussian Landrecht punished the fourth offence as relapse with penal servitude for life. The Imperial code punishes a thief, robber, *quasi* robber, or receiver on a second relapse for simple theft with penal servitude up to ten years, and for serious theft with penal servitude for not less than two years. Extenuating circumstances may reduce the punishment in the first case to imprisonment with labour for not less than three months, in the second case for not less than one year. Relapse thus forms an intermediate stage between simple and serious theft. The latter is treated in § 243.

Theft committed in a church was punished as sacrilege in the Carolina with death. Under § 243, i. theft is punished when committed in any building devoted to divine service, or of any object used in divine service, such as altar-cloths, chalices, &c. The second paragraph threatens all theft committed by entering a building or enclosed space in an unusual manner. The building need not be locked; it must be immovable as a whole, and large enough to allow a man to enter. A space is enclosed when it offers any considerable obstacle to a man breaking into it, but it is not necessary that the access should be locked. The theft must, further, be committed by entry in some unusual way, as, for instance, by climbing over a wall, or by breaking open a receptacle. The next two paragraphs deal with thefts committed by means of false keys, and thefts committed on things in course of transport at railway stations or other such places. The three last sections are aimed at thefts committed by men bearing arms, or by bands of men, or at night-time. The term 'arms' includes anything which the criminal uses as such or could use as such, for the code oddly enough places the genus under the species in this instance. According to Professor Berner the term 'theft at night' was intended by the legislature to mean the time at which men sleep. The Supreme Court at Leipsic has, however, declared it to be the space of darkness between sunset and sunrise. Further, the offence was, in Professor Berner's view, intended to make secret entry and self-concealment constitute part of the offence, while the Court at Leipsic holds that such secrecy cannot qualify theft. Creeping in only requires entry effected with an avoidance of noise and intentionally escaping the observation of others (Jan. 25th, 1882). The thief need not creep in at night-time, but the theft must be committed at night-time on any building, and includes all buildings attached to a house, or on an inhabited ship.

Embezzlement (§§ 246—248) was dealt with under Roman law as theft. The Carolina distinguished two cases of embezzlement—where the property had been intrusted to the offender's care, and where no such trust existed. It was a moot point under the common law whether taking what was found knowing it not to be one's own should be cause for a criminal or only for a civil action. The difference between the thief and the embezzler lies in the fact that the former takes, and the latter retains, what is already in his custody. Custody implies that the offender has come by the property in no illegal manner. The property must be a material object and not merely a right. The intent required is not the intent to enrich oneself, but the intent to appropriate. The code avoids an enumeration of the different kinds of embezzlement, because under the Prussian code such a catalogue led to doubt whether the list was complete or not, and further, because many cases, as, for instance, that of pawning, are best decided *in concreto.*

Robbery (§§ 249-52, 256) was a *delictum privatum* under Roman law, even after the prætor had constituted the *actio vi bonorum raptorum;* but after the Lex Julia de vi robbery committed in arms or accompanied with arson came under the extensive *crimen vis.* Under the later emperors street robbery became also a crime, and robbery by armed men was punished with death. The essential mark of robbery in Roman law was violence, the essential mark in German law publicity; but in practice both ideas were united, as the Carolina omits to define robbery, which it punishes with death. The modern codes have returned to the Roman standpoint, but have often ranked the offence among those against personal liberty. Under the code robbery is theft with violence or threats of immediate danger to life or limb. The person to whom the force is used need not be the owner, or possessor, or even the occupier of the property. The offence is consummated when the property is taken, but the force must be used before the offence as a means to commit it, otherwise we have a concurrence of theft and assault. It is remarkable that robbery with violence is not punished as murder under the code, if the death of the victim ensues, but by penal servitude for more than ten years or for life.

Under the Roman law extortion was treated by several enactments. The *crimen repetundarum* covered cases of public extortion by officials; the *actio quod metus causa* punished appropriation by means of illegal threats. Lastly, extortion by the help of a riot fell under the provisions of the Lex Julia de vi. These, however, proved insufficient, and hence there grew up a series of intermediate cases, treated individually as *concussio*, but for which no general definition was provided. *Concussio* was constituted by extortion *simulato præsidis jussu* by the threat of misuse of official power and of a criminal prosecution. Under the common law and most of the modern codes the term covered a large number of offences, under the Prussian code that of obtaining any unlawful pecuniary advantage by the threat of a felony or misdemeanour. Under the Imperial code extortion is the offence of obtaining money by threatening with any disadvantage whatever, and the offence is complete when the person threatened has committed, suffered, or forborne the act in question. Extortion differs from robbery in that the threat is of future, not immediate, harm; further, the robber takes, the extortioner allows his victim to give; and lastly, robbery is limited to the appropriation of things, extortion extends to all pecuniary advantages whatsoever.

The common law placed the delict of favor by itself and not under participation. Under the Imperial code the same scheme is followed, and favor is punished as such generally and as receiving. In both cases the punishment is lighter or severer, according as the assistance rendered does or does not involve profit to the favorer, a heavier penalty being reserved for the second relapse in this offence.

The twenty-second chapter deals with fraud and breach of trust, a question on which neither the Imperial laws nor the Carolina itself laid down any general principle. The Roman law supplied the gap with its enactments concerning *falsa* and *quasi falsa* and *stellionatus.* The Lex Cornelia de falsis was passed in the time of Sulla against forgery of wills in all forms, and against the counterfeiting of coins and seals. Later the protection afforded to wills was extended by *senatus consulta* to all documents, and the offence of *falsum* was made to cover all use of all forged documents with intent to deceive, all bribery of witnesses and judges, use of false names, fraudulent removal of boundaries, and conspiracy to accuse the innocent. This did not, however, cover all the necessary ground, and hence there arose under the name of *stellionatus* a series of special delicts too trivial to be punished with death and confiscation under *falsum*, and too serious to be left to the civil action. *Stellionatus*, together with *injuria* and the *crimen vis*, was in fact employed to fill up all the gaps in Roman criminal law. The Carolina only deals with the important cases of fraud, such as coining, forgery of letters and seals, the removal of boundaries, starting from the standpoint of Roman law that such acts are offences against the *publica fides.*

In the 18th century an untenable distinction was made by the school of Kant and by Feuerbach between *falsum*, or the injury of the *jus in verum*, and fraud, the injury to property produced by maliciously misleading, the former being the generic and the latter the specific form of the offence. The Imperial code has practically adopted the provisions of the Prussian code: fraud is the unlawful gain of property intentionally made by the offender from the injured person, and to complete the offence it is necessary that the gain should have been intended, and the injury to property have taken place. The man who commits fraud deceives another intentionally by inventing, distorting, or suppressing facts. The offence involves word or deed, mere silence is insufficient; and, further, the words or action must refer to matters of fact, and not to matters of opinion. The damage to property includes all damage to property, to rights or claims which can affect property, including means of proof relating to a lawsuit. The damage to the property must be effected by the deceit, but the person deceived and the person whose property is injured are not necessarily one and the same. There is no responsibility for chance consequences of deceit; the deceiver must have known the possibility of the damage taking place to the property of the other, besides having the intention of unlawful gain for himself or a third person (Leipsic, December 6th, 1880).

The actual invention, distortion, or suppression of facts constitutes attempt, even if neither the damage nor the error has resulted. The offence itself is completed as soon as the damage to property has taken place. Under the code simple fraud constitutes a misdemeanour; repeated fraud, at the second relapse, and fraudulent insurance are felonies. The last named differs from the two former in that for the completion of the crime it is not necessary that the injury to property should have taken place.

§ 266 punishes under the name of breach of trust (*Untreue*) the offences which the Roman law treated as violations of the *mandatum*, *depositum*, *tutela*, and *societas*. The Prussian code confined the offence to persons who are invested with a certain public character, and considered the offence as aggravated if the crime had been committed with the object of gain. The Imperial code follows the Prussian code with two exceptions: it increases the number of persons, and includes not only persons invested with public credit, but persons acting under a private power of attorney (*Privatvollmacht*).

The codes of Wurtemberg and Darmstadt, following the idea of the common law, placed the forgery of documents under fraud as a species, contrasting a forgery of things with a forgery of documents. It became obvious in practice that there is no forgery of things as opposed to a forgery of documents; but where a forgery of things existed, such forgery was as a rule only criminal in so far as it fell under fraud. The Imperial code has, therefore, followed Prussian law, and treats the forgery of documents in a separate chapter[1] on the same footing as the more important attacks on *publica fides*, coining and perjury.

Simple forgery of documents is the forgery of certain documents with unlawful intent, and the use of such documents when forged. According to the Supreme Court at Leipsic (May 19th, 1882), documents in the meaning of the code are "lifeless (*leblose*) objects prepared by hand, which are calculated to prove a fact," and not, as others contend, objects which are intended to prove facts. Public documents differ from private in respect of forgery, in that to constitute criminality the latter must, and the former need not, be of importance for the proof of rights or legal relations. The document may either be forged or fraudulently prepared; in the former case an important change is made in the tenor of a document, in the latter the document is entirely fabricated. If the document is so far altered as to lose its original character, it is said to be destroyed, and this offence is punished under § 274.

Forgery of a document relates to the contents, not to the form thereof. Forgery, in so far as it relates to the form of a document, for instance, forgery of the signature, renders the document counterfeit, and comes under

[1] Chapter xxiii. §§ 267—280.

the head of fraudulent preparation. A distinction is thus made between a document having false contents with a genuine signature and a document which has genuine contents with a forged signature: in the former case the contents, in the latter case the authorship, is spurious. The special case of fraudulent attestation by an official is treated by a later section (§ 348). In forgery as in fraudulent preparation the intent must be unlawful, but it does not cease to be so because the offence is committed to prove a true fact (Leipsic, February 12th, 1880).

The document must have been made and used, or merely used, with knowledge of its falseness, to prove a fact. It is the actual use of the document which constitutes the offence, but this use may be made *per alium*, as in the case of one who sends a telegram in a false name. If the document has not yet been used, but only fabricated, an attempt has been committed; but this is not criminal according to § 43.

The offence is aggravated, if it is committed with the intent of gain to oneself or harm to others. The code further protects the use of paper provided with genuine signatures (*Blankett*) in § 269. The rest of the chapter deals with the use of false or forged documents, causing false attestation to be made, the destruction of documents and landmarks, offences relating to stamped paper, postage stamps, &c., and medical certificates.

The twenty-fourth chapter on bankruptcy is supplied by the bankruptcy law of 1877, under § 2 of the law, which introduced the Imperial code. Under the Roman law and in the middle ages bankruptcy was punished by making the bankrupt the serf of his creditor. Under the common law bankruptcy was punished as theft when the insolvency was fraudulent and with a view to evade creditors, and as fraud or forgery when fictitious.

In the new code the question arose, should the criminal regulations be extended beyond the merchant class? The universal Prussian Landrecht included all classes under the bankruptcy law, and its example was followed by the codes of Saxony (1838 and 1855), Thuringia, Brunswick, and Austria. On the other hand, the Code Pénal confined such provisions to the merchant class, and so also did the codes of Wurtemberg, Hanover, Darmstadt, Baden, Bavaria, and Prussia (1851), and the Imperial code of 1871 (§§ 281—283). The law of 1877 made four alterations in the code of 1871, in extending the penalties to non-merchants, in punishing the debtor for fraudulent preference, and the creditor for selling his vote at meetings of creditors, lastly in extending the regulations as to the joint debtor to the president of commercial societies.

The bankruptcy law requires for bankruptcy in the first place debtors, whether merchants or not, and in the second place, suspension of payment and the opening of proceedings in bankruptcy. Not only has the debtor not sufficient money to meet the obligations he has incurred, not only has he not sufficient money to meet the demands made on him, but he has suspended payment, and as a consequence, though it is not a necessary one, proceedings in bankruptcy have been opened.

Further, to constitute criminal bankruptcy there must have been *culpa* or *dolus*, thoughtless or fraudulent acts. The thoughtlessness may have been in extravagant expenditure, careless management, or rash speculation; such acts constitute simple bankruptcy. The fraudulent acts tend either to diminish the bankrupt's estate, for instance, by the false entry of debts; or to obscure a survey of the estate, for instance, by destroying the books: these acts are closely connected with each other, and constitute fraudulent bankruptcy. The legislator has given no general definition of either simple or fraudulent bankruptcy, but has contented himself with enumerating one by one to avoid confusion the acts, which are criminal. The Supreme Court has decided that several single acts of bankruptcy of § 209 *or* § 210 are one offence and do not form a real concurrence, but that several single acts of § 209 *and* § 210 form an ideal concurrence of offences. The law distinguishes simple bankruptcy (§ 209), fraudulent bankruptcy (§ 210), and independent cognate offences (§§ 211—214). Simple bankruptcy consists in endangering the interests of the creditor by thoughtlessness; such thoughtlessness need not be proved, it is sufficient if one of the acts mentioned can be proved. In fraudulent bankruptcy the intent of prejudicing the creditor is present but, as in simple bankruptcy, the act, not the state of mind, must be proved. In both cases it is necessary that besides the commission of the act the bankrupt should have suspended payment, or be the subject of proceedings in bankruptcy, it being indifferent in the latter case whether the act was committed before or after the suspension of payment or the commencement of proceedings.

The twenty-fifth chapter deals with criminal selfishness and injury to the secrets of others. Games of chance and lotteries are punished from moral as well as state reasons. To constitute criminality the sum at stake must be considerable, so that gambling to pass the time is excluded (Leipsic, October 13th, 1880), and further the game must be pursued as a trade. The permission, whether tacit or not, of gambling in public places of amusement by the proprietor, and the concealment of gambling is also punished, and so too is the institution of public lotteries and raffles without permission of the authorities.

The code protects in this chapter trade-marks on goods or their cases by § 14 of the trade-mark law of 1874.[1] Under that law the name or the form must not be imitated in a trade-mark with changes, which can only be detected by special care, and the mark can only be used even by the firm, to which it belongs, for the goods

[1] Cf. Appendix V.

for which it is registered (Leipsic, May 13th, 1881). The firm which registers the trade-mark must be entered in the commercial register of the place where the firm trades; citizens of foreign countries, who have made special treaties with Germany for the protection of trade-marks, must register at Leipsic. Under § 14 of the law for the protection of trade-marks forgery of the name or form and further exposing for sale or selling articles with such false marks is forbidden. Prosecution only takes place on proposal, and besides the punishment the injured person can demand compensation up to 5000 shillings, in which case as usual all other compensation is excluded (§ 15). The injured person can further demand the destruction of the false trade-marks, and if successful in his suit the publication of the fact at the cost of the defendant.

Poaching[1] is looked upon as an infringement of the right of occupation, and not of the right of property, and is constituted by any act, which has for its object the taking of game on the hunting-ground of another with the knowledge that it belongs to another; this includes even following game, which has been wounded over the boundary. Taking possession is not necessary for the completion of the offence, and the beaters are not participators but assistants in the offence. The offence is considered to be aggravated if other means are used for taking the game than firearms or hounds, or if it is committed within close time, in woods at night, and above all if it is pursued as a trade. In any case the dogs, guns, &c. are confiscated, even if they do not belong to the person concerned.

The same view is taken of fishing for crabs and fish in waters, where the fisher has no right. In its simple form this is a minor offence, but becomes a misdemeanour when committed at night, or by torchlight, or with the help of noxious or explosive materials. The

[1] §§ 292—295.

offence can amount to theft when committed in private waters on fish which are such that they can be said to be the property and in the custody of the injured person.

Under the same chapter the code punishes certain cases of giving credit to minors. The offence consists in its simple form in trading on the thoughtlessness and inexperience of the minor with knowledge of his age, and in the aggravated form in the application of tricks to extort the money by the moral compulsion of an oath or word of honour.

A law of 1880 added four sections to the criminal code on the subject of usury. Simple usury consists in exceeding the usual rate of interest, so that according to the circumstances of the case the advantage gained is in striking disproportion to the amount paid. It includes all cases, in which necessity, thoughtlessness, and inexperience have been made an undue source of profit, and extends to delay in exacting a claim as well as to all classes of loans. The efficacy of the provision will depend on the judges, for its provisions are exceedingly vague. The offence may be aggravated by the attempt to conceal the nature of the transaction under some lawful form of business, or if it is committed jointly, or with the extortion of a promise or oath. Further, a severer penalty is provided for those, who knowingly acquire such debts, and either alienate or exact them, and also for usury as a trade; in the last case criminality is constituted by several usurious transactions, not by raising usurious interest several times on the same transaction.

§ 3 of the law of 1880 describes the results of this offence at civil law, which are sufficiently important to excuse mention of them here. "Contracts which infringe §§ 302 *a*, 302 *b* of the criminal code are invalid. All payments in money or kind made by or for the debtor must be repaid to him with interest from the day, on which they were received; for such payment those persons who have been guilty of the usury are liable jointly and separately, but an offender under § 302 *c* is liable only to the amount received by him or by a successor to his rights. The obligation of a third person, who is not guilty of usury is defined according to the regulations of civil law. The right of demanding the property back falls under prescription in three years from the day, on which the delivery took place. The creditor is entitled to demand back that, which was delivered under the invalid contract; for this claim the security given for the contractual claim is liable. The further rights of a creditor against whom, according to the regulations of the civil law, the invalidity of the contract cannot be set up, are not touched hereby."

Other sections of the same chapter punish the frustration of an execution by making away with property, the purloining of the offender's own property from the usufructuary or mortgagee, the use of pawned articles, the appropriation of ammunition which has been shot away, the taking on board contraband articles, and sailors who abscond with their wages. Lastly, under the head of injury to the secrets of others are punished the opening of letters and the unauthorized revelation of the secrets of others. The opening of letters by the post-office authorities is dealt with by a later section (§ 354).

The twenty-sixth chapter deals with damage to property. Under the Roman law this offence was met by the *obligatio ex delicto*, with the Actio Legis Aquiliæ, and the *damnum injuria datum*, and a few extraordinary cases only were met with a public penalty. The Carolina makes no provision here, and hence the common law applied arbitrary penalties in serious cases of malicious injury. The modern codes punished serious malicious injuries to property according to the motive; the Imperial code more logically makes malice the ground of criminality. The offence in its simple form is marked by malice and unlawfulness, and is considered more serious on the one hand if the property injured is of religious or public character, on the other hand if any structure whatever is destroyed. The damage must in each case affect the property corporeally; for instance, it cannot consist in verbal depreciation of its value, and must further be malicious.

The twenty-seventh chapter deals with offences, which involve danger to the public, that is, danger to human beings or to property, or to both human beings and property. The Imperial code here follows the Prussian code closely, only altering the amount of the penalties threatened, and including injuries arising from neglecting the rules of the art of building under this head rather than under that of bodily injury. The Prussian code, presuming malicious intent from the nature of the act, threatened arson, inundation, endangering railway trains, destruction of fire signals, stranding vessels, and poisoning wells with death, when such offences resulted in the death of a human being. The Imperial code, on the other hand, contents itself with threatening penal servitude, except in cases where both malice and deliberation can be proved.

Arson in Roman law was confined to buildings, and was punished less severely when committed on isolated buildings than when committed in a city. Arson in a city was punished by burning alive when committed from desire of gain or *ex hostili animo;* on the other hand, where the fire was due to carelessness, it was only punished in *luxuria* or *culpa dolo proxima.* Under the Carolina the malicious incendiary was threatened with death, a penalty which was later only inflicted in serious cases.

The general principle, which prevails in the common law and in modern legislation, is that the incendiary must be punished in all cases where the person or property of another person is endangered by his act. The Imperial code limits the objects on which the offence can be committed, defines arson in particular cases, and presumes the danger of the act from the nature of the objects on which it is committed. § 306 punishes arson committed on buildings appointed for divine service, or in which men temporarily abide. § 308 punishes arson in so far as it endangers the property of another. In the former case danger is presumed from the nature of the building, in the latter the property must be that of another, or likely to communicate the fire to one of the buildings mentioned in § 306, i.—iii.

Damage of other kinds than that mentioned in these sections is punished under chapter twenty-six; a later section (§ 368, v., vi.) punishes thoughtless use of fire as a minor offence.

At present the law recognizes no extenuating circumstances in connection with the offence. To complete the offence there must be malicious intent together with a knowledge of the nature of the building, and the building must have actually taken fire. The offender is, however, freed from punishment if he himself extinguishes the fire before it is discovered. With regard to fires due to negligence, the code leaves the question of what constitutes criminal negligence to the discretion of the judge.

Criminal inundation bears the same characteristics as arson, namely danger to the persons of others, or public danger of property. Modern legislation and the Imperial code treat this offence on the analogy of arson, the common law containing no penal regulations with regard to it.

§§ 315, 316 punish persons who endanger railway traffic, including under that term not only the forwarding of persons and things, but the arrangement of the train, when such arrangement is effected by the use of the forces of nature,[1] and not by purely manual

[1] *E. g.* steam-power, the application of the laws of gravity.

labour. The offence may be committed by damaging the permanent way, the rolling-stock or any other appurtenances of the railway, or by preparing obstacles by means of false signals, or in any other way. The grounds, on which the offence can be committed, are those connected with the traffic; real danger is not necessary, it need only be probable.

§§ 317, 318 treat of the destruction of telegraphic communications. This offence, which is often merely due to the wanton mischief of boys, may be serious in times of riot or disturbance, when it is important that the central authorities should be well informed. The penalties threatened are less severe than in the preceding instance, because the danger to life and property is not so great. The Prussian code made any official, who was condemned for this misdemeanour incapable for the future for the service of both railways and telegraphs. The Imperial code merely permits the judge to declare the offender incapable for either branch, whether his act be due to malice or negligence, and if the offender be declared incapable, the code provides that the decision shall be enforced (§ 320).

§§ 321—326 provide for the punishment of all those, who shall destroy roads, disturb water-ways, destroy sea-marks, sink or strand ships, or poison wells, &c. Under the first-named heading are included all means for the safety of mines by the Novella of 1876. Under the last-named are included the poisoning of all things appointed for public sale or use;[1] not only things edible, but other substances, as clothes and carpets; and the danger must be connected with the ordinary use to which the things are put. The same section (§ 324) threatens all those who expose for sale or in any way bring into circulation such poisoned things.

§§ 327, 328 enforce the rules, which the authorities may lay down for the suppression or avoidance of certain

[1] Cf. Appendix XI.

diseases. To constitute the offence the act must be malicious and the rule known.

§ 329 provides that certain contracts of delivery, if concluded in time of war, or need, by the authorities, shall be fulfilled at the right time and in the manner agreed upon, whether failure be due to malice or negligence, on pain of punishment. The offender must have known the object of the delivery, and the offence is considered so serious, that it may involve the loss of civil privileges.

Lastly, in § 330, the universally recognized rules of the art of building are enforced by the criminal law. All persons connected with the operation of building can be made responsible, if through their action danger arise to any person, whether he be engaged on the work or not. It is enough if it is proved that the act or omission would have caused danger to any person had the building been continued (Leipsic, Nov. 22nd, 1881).

The twenty-eighth chapter deals with felonies and misdemeanours committed in office. The Roman law punished bribery and extortion under the *crimen repetundarum,* which was originally intended to meet the case of extortion alone, but was later extended to all cases of misuse of official power. The penalty was three times the amount of the peculation proved, together with banishment; but even this severe legislation proved a failure because of the sums exiles were allowed to take with them into exile.

> "Exul ab octava Marius bibit et fruitur dis
> Iratis, at tu victrix provincia ploras."—Juv. i. 50.

The Roman law, however, made no provision for illegal investiture with office, and this gap was filled in the middle ages from the canon law, which treated such offence as committed against the state. Even the canon law failed to supply any general rule to meet all cases, and the result was that the courts in practice had recourse to arbitrary penalties. The service of the courts in this respect was important, inasmuch as they constituted the only check on the ministers of the sovereign and the sovereign himself. In 1848 the idea prevailed that officials should not be cramped in the exercise of their duties; the Prussian code is therefore no model, and the Imperial code is the first attempt at comprehensive legislation on the subject.

Official offences are constituted by the infringement of official duties, which are based either upon a public appointment, or upon the temporary performance of a public function. All infringements of such duties fall either under the disciplinary law of the office, in so far as they affect the order and dignity of such office, and under the criminal law, in so far as they are of a more serious character. The former sanction protects the rights of the service, the latter protects the rights of the public. Both provinces must be carefully limited, and the legislature has elected in the criminal code to extend the class of criminal offences.

Officials in the meaning of this criminal code are defined in § 359 to be all persons, who are employed in the service of the Empire, and all those who are immediately or mediately in the service of one of the federal states, even though the relation be a transitory one, and no oath of office have been exacted. Under the law of March 31st, 1873, imperial officials are defined as those who are appointed by the Emperor, or who are bound to execute the decrees of the Emperor according to the regulations of the constitution of the Empire. Among officials who are in the mediate service of the state are included officials of the community, the hundred, and the province, but not court and other private officials.

Officials of the Empire are bound by the law of 1873 to fulfil the duties of their office conscientiously, according to the Constitution and the laws, and to behave themselves in and out office in such a manner as to show themselves worthy of their position. For the breach of these rules are provided the disciplinary punishments of warning, reprimand, fine, and dismissal, which includes transference to a less important post, and loss of the title and claim to a pension.

Offences may be divided into simple and mixed, according as they are violations of the duties of office alone, or include a common[1] offence. Further such offences may be divided according as they are confined to a certain class of officials, or are common to all officials alike; for instance, in the first place the perversion of justice, in the second receiving a bribe; it is however better to consider the offences individually.

§§ 331—335 deal with bribery, which involves on the one hand the bestowal, and on the other hand the receival of an advantage, by which influence is brought to bear on official activity. It can be committed on the one side by the public, on the other by officials, members of the military or naval forces, or by arbitrators, jurymen, and lay assessors. There must be a relation proved between the act of the briber and an act of the person receiving the bribe concerning his office or service.

On the one side the criminal act consists in receiving, asking, or permitting a promise of an advantage; on the other side in offering, promising, or guaranteeing such advantage. In all cases the amount actually received is confiscated. Under the code bribery may be divided into three classes. Simple bribery is the giving of money for an act not itself contrary to official duty, and is only punished in him that gives. Serious bribery is the giving of money for an act contrary to the rules of the office or service, and is punished both in him that gives and in him that takes, but more heavily in the latter than in the former. Bribery of persons holding a judicial office is punished with penal servitude on

[1] Common = non-official.

both sides, though extenuating circumstances may reduce the penalty to imprisonment with labour in the case of the briber. It is noteworthy that in this case it is indifferent, whether the person has received the money with a view to an act permitted by the duties of his office or not. The code includes under §§ 331, 332 as bribery, the giving money after as well as before the official act, but the Supreme Court has excluded from criminality the receiving money as a recognition of personal qualities, or as actual proof of thanks or piety[1] (*Pietät*). Receiving small gratuities is not punishable, but the law prevents the payment of any considerable sum for official acts from becoming customary, a custom which often arises in countries where bureaucracy prevails.

§ 336 punishes perversion of justice in the conduct or decision of civil or criminal cases. To constitute the offence wrongful intent is necessary, and the offence may be committed by arbitrators as well as judges, but not by jurymen and lay assessors. If there is concurrent bribery, a punishment of as much as fifteen, instead of five years' penal servitude can be inflicted. But it is noticeable that while the judge, who only receives the bribe and does not commit an act contrary to the duties of office, can be punished with fifteen years' penal servitude, the judge, who perverts the course of justice from other motives than bribery, can only be sentenced to five years' penal servitude.

§§ 337, 338 deal with the solemnization of marriage. Ministers of the Christian or other religions are to be punished, if they perform the ceremony of marriage before receiving proof that the civil marriage has taken place, or with the knowledge that the marriage of which they are performing the ceremony, is bigamous. In the first case, the fact that the minister was deceived, but acted in good faith, excludes criminality.

[1] November 19th, 1879.

In § 339 the code provides against illegal compulsion by means of the mere threat of a definite misuse of official power, whereas the Prussian code prohibited only the actual misuse of official power with intent to compel.

§§ 340—347 deal with different acts of misuse of official power, including bodily injury, unlawful imprisonment, and the conduct of criminal cases.

§§ 348, 349 punish false attestations made by an official authorized to receive public documents, and competent in the particular case; and further all malicious damage or falsification of public documents by the officials, who have access to or the care of such documents. The code requires the intent to damage another to constitute the offence, not, as the Prussian code did, the intent of gain.

The official embezzlement threatened in § 350 is similar to the embezzlement of § 246, but the minimum penalty is higher, and extenuating circumstances are excluded.

§ 351 punishes incorrect book-keeping, and the next two sections the raising of undue taxes.

§ 353 *a*, to which the Arnim incident gave rise, is directed against future infringements of official secrecy and disobedience to official superiors. The next two sections protect letters and telegrams, and the last two sections of the chapter provide against unlawful advice being given by the legal advisers of one side to the other side in a suit, and the misleading of official inferiors by their superiors, together with the connivance of superiors at the unlawful acts of their inferiors.

The twenty-ninth chapter deals with a series of minor offences which belong to administrative rather than to the criminal law; they are rather questions concerning the welfare and convenience of the public than offences endangering the security of the state. The general rules, therefore, which apply to the rest of the code do not apply here. The difference between malice and negligence is no longer important.

Attempt, assistance, and favor are free from punishment. Relapse and concurrence of offences do not raise the penalties attached to them, but in real concurrence the penalties are accumulated; prosecution falls under prescription in three months, execution of the sentence in two years. As a rule only minor offences committed in German territory are punished (cf. § 6). The withdrawal of civil privileges and the admission of extenuating circumstances are excluded. The system of punishment is peculiar: the smallest amount of a fine is one shilling, the largest one hundred and fifty shillings. Fines which the offender cannot pay are converted into arrest, in the proportion of one day's arrest to any sum of from one to fifteen shillings. Arrest can be inflicted for periods of from one day to six weeks. In the case of dissolute persons, labour during arrest, or a subsequent arrest with labour, is permitted for correctional purposes.

§ 360 treats of minor offences akin to treason and forgery, and further among other less important matters of cruelty to animals. Cruelty to animals, which was first punished by the Saxon code of 1838 and the Thuringian code, was defined in the Prussian code as spiteful public torture or cruel ill-treatment. The Saxon code of 1855 defined the offence as wanton ill-treatment, or cruel treatment such as to give public scandal. The Imperial code combines the two, and requires spiteful torture, or cruel ill-treatment such as to cause public scandal; the former including cases where there is no provocation, the latter cases where the offender is angered by the opposition of the animal to his wishes.

It is noticeable, with regard to § 361, that immorality as a trade is punished, if not under police supervision, and also when under such supervision, if the police rules for the preservation of public health, order, and decency are not observed. The same section punishes those, who have the duty of the supervision of children and others for thefts and certain other minor offences of those under them.

The rest of the sections require no particular notice except perhaps § 367, xi., xiii., as to the keeping of wild beasts, and as to the conduct of building operations.

INTRODUCTORY LAW.

1. The criminal code for the German Empire comes into force throughout the federal territory on January 1st, 1872.

2. On the same day the criminal laws of the Empire and of the federal states are repealed, in so far as they cover the same ground as the criminal code for the German Empire.

The particular regulations of the criminal laws of the Empire and the federal states remain in force; namely, those with regard to the criminal violation of the laws as to the press, taxes, customs, fishing, hunting, forests and fields, the misuse of the rights of association and meeting, and the theft of wood (in forests).[1]

3. If reference be made in the laws of the federal states to penal regulations which are repealed by the criminal code for the German Empire, the corresponding regulations of the latter take the place of the former.

4. Till the issue of the Imperial laws for which reservation is made in Articles 61 and 68 of the Constitution of the German Empire, the felonies which are threatened with penal servitude for life in §§ 81, 88,

[1] A third paragraph, providing that the local criminal laws with regard to bankruptcy should remain in effect till the issue of the Bankruptcy Act for the Empire, became obsolete on the passing of that act, February 2nd, 1877.

90, 307, 311, 312, 315, 322, 323, 324 of the criminal code for the German Empire, are to be punished with death, if they be committed in a part of the federal territory which the Emperor has declared to be in a state of siege (Article 68 of the Constitution), or on the scene of operations during a war which has broken out against the German Empire.

Note.—Article 61 (ii.) of the Constitution. "After the uniform introduction of the military organization of the German army a comprehensive military code for the Empire shall be laid before the Imperial Parliament and the Federal Council with the object of arriving at a constitutional conclusion."

Article 68. "If public security be threatened in the federal territory, the Emperor can declare any part of the same to be in a state of siege. Till the issue of an Imperial law regulating the conditions, the form of publication, and the operation of such a declaration, the regulations of the Prussian law of June 24th, 1851, take its place."

For Bavaria the Imperial law of April 4th, 1871, decrees that instead of the regulations of the aforesaid Introductory Law, the matter remain till further notice subject to the directions of the military penal code, which also applies to the legal regulations with regard to martial law. The Imperial law mentioned in Article 61 was passed on May 2nd, 1874, but the law mentioned in Article 68 has not yet been issued, so that this section (4) is still in force.

5. In the regulations of the laws of the federal states, which do not come under the criminal code for the German Empire, the following penalties alone may be threatened: imprisonment with labour up to two years, arrest, fines, the confiscation of particular objects, and the deprivation of public offices.

Note.—This section relates only to future laws; existing laws remain in force according to § 6, even when they contain severer penalties, as for instance the regulations in Prussia as to the slave trade.

6. From the 1st of January, 1872, judgment must only be given according to the kinds of punishment contained in the criminal code for the German Empire.

If in the laws of the several states instead of the penalties of imprisonment or fining, labour in the forest or the parish be threatened or allowed as an abatement, such regulations retain their force.

7. Infractions of the regulations with regard to the payment of the taxes on brandy and beer, and of post dues, fall under prescription in three years from January 1st, 1872.

8. It is reserved for the legislation of the federal states to adopt transitional provisions to bring their criminal laws, which still remain in force, into harmony with the regulations of the criminal code for the German Empire.

NOVELLA OF FEBRUARY 26TH, 1876.

(THE alterations introduced by this supplementary law will be noticed in their place.)

Article I. alters the following sections of the code:— 4, 55, 64, 70 (ii., iii.), 88, 95, 102, 104, 108, 113, 114, 117, 130 *a*, 135, 140, 144, 145, 176, 177, 178, 183, 194, 200, 208, 223, 228, 232, 240, 241, 247, 263, 275 (ii.), 292, 296, 303, 319, 321, 360 (iii., iv., vii., xii), 361 (vi.), 363, 366 (iii., viii., ix., x.), 367 (v., viii., x.), 369, 370.

II. After §§ 49, 103, 223, 296, 353, and 366 of the criminal code the following new sections are added:— 49 *a*, 103 *a*, 223 *a*, 296 *a*, 353 *a*, 366 *a*. After 361 (viii.) another paragraph (ix.) is added.

III. In regard to acts committed before the law

comes into force, the necessity of the proposal to prosecute and the permissibility of the withdrawal shall be judged according to the hitherto existent laws.

IV. In cases in which in the criminal code the amount of a fine or mulct is expressed in thaler coinage, the corresponding amount in the Imperial coinage takes its place.

Note.—The fines &c. were expressed in the old thaler coinage, the place of which was taken by the new mark[1] coinage (July 9th, 1873).

V. The Chancellor of the Empire is empowered to make known the text of the criminal code according to the changes introduced by Articles I., III., IV., with the omission of §§ 287, 337, by means of the Imperial Law Gazette.

[1] 'Mark' has been throughout translated by 'shilling.' Accurately speaking twenty shillings are worth $3\frac{1}{2}d.$ more than twenty marks.

THE CRIMINAL CODE FOR THE GERMAN EMPIRE.

INTRODUCTORY PROVISIONS.

1. An act, which is threatened with death, with penal servitude, or with confinement in a fortress for more than five years, is a felony.

An act, which is threatened with confinement in a fortress up to five years, with imprisonment with labour, or with a fine of more than 150 shillings is a misdemeanour.

An act, which is threatened with arrest or with a fine up to 150 shillings, is a minor offence.

2. An act, can only be met with a punishment in those cases, in which such punishment was appointed by law before the act was committed.

If the law change between the time, at which the act was committed, and that, at which the act was judged, the milder law is to be applied.

3. The criminal laws of the German Empire are applicable to all criminal acts committed in German territory, even if the author is a foreigner.

Note.—The districts of German consular courts are German territory within the meaning of this section.

4.[1] As a rule no prosecution takes place with regard to felonies and misdemeanours committed in a foreign country. (Cf. §§ 102, 298.)

Nevertheless a prosecution according to the criminal laws of the German Empire can be brought against:—

(i.) A German or a foreigner, who has committed in

[1] Novella of 1876.

a foreign country an act of high treason against the German Empire, or one of the federal states, or a coinage felony, or who, as an official of the German Empire or one of the federal states, commits an act which is to be considered as an official felony or misdemeanour according to the laws of the German Empire.

Note.—It is not necessary that the coinage felony should be committed against the Empire or a federal state. (With (i.) cf. §§ 80—86, 146, 147, 149, 331 and foll.)

(ii.) A German who has committed in a foreign country an act of treason against the German Empire or one of the federal states, or an insult against one of the federal princes.

(iii.) A German who has committed in a foreign country an act which is to be looked on as a felony or misdemeanour according to the laws of the German Empire, and which is threatened with punishment by the laws of the place in which the act was committed.

Prosecution is also permissible if the author was not yet a German at the time he committed the act. In this case however a proposal to prosecute must be made by a competent magistrate of the country in which the criminal act was committed, and the foreign law is to be applied in so far as it is milder.

5. In cases under § 4 (iii.) prosecution is excluded if:—

(i.) A foreign court has given a valid decision with regard to the act, and either an acquittal has followed or the sentence passed has been carried into effect. (Cf. § 37.)

(ii.) The criminal prosecution or the execution of the punishment falls under prescription, or the penalty is remitted.

(iii.) If the proposal on the part of the injured person, which is necessary according to the laws of the foreign country to make prosecution for the act possible, has not been made.

6. Minor offences committed in a foreign country are only to be punished in cases where provision is made for such punishment by means of particular laws or by treaties.

7. A punishment suffered in a foreign country is to be reckoned in considering the punishment to be awarded if a fresh condemnation ensues in the territory of the German Empire for the same act. (Cf. §§ 3, 4, i., ii., iii.)

8. Foreign country within the meaning of this criminal code is every territory which does not belong to the German Empire.

9. A German must not be delivered up to a foreign government for prosecution or punishment.

Note.—Extradition treaties exist between the Empire and Italy, Great Britain, Switzerland, Belgium, Luxemburg, Brazil, Sweden and Norway, Spain, and for Alsace-Lorraine with France.

10. The universal criminal laws of the Empire are applicable to members of the German military service so far as the military laws do not enact otherwise.[1]

11. No member of a parliament or chamber of a state belonging to the Empire can be made responsible outside the assembly, to which he belongs, for his vote or for expressions used in the practice of his vocation.

12. Truthful reports of the proceedings of a parliament or chamber of a state belonging to the Empire are free from all responsibility.

[1] The military criminal code of June 20th, 1872, is now in force throughout the Empire for members of the military service.

FIRST PART.

OF THE PUNISHMENT OF FELONIES, MISDEMEANOURS, AND MINOR OFFENCES IN GENERAL.

FIRST CHAPTER.

PUNISHMENTS.

13. THE punishment of death is to be carried into effect by means of decapitation.

14. The punishment of penal servitude is either lifelong or temporary.

The longest term of temporary penal servitude is fifteen years, the shortest term one year.

Where the law does not expressly threaten the punishment of penal servitude as lifelong it is temporary. (Cf. § 19.)

15. Persons condemned to the punishment of penal servitude, are to be kept in the penal institution at the appointed work.

They can also be employed on work outside the institution, especially on public works or works under the supervision of a public magistrate. This kind of employment is only permissible, if the prisoners are therein kept separate from the free labourers.

16. The longest term of imprisonment with labour is five years, the shortest term one day. (Cf. §§ 57, 74.)

Persons condemned to imprisonment with labour, can be employed in a prison institution according to their capacities and circumstances; at their request they are to be employed in this manner.

Employment outside the institution (§ 15) is only permissible with their consent.

17. Confinement in a fortress is either lifelong or temporary.

The longest term of temporary confinement in a fortress is fifteen years, the shortest term one day.

Where the law does not expressly threaten confinement in a fortress as lifelong, such confinement is temporary.

The punishment of confinement in a fortress consists in the withdrawal of freedom, together with supervision of the employment and mode of life of the prisoner; it will be carried into effect in fortresses or in other places appointed for that purpose.

18. The longest term of arrest is six weeks, the shortest term one day. (Cf. §§ 77, 78.)

The punishment of arrest consists in the mere withdrawal of freedom.

19. In punishments of imprisonment the day will be reckoned as twenty-four hours, the week as seven days, and the month and year according to the calendar.

The length of a term of penal servitude may only be measured according to complete months, the length of other terms of imprisonment only according to complete days. (Cf. § 74, *note.*)

20. Where the law gives the choice between penal servitude and confinement in a fortress, penal servitude must only be awarded, if it is proved that the act which has been found to be criminal arose from a dishonourable disposition. (Cf. §§ 82—86, 88, 89, 94, 96, 98, 100, 105, 106.)

21. Eight months' penal servitude is to be considered as equivalent to one year's imprisonment with labour; eight months' imprisonment with labour as equivalent to one year's confinement in a fortress.

22. The punishment of penal servitude and imprisonment with labour can be carried into effect in solitary

confinement for the whole or part of the term of the sentence in such a manner that the prisoner be kept continually separate from the other prisoners.

No prisoner must be sentenced to solitary confinement for more than three years without his consent.

23. Persons condemned to a longer term of penal servitude or imprisonment with labour may with their consent be provisionally released when they have completed three-fourths, but at least one year, of the punishment imposed on them, if they have conducted themselves well during this period.

24. The provisional release can be revoked at any moment, if the released prisoner conducts himself ill or acts contrary to the duties imposed on him at his release.

The revocation has the effect that the time, which has elapsed from his provisional release till he is re-committed, is not reckoned as part of the appointed term of punishment.

25. The decision with regard to the provisional release, and also the revocation of the same, issues from the supreme officials for the supervision of justice. Before the decision with regard to the provisional release the prison authorities are to be heard.

A prisoner who has been provisionally released may, if the public welfare urgently require, be temporarily apprehended by the police magistrate of the place at which he resides. Application must be immediately made for the decision with regard to the final legal revocation.

If the temporary apprehension leads to a revocation, such revocation dates as if it had ensued on the day of the apprehension.

26. If the appointed term of punishment has expired without the provisional release being revoked, the punishment of imprisonment is held to be expiated (*verbüsst*).

27. The smallest amount of a fine is in the case of

felonies and misdemeanours three shillings, and in the case of minor offences one shilling.

28. A fine, which cannot be levied, is to be converted into imprisonment with labour, and if it has been awarded for a minor offence into arrest.

If in the case of a misdemeanour a fine is threatened alone, or in the first instance or optionally with arrest, the fine can be converted into arrest, if the punishment awarded does not exceed the amount of 600 shillings, and the punishment of imprisonment which takes its place does not exceed a term of six weeks.

If penal servitude be awarded together with the fine, the punishment of imprisonment with labour which takes its place is to be converted into penal servitude according to the standard of § 21.

The person condemned can free himself from the last by payment of the amount of the fine so far as such punishment is not yet discharged by the punishment of imprisonment which has arisen therefrom.

Note. — The omission of a reference to the source or name of an author in a scientific or literary work makes the person who occasions or allows it liable to a fine of not more than sixty shillings, which may not be converted into imprisonment (law of June 11th, 1870). Further a fine may not be converted in cases under § 15 of the law of June 6th, 1869.

29. In the conversion of a fine awarded for a felony or misdemeanour, a day's imprisonment is to be held equivalent to an amount of from three to fifteen shillings; in the conversion of a fine awarded for a minor offence it is to be held equivalent to an amount of from one to fifteen shillings.

The shortest term of a punishment of imprisonment which takes the place of a fine is one day; the longest term in the case of arrest, six weeks, in the case of imprisonment with labour, one year. If, however, a punishment of imprisonment, which is threatened optionally with the fine, does not reach in duration the longest term above provided, the punishment of imprisonment which takes the place of such fine cannot exceed the longest term threatened of that punishment of imprisonment.

30. A fine can only be exacted from an inheritance, if the judgment became valid during the lifetime of the person condemned.

31. Condemnation to penal servitude involves permanent incapacity to serve in the German army and the Imperial navy, as well as the incapacity to hold public judicial offices.

Under public offices in the meaning of this criminal code are included those of advocate, attorney (*Anwalt*), and notary, as well as the services of juryman and lay-assessor.

Note.—In § 359 *infra* the code distinguishes from the above public offices the position held by state servants (*Beamte*).

32. To the punishment of death and that of penal servitude may be added the forfeiture of civil privileges. To the punishment of imprisonment with labour such forfeiture may only be added, if the length of the punishment awarded reaches three months, and either the law expressly permits the forfeiture of civil privileges, or the punishment of imprisonment with labour is the sentence passed on account of the admission of extenuating circumstances.

The duration of such forfeiture is in cases of penal servitude two years at the least and ten years at the most, in the case of imprisonment with labour at the least one year and at the most five years.

Note.—In cases of perjury (§ 161), aggravated procuring (§ 181), and usury as a trade (§ 302), the loss of civil privileges is a necessary consequence of conviction. This forfeiture is expressly permitted by the code in §§ 49 *a*, 108, 109, 133, 142, 143, 150, 160, 161, 164, 168, 173,

175, 180, 183, 248, 256, 262, 263, 266, 280, 284, 289, 294, 302, 304, 329, 333, 350. In cases of attempt cf. § 45; youthful criminals, § 57 (v.); and concurrence, § 76.

33. The sentence of withdrawal of civil privileges involves the permanent forfeiture of the rights derived by the person condemned from public election, and in like manner the permanent loss of public offices, dignities, titles, orders, and insignia of honour.

34. The sentence of withdrawal of civil privileges further involves during the period appointed in the sentence, incapacity—

(i.) To wear the national cockade.

(ii.) To enter the German army or the Imperial navy.

(iii.) To acquire public offices, dignities, titles, orders, and insignia of honour.

(iv.) To vote on public affairs, to elect or be elected, or exercise other political rights.

(v.) To act as witness at the admission of documents.

(vi.) To act as trustee, co-trustee, curator, counsel at law, or member of a family council, even when it is a question of a relation in the descending line and the supreme official trustee or the family council gives its sanction.

35. With a sentence of imprisonment, with which a sentence of withdrawal of civil privileges could have been united at all, a further sentence of incapacity to hold public offices for a term of from one to five years can be pronounced.

The sentence of withdrawal of the capacity to hold public office involves the permanent forfeiture of judicial offices held. (Cf. §§ 128, 129, 331, 339—341, 352—355, 357, 358.)

36. The effect of the sentence of withdrawal of civil privileges in general, no less than that of the capacity to hold public office in particular, comes into operation as soon as the decision is legally valid. The term will

be reckoned from the day, on which the punishment of imprisonment, with which the sentence of withdrawal was pronounced, was completed, fell under prescription, or was remitted.

37. If a German has been punished in a foreign country for a felony or misdemeanour, which, according to the laws of the German Empire, involves or can involve the forfeiture of civil privileges in general or in particular, fresh criminal proceedings are permissible to give an award on that issue against the person declared guilty in the former proceedings.

38. With a punishment of imprisonment the sentence may also in certain cases, for which provision is made by the law, permit police supervision.

(Cf. §§ 44, 49 *a*, 115, 116, 122, 125, 146, 147, 180, 181, 248, 256, 262, 294, 325; also 45, 57 (v.), and 76.)

The higher police magistrates in the different states receive through such a decision the competence, after referring to the administrative officials of the prison, to place the convict under police supervision for a period at the most of five years.

This period is reckoned from the day on which the punishment of imprisonment was completed, fell under prescription, or was remitted.

39. Police supervision has the following effects:—

(i.) The convict may be forbidden to reside at certain definite places by the higher police magistrates of the different states.

(ii.) The higher police magistrates of the different states are authorized to expel a foreigner from the federal territory.

(iii.) There is no restriction as regards the time at which houses may be searched.

40. Objects which are produced by a deliberate felony or misdemeanour, or which are used or intended for committing a deliberate felony or misdemeanour, can be confiscated in so far as they belong to the author

or a participator. The confiscation is to be pronounced in the judgment.

Note.—Confiscation is obligatory in §§ 152, 295, 369. There are special directions for certain minor offences: cf. §§ 360, 367, 369 (ii.).

41. If the contents of a writing, drawing, or representation are criminal, it must be announced in the judgment that all copies, as well as the plates and types intended for their production, are to be rendered useless.

This direction however refers only to the copies in the possession of the author, the printer, editor, publisher, or bookseller, and those which are openly exposed or offered for sale.

When only one part of the writing, drawing, or representation is criminal, then so far as a distinction is possible, announcement must be made in the judgment that only those criminal passages and that part of the plates and types, in which these passages are found, are to be rendered useless.

Note.—The Supreme Court of Berlin decided no less than four times that such writings could be seized even if no criminal act existed, that is, no person to be prosecuted. This has not yet been confirmed by the Supreme Imperial Court at Leipsic. With regard to immoral pictures cf. § 184.

42. If in the cases mentioned in §§ 40, 41 the prosecution or condemnation of a definite person cannot be carried into effect, the measures there provided can be decided on independently. (Cf. § 152.)

Note.—This provision is only to be applied, if the prosecution of a certain person really is not feasible, not when it is impossible on legal grounds, for instance, for the want of a proposal to prosecute.

SECOND CHAPTER.

ATTEMPT.

43. A PERSON who has realized the intent to commit a felony or misdemeanour by acts, which involve a commencement of the execution of such felony or misdemeanour, is to be punished for attempt if the proposed felony or misdemeanour did not reach consummation.

Attempt to commit a misdemeanour shall, however, only be punished in those cases, in which the law expressly directs such punishment.

Note.—Attempt is liable to punishment in the following misdemeanours: §§ 107, 120, 141, 148, 150, 168, 169, 240, 242, 246, 253, 263, 289, 303—305, 339, 350, 352. In minor offences attempt is free from punishment.

44. An attempted felony or misdemeanour is to be punished less severely than one which has been consummated.

If the felony when consummated is threatened with death or penal servitude for life, penal servitude for not less than three years takes place, and with this the sentence may also permit police supervision.

If the felony, when consummated, is threatened with confinement in a fortress for life, confinement in a fortress for not less than three years takes place.

In all other cases the punishment can be lessened down to a quarter of the smallest amount of punishment, whether of imprisonment or fine, with which the felony or misdemeanour if consummated was threatened. If in this manner penal servitude for less than one year is incurred, such penal servitude is to be converted into imprisonment with labour according to § 21.

Note.—Exceptional cases, in which the full punishment is awarded for theft, occur in the Prussian law of April

4th, 1878, with regard to forest thefts, and the Prussian law of January 4th, 1880, with regard to the police of field and forest. It has been decided at Leipsic that a quarter of a month is eight days, not one week (February 13th, 1882).

45. If together with the punishment for the consummated felony or misdemeanour the sentence of withdrawal of the civil privileges is permitted or directed, or if the sentence permits police supervision, the same holds good with regard to the punishment for attempt.

46. Attempt as such remains unpunished—

(i.) If the author has given up the execution of the intended act, without having been hindered in such execution by circumstances which were independent of his will; or

(ii.) If he, at a time at which the act was not yet discovered, has by his own activity averted the occurrence of the result requisite to the consummation of the felony or misdemeanour.

THIRD CHAPTER.

PARTICIPATION.

47. If several persons carry out a criminal act with a common intention, each shall be punished as author.

48. A person who has deliberately determined another person to the criminal act committed by such other person by gifts or promises, by threat, by misuse of authority or power, by intentionally producing or promoting an error, or by other means, shall be punished as abettor.

The punishment of the abettor is to be decided according to the law which is applied to the act in which he has knowingly abetted another.

Note.—Abetting is criminal in all three classes of offences. Cf. special cases of abetting, §§ 85, 110, 111, 159, 160.

49. The person who by word or deed has knowingly rendered help to the author in the commission of a felony or misdemeanour shall be punished as an assistant.

The punishment of assistants is to be decided according to the law, which is applied to the act to which he has knowingly rendered assistance; such punishment is however to be lessened according to the principles set forth for the punishment of attempt.

Note.—Assistance to a minor offence is free from punishment.

It is not necessary that the offender should know of the assistance (Leipsic, September 23rd, 1880), even if the act of assistance produced no result (Leipsic, April 20th, 1882).

An exception is made to this section under § 143. Exceptions are made for Prussia by laws relating to thefts committed in forests (March 18th, 1878), and the police for fields and forests (April 4th, 1880).

49 *a.*[1] Any one who invites another to commit a felony or to participate in a felony, or any one who accepts such an invitation, shall, in so far as the law does not threaten another punishment, be punished by not less than three months' imprisonment with labour if the felony is threatened with death or penal servitude for life, by imprisonment with labour up to two years or with confinement in a fortress for a like period if the felony is threatened with a lighter punishment.

A like punishment is incurred by the person who proffers himself for the commission of a felony, or for participation in a felony, as well as the person who accepts such a proffer.

However invitation or proffer merely expressed by

[1] Novella of 1876.

word of mouth, and the acceptance of such invitation or proffer, shall only be punished in cases in which the invitation or proffer is united to the promise of any advantages whatsoever.

To the punishment of imprisonment with labour the sentence may add the withdrawal of civil privileges and may further permit police supervision.

50. If the law raises or lessens the criminality of an act according to the personal qualities or circumstances of the person, who has committed that act, these peculiar conditions are to be imputed to that author or that participator (joint author, instigator, or assistant) in whom they exist. (Cf. §§ 215, 217, 221, 223, 340, 341, 343, 348, 349, 351, and §§ 57, 157, 158.)

FOURTH CHAPTER.

GROUNDS WHICH EXCLUDE OR EXTENUATE PUNISHMENT.

51. There is no criminal act, if the author was at the time he committed the act in a state of unconsciousness (*Bewusstlosigkeit*), or morbid disturbance of the activity of his mind, through which free volition on his part was precluded.

52. There is no criminal act, if the author has been compelled by irresistible power or by a threat, which was joined with immediate danger, which could not otherwise be averted, to the life or limb of himself or one of his relatives (*Angehörige.*)

Relations[1] and connections by marriage[2] in the ascending and descending line, adoptive and foster parents and children, husbands and wives, brothers

[1] This includes legitimate and illegitimate relations.

[2] This includes parents and children-in-law, step-parents and step-children.

and sisters and their wives and husbands, and betrothed persons are to be considered relatives within the meaning of this criminal law. (Cf. §§ 54, 213, 247, 258, 263.)

53. There is no criminal act if the act was demanded by self-defence (*Nothwehr*).

Self-defence is the defence, which is requisite to avert an immediate unlawful assault from oneself or another.

To exceed self-defence is not criminal, if the author has gone beyond the limits of defence through confusion, fear, or terror.

Note.—The second paragraph contains ground of justification, the third merely ground for excuse. The common assumption of both paragraphs is the defence of one's rights.

According to the Imperial code of criminal procedure, the question whether there has been excess in self-defence is one for the court, not for the jury, because the main question of guilt is decided in the negative.

54. There is no criminal act, if the act beyond the case of self-defence was committed in unmerited and inevitable stress (*Nothstand*), for the preservation of the author, or a relative of his, from an immediate danger to life or limb.

55. A person, who at the time he committed the act had not completed his twelfth year, cannot be prosecuted for such act according to the criminal law.

Against such a person, however, the measures suitable for his improvement and supervision can be taken according to the regulations of the different states. In particular, such a person can be quartered in an institution for education and improvement after that the commission of the act has been proved, and such quartering declared permissible by decree of the official guardians.

Note.—The first paragraph applies also to the laws of the several states, the second was added by the Novella of 1876.

56. An accused person, who has committed a criminal act, at a time when he had completed his twelfth but not his eighteenth year, is to be acquitted, if at the time he committed such act he did not possess the intelligence necessary to the knowledge of its criminality.

(*Note.*—This is a question for the jury.)

The judgment must direct whether the accused shall be intrusted to his family, or be conveyed to an institution for education or improvement. In the institution he is to be detained so long as the administrative magistrate at the head of the institution considers such detention necessary; not, however, after he has completed his twentieth year. (Cf. § 361, ix.)

57. If an accused person, who has committed a criminal act, at a time when he had completed his twelfth but not his eighteenth year, possessed at its commission the intelligence necessary to the knowledge of its criminality, the following directions come into operation against him:—

(i.) If the act is threatened with death or penal servitude for life, imprisonment with labour for from three to fifteen years is to be awarded.

(ii.) If the act is threatened with confinement in a fortress for life, confinement in a fortress for from three to fifteen years is to be awarded.

(iii.) If the act is threatened with penal servitude or another kind of punishment, the punishment is to be determined between the legal minimum of the kind of punishment threatened and half of the maximum of the punishment threatened.

If the punishment so determined is penal servitude, the punishment of imprisonment with labour of equal duration takes its place.

(iv.) If the act is a misdemeanour or minor offence, then in particularly unimportant cases a reprimand may be inflicted.

(*Note.*—The reprimand is, failing special legislation,

left to the discretion of the judge, who can administer it in writing or by word of mouth.[1])

(v.) The sentence may not include the forfeiture of civil privileges in general, or of particular civil privileges, and the permissibility of police supervision.

The punishment of imprisonment is to be carried into effect in particular institutions or places appointed for the expiation of punishment by young persons.

58. A deaf mute, who did not possess the intelligence necessary to the knowledge of the criminality of an act committed by him, is to be acquitted.

Note.—This is a question for the jury. Cf. the code of criminal procedure, § 298.

59. If a person in committing a criminal act was ignorant of the presence of circumstances in the case, belonging to the body of facts which constitute criminality in the eyes of the law (*corpus delicti*), or which augment the criminality, such circumstances are not to be imputed to him.

In punishing acts committed from negligence this direction only holds good, so far as the ignorance itself is not caused by negligence.

60. When judgment is given the arrest, which has been undergone during the inquiry, can be reckoned wholly or partially as fulfilment of the punishment.

61. An act, the prosecution of which only takes place on a proposal, cannot be prosecuted, if the person, who has the right to make the proposal, omits to make the proposal within three months. This term begins to run from the day, on which the person who has the right to make the proposal, has had knowledge of the act and of the personality of the author.

Note.—The following criminal acts require a proposal:— §§ 102, 103, 104, 123, 170, 172, 179, 182, 189, 194, 195, 196, 232, 236, 237, 247, 263, 288, 289, 292, 293, 299, 300, 301, 302, 303, 370 (v., vi.).

[1] Cf. Appendix I., Introductory Law for Alsace-Lorraine, § 12.

Cf. also the Imperial laws as to pirated editions, sailors, the press, patents, trade-marks, rights of authors. The following decisions have been given by the Supreme Court at Leipsic. No presumption of knowledge will be made, but earlier knowledge can be proved. On the other hand, a proposal for criminal proceedings made without the knowledge of the author of the act is effectual. The name of the author of the act need not be stated.

62. If several persons have a right to make the proposal, and one of them allows the term of three months to pass, the right of the rest is not thereby precluded. (Cf. §§ 198, 222.)

63. The proposal cannot be divided. The legal proceedings take place against all persons, who have participated in the act (authors and participators), as well as against the favorer, even if the proposal for punishment is only made against one of these persons.

Note.—For favorers (accessories after the fact) cf. § 257.

Exceptions from the above are to be found in §§ 247, 263, 292, 303.

64. The withdrawal of the proposal is only permissible in the cases, for which the law has made especial provision, and only till the publication of a judicial sentence.

The timely withdrawal of the notice against one of the persons previously indicated involves the suspension of proceedings against the others also.

Note.—The Novella of 1876 qualified the permission to withdraw such proposals, which was formerly universally allowed. Such withdrawal is now only possible under §§ 102, 103, 104, 194, 232, 247, 263, 292, 303, and 370.

Withdrawal before a competent official cannot be revoked. Compromise or mere renunciation without withdrawal of the proposal before the magistrate, or before making the proposal, and even judicial renunciation are ineffectual.

Costs are borne by the maker of the proposal in cases where it is withdrawn (code of criminal procedure, § 502).

From the withdrawal of the proposal, (which is also necessary for the public action,) must be distinguished the withdrawal of the private action in cases of insult and bodily injury (code of criminal procedure, § 431). The last-mentioned action can be withdrawn till the judgment of the court of second instance is pronounced.

65. The injured person, who has not completed his eighteenth year, has the independent right to make the proposal for punishment.

So long as the injured person is a minor, his legal representative has the right to make the proposal independently of the special authorization of the injured person.

For insane persons and deaf mutes who are provided with a guardian, the guardian has the right to make the proposal.

Note.—If the legal representative of sick persons is himself author or participator in the act, a special representative must be appointed for the injured party. The term of three months (§ 61) begins to run from the day on which the curator has knowledge of the injury.

66. Criminal prosecution and the carrying the punishment into effect will be precluded by prescription.

67. Criminal prosecution of felonies falls under prescription—

(i.) In twenty years, if such felonies are threatened with death or penal servitude for life.

(ii.) In fifteen years, if threatened at the utmost with imprisonment for more than ten years.

(iii.) In ten years, if threatened with a shorter term of imprisonment.

Criminal prosecution of misdemeanours, which are

threatened at the utmost with a longer term of imprisonment than three months, falls under prescription in five years, that of other misdemeanours in three years.

Criminal prosecution of minor offences falls under prescription in three months.

Prescription begins with the day on which the act is committed, without regard to the date at which the result came to pass.

Note.—Special periods are enacted in the press law, § 22; the seaman's ordinance, § 100; trade ordinance, § 145. (Cf. Introductory Law, § 7.)

In offences of omission prescription does not begin so long as the corresponding duty lasts. With regard to criminal organizations prescription begins when they cease to exist (Leipsic, September 16th, 1880, March 5th, 1881).

68. Any proceeding of the judge, which is directed against the author for the act committed, interrupts the prescription.

The interruption only takes place with regard to the person, against whom the proceeding is taken.

After the interruption a fresh prescription begins.

Note.—Prescription is interrupted, in the case of minor offences, by the provisional settlement of the punishment by the police, and by the decision of the administrative magistrates in the case of offences against the tax regulations. In the embezzlement cases under the stamp act any official act interrupts prescription.

69. If the commencement or continuance of certain criminal proceedings depends on a preliminary question, which must be decided in other proceedings, prescription does not commence till the end of such proceedings. (Cf. §§ 164, 171, 172, 191.)

70. The execution of a legally-awarded punishment falls under prescription—

(i.) In thirty years, if death, penal servitude for life, or confinement in a fortress for life was awarded.

(ii.[1]) In twenty years, if penal servitude or confinement in a fortress for more than ten years was awarded.

(iii.[1]) In fifteen years, if penal servitude up to ten years, or confinement in a fortress for from five to ten years, or imprisonment with labour for more than five years was awarded.

(iv.) In ten years, if confinement in a fortress, or imprisonment with labour for from two to five years, or a fine of more than 6000 shillings was awarded.

(v.) In five years, if confinement in a fortress, or imprisonment with labour up to two years, or a fine from 150 to 6000 shillings was awarded.

(vi.) In two years, if arrest or a fine up to 150 shillings was awarded.

The prescription begins on the day, on which the judgment became valid at law.

Note.—The forfeiture of civil privileges and police supervision do not fall under prescription with the chief punishment. (Cf. §§ 36, 38.)

71. The carrying into effect of a fine, awarded for the same act together with a term of imprisonment, does not fall under prescription before the carrying into effect of the term of imprisonment.

72. Every act towards carrying the punishment into effect committed by the magistrate, whose duty it is to carry such punishment into effect, and also the apprehension of the person condemned with a view to carrying the punishment into effect, interrupts the prescription.

After the interruption of the carrying of the punishment into effect a fresh prescription begins.

[1] Novella of 1876.

FIFTH CHAPTER.

CONCURRENCE OF SEVERAL CRIMINAL ACTS.

73. If one and the same act infringes several criminal laws, that law only is to be applied, which threatens the severest punishment, and where the kinds of punishment are dissimilar, that law which threatens the severest kind of punishment.

Note.—If one criminal law requires a proposal and another does not, the first is only to be applied, if the proposal has been made (Berlin, January 22nd, 1872).

74. To such persons, as have through several independent acts committed several felonies or misdemeanours, or the same felony or misdemeanour several times, and thus incurred several terms of imprisonment, a collective punishment must be awarded, which consists in augmenting the severest punishment incurred.

On the concurrence of dissimilar punishments of imprisonment, this increase takes place in the punishment which is severest in character.

The amount of the collective punishment must not reach the total of the individual punishments incurred, and must not exceed fifteen years' penal servitude, ten years' imprisonment with labour, or fifteen years' confinement in a fortress.

Note.—§§ 74—76 only relate to felonies and misdemeanours, not to minor offences, and further, only to temporary punishments of imprisonment. The punishments of death, fine, reprimand, the forfeiture of civil privileges, and arrest are excluded from collective punishment. The amount of the individual punishments incurred must appear in the reasons for the sentence; the hardest of such individual punishments must be raised according to the first paragraph of this section. Each individual punishment must not sink below the legal minimum. The minimum punishment of the most serious offence must always be exceeded. Less than one month's penal servitude may be awarded on the conversion of imprisonment with labour into penal servitude, but not in cases where there are several offences which are to be punished with penal servitude (Leipsic, April 13th, 1881, January 29th, 1883).

75. If confinement in a fortress is concurrent only with imprisonment with labour, each of these punishments must be awarded apart.

If confinement in a fortress or imprisonment with labour is incurred several times, the several punishments of a similar kind must be dealt with as if the same were alone incurred.

The collective term of the punishment must not exceed fifteen years in these cases.

76. Condemnation to a collective punishment does not preclude the withdrawal of civil privileges, even if this is permitted or commanded only with one of the individual punishments incurred.

In like manner police supervision may be permitted by the sentence, even if this is only admissible for one of the several criminal actions.

Note.—It has been decided that civil privileges can only be withdrawn, if one of the individual punishments amounts to three months' imprisonment with labour (Leipsic, February 5th, 1880).

77. If arrest is concurrent with another punishment of imprisonment, the first-named must be awarded apart.

If arrest has been incurred several times, a term must be awarded according to its collective amount, but not, however, a term of more than three months. (Cf. § 18.)

Note.—The first paragraph holds good even with the misdemeanour of insult (§§ 185, 186).

78. Fines incurred for several criminal acts, either alone or jointly with a punishment of imprisonment, are to be imposed to their full extent.

If several fines are converted, the maximum of the term of imprisonment, which takes their place, is two years' imprisonment with labour; and, if the several fines have only been awarded for minor offences, three months' arrest. (Cf. § 29.)

Note.—It has been decided that terms of imprisonment substituted for fines are not to be converted into a collective punishment (Leipsic, March 4th, 1882).

79. The regulations of §§ 74 to 76 are applicable, even if before a punishment awarded has been expiated, has fallen under prescription, or has been remitted, condemnation takes place for a criminal act which had been committed before the earlier condemnation.

Note.—The code of criminal procedure, § 492, enacts that if any one has been condemned to punishment by several valid judgments, and if the regulations of § 79 of the criminal code with regard to the adjudication of a collective punishment have thus remained out of consideration, the punishments awarded must be reduced to a collective punishment by means of a supplementary judicial decision. It has been decided that the new collective penalty can be as high as the old (Leipsic, April 13th, 1882). The words "earlier condemnation" presuppose only the publication of the decision.

If the conditions required by § 79 are not present, the punishment of penal servitude can exceed fifteen years (Leipsic, April 15th, 1881).

SECOND PART.

OF THE INDIVIDUAL FELONIES, MISDEMEANOURS, AND MINOR OFFENCES, AND THEIR PUNISHMENT.

FIRST CHAPTER.

HIGH TREASON AND TREASON.

80. (J.[1]) MURDER and attempted murder committed on the Emperor, on the sovereign of the offender's own state, or during the stay of the offender in a federal state on the sovereign of that state, shall be punished as high treason with death. (Cf. § 93.)

Note.—In cases of high treason against the Emperor and the Empire, the Supreme Court of the Empire at Leipsic is competent. Otherwise cases of high treason come before a jury. This section was adopted by the Imperial Parliament on May 24th, 1870, by 128 to 107 votes.

81. (J.) Any one who, besides cases under § 80, undertakes :—

(i.) To slay, take prisoner, deliver into an enemy's power, or make incapable of government, a federal sovereign;

(ii.) To change by violence the constitution of the German Empire or of a federal state, or the succession to the throne existing in the same;

(iii.) To incorporate by violence the federal territory either wholly or partly with another state, or forcibly to sever any part of the same from the whole;

(iv.) To incorporate by violence the territory of one

[1] Sections under which the criminal is tried by a jury will be marked with a J.

federal state wholly or partly with another federal state, or forcibly to sever one part of the same from the whole, —shall be punished for high treason with penal servitude for life or confinement in a fortress for life. (Cf. § 20.)

If extenuating circumstances exist, confinement in a fortress for not less than five years takes place. Together with confinement in a fortress the sentence may include the forfeiture of public offices held, and also the rights which have accrued from public elections.

82. Every act, through which the design must be carried immediately into effect, is to be considered as an undertaking, through which the felony of high treason is consummated.[1]

83. (J.) If several persons have agreed to carry into effect a highly treasonable undertaking, and such act does not come to the beginning of an act criminal under § 82, such persons shall be punished with penal servitude for not less than five years, or with confinement in a fortress for a like period. If extenuating circumstances exist, confinement in a fortress for not less than five years takes place. Together with confinement in a fortress the sentence may include the forfeiture of public offices held, and also of the rights which have accrued from public elections. (Cf. § 93.)

84. (J.) The penal regulations of § 83 apply also against those who, with a view to the preparation of an act of high treason, either enter into communication with the Government of another state, or misuse the power intrusted to them by the Empire or one of the federal states, or either levy troops or train them in the use of arms.

Note.—Cf. § 93. The Government of another state (*auswärtige Regierung*) is here used instead of (*ausländ-*

[1] The Supreme Court of the Empire at Leipsic decided that this definition of undertaking only applies to high treason (November 9th, 1880).

ische) foreign, in order to include the Governments of the different federal states.

85. (J.) Any one who invites the execution of an act criminal under § 82, publicly in the presence of a crowd of men, or by the distribution or posting in public or public exhibition of writings or other representations, shall be punished with penal servitude up to ten years, or with confinement in a fortress for a like period. If extenuating circumstances exist, confinement in a fortress for from one to five years takes place. (Cf. §§ 110, 111.)

86. (J.) Every other act, which is preparatory to undertaking high treason, shall be punished with penal servitude up to three years, or confinement in a fortress for a like period. If extenuating circumstances exist, confinement in a fortress for from six months to three years takes place.

87. (J.) A German who enters into communication with the Government of another state, to induce the same to make war on the German Empire, shall be punished for treason with penal servitude for not less than five years, and if the war has broken out, with penal servitude for life. If extenuating circumstances exist, confinement in a fortress for from six months to five years takes place, and if the war has broken out, confinement in a fortress for not less than five years. With the confinement in a fortress the sentence can also include the forfeiture of public offices held, as well as of the rights which have accrued from public elections. (Cf. §§ 31, 35.)

88. (J). A German who, during a war, that has broken out against the German Empire, takes service in the hostile army, or bears arms against the German Empire or its allies, shall be punished for treason with penal servitude for life, or confinement in a fortress for life. If extenuating circumstances exist, confinement in a fortress for not less than five years takes place.

A German, who was already at an earlier period in a foreign military service, shall, if after the outbreak of the war he remain in the hostile army, or bear arms against the German Empire or its allies, be punished for treason with penal servitude for from two to ten years, or with confinement in a fortress for a like period. If extenuating circumstances exist, confinement in a fortress up to ten years takes place.

With the confinement in a fortress the sentence may include the forfeiture of public offices held, as well as of the rights which have accrued from public elections.

Note.—This section was added by the Novella of 1876.

89. (J.) A German, who during a war, which has broken out against the German Empire, deliberately renders assistance to a hostile power, or causes damage to the troops of the German Empire or the allies of the same, shall be punished for treason with penal servitude up to ten years, or with confinement in a fortress for a like period. If extenuating circumstances exist, confinement in a fortress up to ten years takes place. With the confinement in a fortress the sentence can also include the forfeiture of public offices held, as well as of the rights which have accrued from public elections.

90. (J.) A German is liable to penal servitude for life if he deliberately, during a war which has broken out against the German Empire :—

(i.) Brings into the enemy's power fortresses, passes, garrisoned places, or other posts of defence, and in like manner German or allied troops, or individual officers or soldiers.

(ii.) Brings into the enemy's power fortress-works, ships or other vessels of the navy, military chests, arsenals, magazines or other stores of arms, ammunition or other necessaries of war, or, to the advantage of the enemy, destroys or renders useless the same, as well as bridges and railways.

(iii.) Supplies the enemy with troops, or beguiles the

soldiers of the German or the allied army to go over to the enemy.

(iv.) Communicates plans of operations or plans of fortresses or strong positions to the enemy.

(v.) Serves the enemy as spy, or harbours, conceals, or assists the enemy's spies.

(vi.) Stirs up a mutiny among the German or allied troops.

If extenuating circumstances exist, confinement in a fortress for not less than five years takes place. With the confinement in a fortress the sentence may include the loss of public offices held, as well as of the rights which have accrued from public elections.

91. Against a foreigner proceedings must be taken for the acts mentioned in §§ 87, 89, 90, according to the usages of war.

(J.) But if foreigners commit such acts, while they are residing within the federal territory under the protection of the German Empire or of a federal state, the punishments appointed in §§ 87, 89, 90 may be inflicted.

92. (J.) Any one shall be punished by penal servitude for not less than two years who deliberately—

(i.) Communicates to another Government or makes publicly known state secrets, or plans of fortresses, or such documents, papers, or news of which he knows that to keep them secret is necessary for the welfare of the German Empire or a federal state as against that other Government.

(ii.) Destroys, forges, or suppresses, to the endangering of the rights of the German Empire or a federal state in relation to another Government, the documents or means of proof which refer to such rights.

(iii.) Conducts a negotiation which has been intrusted to him on behalf of the German Empire or a federal state with another Government, to the disadvantage of the body which has given him the commission.

If extenuating circumstances exist, confinement in a fortress for not less than six months takes place.

93. If in cases under §§ 80, 81, 83, 84, 87—92 the inquiry is opened, the property, which the accused possesses or which subsequently falls to him, can be sequestrated till the valid determination of such inquiry.

SECOND CHAPTER.

INSULTING THE SOVEREIGN OF A FEDERAL STATE.

94. (J.) Any one who is guilty of an act of violence against the Emperor, against the sovereign of his own state, or during his stay in a federal state of an act of violence against the sovereign of that federal state, shall be punished by penal servitude for life or confinement in a fortress for life, or in less serious cases by penal servitude for not less than five years or confinement in a fortress for a like period. Together with confinement in a fortress the sentence may include the forfeiture of public offices held, as well as of the rights which have accrued from public elections. If extenuating circumstances exist, confinement in a fortress for not less than five years takes place. (Cf. § 4, ii.)

95. (L.) Any one who insults the Emperor, the sovereign of his own state, or during his stay in a federal state the sovereign of that state, shall be punished by imprisonment with labour for not less than two months, or by confinement in a fortress for from two months to five years. (Cf. § 4, ii.; Press Law, § 23.)

With the imprisonment with labour the sentence may include the forfeiture of public offices held, as well as of the rights which have accrued from public elections.

Note.—This section was introduced by the Novella of 1876.

Sections which are marked L. are within the competence of the Landgericht or provincial court, the extent of which is explained in Appendix II.

96. (J.) Any one who is guilty of an act of violence against a member of the royal house of his state or against the regent of his state, or during his stay in a federal state, of an act of violence against a member of the royal house of that state, or of the regent of that state, shall be punished by penal servitude for not less than five years, or by confinement in a fortress for a like period; in less serious cases, by penal servitude up to five years, or by confinement in a fortress for a like period. If extenuating circumstances exist, confinement in a fortress for from one to five years takes place.

97. (L.) Any one who insults a member of the royal house of his own state or the regent of his state, or during his stay in a federal state, a member of the royal house of that state or the regent of that state, shall be punished by imprisonment with labour for from one month to three years, or by confinement in a fortress for a similar period.

THIRD CHAPTER.

INSULTING FEDERAL PRINCES.

98. (J.) Any one who, besides cases under § 94, is guilty of an act of violence against a federal prince, shall be punished with penal servitude for from two to ten years, or with confinement in a fortress for a similar period. (Cf. § 4, ii.) If extenuating circumstances exist, confinement in a fortress for from six months to ten years takes place.

99. (L.) Any one who, besides cases under § 95, insults

a federal prince, shall be punished by imprisonment with labour for from one month to three years, or by confinement in a fortress for a like period. (Cf. §§ 4, ii., 185.)

Prosecution is only commenced with the authorization of the person insulted.

100. (J.) Any one who, besides cases under § 96, is guilty of an act of violence against a member of the house of a federal prince or the regent of a federal state shall be punished by penal servitude up to five years, or by confinement in a fortress for a similar period. If extenuating circumstances exist, confinement in a fortress for from one month to three years takes place.

101. (L.) Any one who, besides cases under § 97, insults the regent of a federal state, shall be punished by imprisonment with labour for from one week to two years, or by confinement in a fortress for a like period.

Prosecution is only commenced with the authorization of the person insulted.

FOURTH CHAPTER.

HOSTILE ACTS AGAINST FRIENDLY STATES.

102.[1] (J.) A German, who either at home or abroad, or a foreigner who during his stay in Germany, undertakes against a state, which does not belong to the German Empire, or against the sovereign of such state, an act, which would be liable to punishment, if it had been committed against a federal state or a sovereign of a federal state according to the directions of §§ 81—86, shall in the cases of §§ 81—84 be punished by confinement in a fortress for from one to ten years, or,

[1] Novella of 1876.

if extenuating circumstances exist, by confinement in a fortress for from six months to ten years, and in the cases of §§ 85, 86 (L.) by confinement in a fortress for from one month to three years, so far as reciprocity is guaranteed to the German Empire in the other state.

Prosecution commences only on the proposal of the foreign Government. The withdrawal of the proposal is permissible.

Note.—It has been held that the judge must decide whether reciprocity exists (Leipsic, July 2nd, 1881).

103.[1] (L.) Any one who is guilty of an insult to the sovereign or regent of a state, which does not belong to the German Empire shall be punished by imprisonment with labour for from one week to two years, or by confinement in a fortress for a similar period, so far as reciprocity is guaranteed to the German Empire in such other state.

Prosecution commences only on the proposal of the foreign Government. The withdrawal of the proposal is permissible.

103 *a.*[1] (L.) Any one who maliciously takes away, destroys, injures, or commits insulting mischief on a public emblem of the authority of a state, which does not belong to the German Empire, or an emblem of the majesty of such a state, shall be punished by a fine up to 600 shillings, or by imprisonment with labour up to two years.

104.[1] (L.) Any one who is guilty of an insult to an envoy or *chargé-d'affaires* accredited to the Empire, the court of a federal sovereign, or the senate of one of the free Hanse towns, shall be punished by imprisonment with labour up to one year, or by confinement in a fortress for a similar period.

Prosecution takes place only on the proposal of the person insulted. The withdrawal of the proposal is permissible.

[1] Novella, 1876.

FIFTH CHAPTER.

FELONIES AND MISDEMEANOURS IN RELATION TO THE USE OF CIVIL RIGHTS.

105. (J.) ANY one who undertakes to set violently at variance the senate or civic body of one of the free Hanse towns, a legislative assembly of the Empire, or of a federal state, to compel the passing or omission of resolutions, or to remove members by force from them, shall be punished by penal servitude for not less than five years, or by confinement in a fortress for a similar period. If extenuating circumstances exist, confinement in a fortress for not less than one year takes place.

106. (J.) Any one who hinders a member of one of the above-mentioned assemblies by force or by a threat of a criminal act from betaking himself to the place of assembly or from voting, shall be punished by penal servitude up to five years, or by confinement in a fortress for a similar period. (Cf. § 339, iii.) If extenuating circumstances exist, confinement in a fortress up to two years takes place.

107. (L.) Any one who hinders a German by force or by a threat of a criminal act from electing or voting in the exercise of his civil rights shall be punished by imprisonment with labour for not less than six months, or by confinement in a fortress up to five years. (Cf. § 339, iii.) The attempt to commit this offence is criminal.

108. Any one who is intrusted in a public matter with the collection of tickets or tokens of election or voting, or with the conduct of their authentication, and deliberately brings about an erroneous result of the election, or falsifies the result, shall be punished by imprisonment with labour for from one week to three years.

If the act is committed by any one, who is not intrusted with the collection of tickets or tokens, or any other function in the business of the election, then imprisonment with labour up to two years takes place.

The sentence may also include the forfeiture of civil privileges.

109. (L.) Any one who in a public matter buys or sells a vote, shall be punished by imprisonment with labour for from one month to two years. The sentence may also include the forfeiture of civil privileges.

SIXTH CHAPTER.

RESISTANCE TO THE STATE'S AUTHORITY.

A DECISION of the Supreme Court of the Empire at Leipsic (February 15th, 1883,) assumes that this chapter extends to resistance to foreign authorities and officials, if corresponding penal regulations exist in such foreign country. (Cf. § 4, iii.)

110. (L.) Any one who publicly before a crowd of people, or any one who by distributing or publicly posting or publicly exhibiting writings or other representations, invites disobedience to the laws or valid[1] ordinances, or to the directions issued by the magistrates within their competence,[2] shall be punished by a fine up to 600 shillings, or by imprisonment with labour up to two years.

111. (L.) Any one who in the manner before mentioned invites the commission of a criminal act, is to be

[1] 'Valid' inserted by Lasker because all the ordinances which are issued in Germany are not valid, though formally correct.

[2] This according to Planck implies that the judge has to decide whether the magistrates have acted within their power in issuing such ordinances.

punished as the abettor, if the invitation has resulted in the criminal act or in an attempt to commit the same. (Cf. § 48.)

If the invitation has remained without result, a fine up to 600 shillings or imprisonment with labour up to one year takes place. The punishment must, however, in kind and amount be no severer than that, which is threatened for the act itself. (Cf. §§ 85, 110. Cf. Press Law, § 23.)

112. (L.) Any one who invites or entices a person of the military class, whether of the German army or the Imperial navy, to disobey the command of his superiors, especially any one who invites or entices any one belonging to the class of those on furlough not to comply with the summons to serve, shall be punished by imprisonment with labour up to two years.

113.[1] (L. or A.[2]) Any one who resists an official, who is appointed to carry into effect laws, commands, directions of the administrative magistrates, or judgments and mandates of the courts of law, in the lawful exercise of his office, by force or threats combined with force, and any one who violently assaults such an official in the lawful exercise of his office, shall be punished by imprisonment with labour for from fourteen days to two years. If extenuating circumstances exist, imprisonment with labour up to one year or a fine up to 1000 shillings takes place.[3]

The same penal regulations come into force, if the act is committed against persons, who were called in to support the official, or against the troops of armed authority, or against the troops of the community, police, or citizen forces in the exercise of their duty.

[1] Inserted by the Novella of 1876.

[2] A = *Amtsgericht* and *Schöffengericht*, the two lowest criminal courts. See Appendix II., § 75.

[3] 'Takes place' (*eintreten*), an incorrect expression for 'can be inflicted,' derived from the Code Pénal.

Note. — For 'officials' cf. § 359. The executive official who has to carry out commands, acts in the lawful exercise of his duty (Leipsic, November 1st, 1880).

114.[1] (L. or A.) Any one who undertakes by force or threat to compel a magistrate or an official to do or forbear an official act shall be punished by imprisonment with labour for not less than three months. If extenuating circumstances exist, imprisonment with labour up to two years takes place.

115. (L.) Any one who takes part in a public tumultuous assembly, in which one of the acts designated in §§ 113 and 114 is committed by combined force, shall be punished for riot by imprisonment with labour for not less than six months.

(J.) The ringleaders as well as those rioters, who commit one of the acts designated in §§ 113 and 114, shall be punished by penal servitude up to ten years. The sentence may further permit police supervision. If extenuating circumstances exist, imprisonment with labour for not less than six months takes place.

116. (L. or A.) If a crowd of men assembled in the public roads, streets, or places, is invited to withdraw by the competent official or the commander of armed authority, every one of the persons assembled, who does not withdraw on the third invitation, shall be punished for tumult by imprisonment with labour up to three months, or by a fine up to 1500 shillings.

(L. or J.) If in a tumult violent resistance with combined force has been made to officials or armed authority, or if force has been used, the punishments for riot come into force against those, who have taken part in such acts.

117.[1] (L. or A.) Any one who by force or by threat combined with force resists a forest or a venery official, a proprietor of woods, or a person who has forest or venery rights, or a keeper appointed by one of these persons,

[1] Inserted by the Novella of 1876.

in the lawful exercise of his office or right, or any one who violently assaults one of such persons in the exercise of their office or right, shall be punished by imprisonment with labour for from fourteen days to three years.

(L.) If the resistance or assault is accompanied by threats, with firearms, axes, or other dangerous implements, or with violence to the person, imprisonment with labour for not less than three months takes place.

If extenuating circumstances exist, then in cases under the first paragraph of this section, imprisonment with labour up to one year takes place; in cases under the second paragraph of this section imprisonment with labour for not less than one month takes place.

118. (J.) If through such resistance or assault a bodily injury has been caused to the person against whom the act is committed, penal servitude up to ten years is to be awarded. If extenuating circumstances exist, imprisonment with labour for not less than three months takes place.

119. (J.) If one of the acts designated in §§ 117 and 118 is committed by several persons in common, the punishment can be raised to half as much again as the maximum threatened, but the term of imprisonment with labour must not exceed five years.

120. (L. or A.) Any one who deliberately frees or deliberately assists a prisoner to free himself from the prison establishment, or from the power of armed authority, from the official or the person, under whose superintendence, escort, or custody he is, shall be punished by imprisonment with labour up to three years. The attempt to commit this offence is criminal.

121. (L.) Any one who deliberately permits to escape or aids in freeing a prisoner, with the superintendence or escort of whom he is intrusted, shall be punished by imprisonment with labour up to three years. (Cf. § 347.)

(A.) If such escape is aided by negligence, imprisonment up to three months or a fine up to 300 shillings takes place. (Cf. § 347.)

122. (L.) Prisoners who tumultuously assemble and with combined force assault, resist, or undertake to compel to acts or forbearances the officials of the prison or the persons intrusted with the superintendence, shall be punished for mutiny by imprisonment with labour for not less than six months.

A similar punishment takes place, if prisoners tumultuously assemble and with combined force undertake a violent outbreak.

(J.) Such mutineers, as commit acts of violence on the prison officials or the persons intrusted with the superintendence, shall be punished by penal servitude up to ten years. The sentence may further permit police supervision.

SEVENTH CHAPTER.

FELONIES AND MISDEMEANOURS AGAINST THE PUBLIC ORDER.

123. (A.) Any one who unlawfully breaks into the dwelling, the business rooms, or the enclosure of another, or into closed rooms appointed for public service, or any one who unwarrantably abides therein and does not withdraw on the demand of the person entitled to make such demand, shall be punished for a breach of the domestic peace by imprisonment with labour up to three months, or with a fine up to 300 shillings.

Prosecution only takes place on proposal.

(L. or A.) If the act has been committed by a person provided with arms or by several persons in common, imprisonment with labour for from one week to one year takes place.

Note.—For officials cf. §§ 50 and 342. In the case of paragraph iii. of this section a proposal is not necessary. It has been decided that 'arms' include dangerous implements (Leipsic, January 18th, 1883).

124. (L.) If a crowd of men publicly and tumultuously assembles, and with the intent to commit acts of violence on persons or property (*Sachen*) with combined force breaks into the dwelling, business rooms, or enclosed property of another, or into closed rooms appointed for public service, every one who takes part in these acts shall be punished by imprisonment with labour for from one month to two years.

125. (L.) If a crowd of men publicly and tumultuously assembles and with combined force commits acts of violence on persons or property, every one who takes part in such tumultuous assembly shall be punished for a breach of the peace by imprisonment with labour for not less than three months.

(J.) The ringleaders as well as all persons who have committed acts of personal violence, have plundered, demolished, or destroyed property, shall be punished by penal servitude up to ten years. The sentence may further permit police supervision. If extenuating circumstances exist, imprisonment with labour for not less than six months takes place.

126. (L). Any one who disturbs the public peace by threatening to commit a felony involving danger to the public shall be punished by imprisonment with labour up to one year. (Cf. §§ 241, 254, 306, and foll.)

127. (L.) Any one who unwarrantably forms, or commands, or provides with arms or necessaries of war a force, which he knows to be assembled without lawful warrant, shall be punished by imprisonment up to two years.

Any one who joins such an armed band shall

be punished by imprisonment with labour up to one year.

128. (L.) Participation in an association, of which the existence, constitution, or object is to be kept secret from the Government of the state, or in which obedience to an unknown commander or unconditional obedience to a known commander is promised, is to be punished in the members by imprisonment with labour up to six months, in the founders and managers of the association by imprisonment with labour from one month to one year.

Against officials the sentence may include the forfeiture of the capacity to hold public offices for a period of from one to five years.

Note.—(Cf. §§ 35, 36.) It has been decided that a founder need not be a member (Leipsic, May 1st, 1882).

129. (L.) Participation in an association, to the objects or business of which it belongs to hinder or weaken by unlawful means measures of the administration or the execution of laws, is to be punished in the members by imprisonment with labour up to one year, in the founders and managers of the association by imprisonment with labour for from three months up to two years.

Against officials the sentence may include the forfeiture of the capacity to hold public office for from one to five years. (Cf. §§ 35, 36, and Appendix, Law relating to Socialists.)

130. (L.) Any one who publicly, in a manner dangerous to the public peace, incites different classes of the population to acts of violence against each other shall be punished by a fine up to 600 shillings, or by imprisonment with labour up to two years. (Cf. Press Law, § 23.)

130 *a.* (L.) A clergyman or any other servant of religion, who in the exercise or occasion of exercising his calling, publicly before a crowd of men, or in a

church, or in any other place appointed for religious assemblies, makes several matters of state policy the subject of an announcement or disquisition in a manner to endanger the public peace, shall be punished by imprisonment with labour or by confinement in a fortress up to two years.

Similar punishment is incurred by those clergymen or other servants of religion who in the exercise or occasion of exercising their calling issue or publish writings, in which matters of state policy are made the subject of an announcement or disquisition in a manner to endanger the public peace.

Note.—The first paragraph was enacted in a law to supplement the criminal code of December 10th, 1871. On the second reading the bill was only supported by 179 to 108 votes, but on the third reading it passed with a large majority. It is a fair reply to the encroachments of the Ultramontanes. The second paragraph was added by the Novella of 1876.

131. (L.) Any one who publicly makes or publishes fabricated or distorted statements (*Thatsachen*), knowing them to be fabricated or distorted, with the intent thereby to bring into contempt state arrangements or regulations of the authorities, shall be punished by a fine up to 600 shillings, or by imprisonment with labour up to two years.

Note.—The Prussian code, § 101, was less precise in its terminology, and did not require libellous intent. (Cf. § 59.)

132. (L.) Any one who unwarrantably busies himself with the exercise of a public office, or undertakes an act which ought only to be undertaken in virtue of a public office, shall be punished by imprisonment with labour up to one year, or by a fine up to 300 shillings.

Note.—Public office is defined in § 31. The keynote of § 132 is the word 'unwarrantably.'

133. (L.) Any one who deliberately destroys, makes

away with, or damages a document, register, record, or any other object which is being officially preserved in a place thereto appointed, or which has been officially handed over to an official or a third person, shall be punished by imprisonment with labour. (Cf. §§ 303, 348.)

If the act is committed from motives of lucre, imprisonment with labour for not less than three months takes place; the sentence may also include the forfeiture of civil privileges.

134. (L. or A.) Any one who maliciously tears down, injures, or defaces advertisements, ordinances, commands, or notices, which have been publicly posted up by officials, shall be punished by a fine up to 300 shillings, or by imprisonment with labour up to six months.

135.[1] (L.) Any one who maliciously removes, destroys, injures, or commits insulting mischief on a public emblem of the authority of the Empire, or of a federal sovereign, or an emblem of the majesty of a federal state, shall be punished by a fine up to 600 shillings, or by imprisonment with labour up to two years.

136. (L. or A.) Any one who unwarrantably breaks, detaches, or injures an official seal which has been affixed by a magistrate or an official to close, mark, or seize property, or who removes the official lock formed by such a seal, shall be punished by imprisonment with labour up to six months.

Note.—It has been decided that seal includes seal-mark (Leipsic, April 4th, 1880).

137. (L. or A.) Any one who deliberately makes away with, destroys, or in any other way withdraws wholly or partially from attachment property distrained or seized by the competent magistrates or officials, shall be punished by imprisonment with labour up to one year.

[1] Novella of 1876.

Note.—(Cf. §§ 288, 289.) Attachment (*Verstrickung*) includes the sequestration of landed property.

138. (A.) Any one who is summoned as witness, juryman, or lay assessor and pleads an untruth in excuse shall be punished by imprisonment with labour up to two months.

The same holds good with regard to an expert, who is bound by law to appear.

The punishments affixed to such non-appearance in the interest of order are not precluded by the preceding penal regulation.

139. (L.) Any one who has credible knowledge of the purpose to commit high treason, treason, a coinage felony, murder, robbery, kidnapping, or a felony dangerous to the public at a time at which the prevention of the felony is possible, and omits to give notice thereof in time to the magistrate or the person who is threatened by the felony, shall be punished by imprisonment with labour if the felony or a criminal attempt thereat is committed.

Note.—Even those persons are bound to give information, who in virtue of personal ties are not bound to give evidence (Leipsic, May 15th, 1880).

140.[1] (L.) For a breach of the duty to serve punishment shall be inflicted on:—

(i.) Persons bound to serve in the militia who, intending to withdraw themselves from entering the service of the standing army or the fleet without permission, either leave the federal territory, or, after reaching the age at which they are bound to military service, remain outside the federal territory, by a fine of from 150 to 3000 shillings, or by imprisonment with labour for from one month to one year.

(ii.) Officers, or medical men holding the rank of officers, on furlough who emigrate without permission,

[1] Novella of 1876.

by a fine from 150 up to 3000 shillings, or by arrest, or by imprisonment with labour up to six months.

(iii.) Every one who is bound to serve in the militia and who, after public proclamation by the Emperor of a special regulation for the time of a war or danger of war, emigrates contrary to such proclamation, by imprisonment with labour up to two years, a sentence which may include a fine up to 3000 shillings.

The attempt to commit this offence is criminal. The property of the accused can be seized, so far as is necessary in the opinion of the judge, to cover the highest fine, which can possibly be inflicted on the accused, together with the costs of the proceedings.

Note.—Every German is bound to serve in the militia. The duty commences on the completion of the seventeenth year and lasts till the end of the forty-second year. Every German is bound to serve in the army, that is, is liable to be selected for such service, after the 1st of January, on which he has completed his twentieth year. Prescription begins to run from the time when the duty ceases, or on the return of the person to Germany. Emigrated Germans, who have become naturalized in the United States, are not liable to punishment on return, and sentences already pronounced must remain unexecuted under a treaty between the North German Confederation and the United States, dated February 22nd, 1868. Similar treaties were concluded in the same year between the United States and Bavaria, Wurtemberg, Baden, and Hesse.

141. (L.) Any one who solicits a German to enter the military service of a foreign power, or procures the enrolment of the same, in like manner any one who deliberately misleads a German soldier to desert, or deliberately furthers the desertion of the same, shall be punished by imprisonment with labour for from three months to three years. The attempt to commit these offences is criminal.

142. (L.) Any one who deliberately makes himself unfit for the fulfilment of his duty to serve in the militia by self-multilation, or allows another to make him so unfit, shall be punished by imprisonment with labour for not less than one year. The sentence may also include the forfeiture of civil privileges.

The same punishment meets the person, who makes another at his request unfit for the fulfilment of the duty to serve in the militia.

143. (L.) Any one who, with the intention to withdraw himself either wholly or partially from the fulfilment of the duty to serve in the militia, uses means calculated to deceive, shall be punished by imprisonment with labour. The sentence may include the forfeiture of civil privileges.

The same penal regulation is applicable to participators. (Cf. §§ 48, 49.)

144. (L.[1]) Any one who makes it his business to mislead Germans into emigrating by the illusory representation of false facts, or knowingly by unfounded statements or by other means calculated to deceive, shall be punished with imprisonment with labour for from one month to two years.

145. (L. or A.[1]) Whoever trangresses the ordinances issued by the Emperor (*a*) for the prevention of collisions of ships at sea, (*b*) for the conduct of captains after a collision of ships at sea, or (*c*) in regard to signals of distress, and for pilots for ships at sea, or in the seas adjacent to the coast, shall be punished by a fine up to 1500 shillings.

Note. — Such Imperial ordinances were issued on (*a*) January 7th, 1880 ; February 16th, 1881 ; (*b*) August 15th, 1876 ; (*c*) August 14th, 1876.

[1] Novella of 1876.

EIGHTH CHAPTER.

FELONIES AND MISDEMEANOURS RELATING TO THE COIN.

146. (J.) ANY one who counterfeits home or foreign metal or paper money, in order to use the counterfeit money as genuine or otherwise to bring it into circulation, or any one who with similar intent gives to genuine money, by altering the same, the appearance of a higher value, or to money, which has been condemned, by altering the same, the appearance of money which is still lawfully current, shall be punished by penal servitude for not less than two years. Police supervision is also permissible.[1] If extenuating circumstances exist, a sentence of imprisonment with labour takes place.

147. (J.) The same penal regulations are applicable to the person, who brings into circulation as genuine counterfeit or debased money, which he has made without the above-mentioned intention, as well as to the man who procures counterfeit or debased money, and either brings such money into circulation or with the object of uttering imports it from a foreign country.

148. (A.) Any one who receives counterfeit or debased money as genuine, and after recognizing its spuriousness brings it into circulation as genuine, shall be punished by imprisonment with labour up to three months, or by a fine up to 300 shillings. The attempt to commit this offence is criminal.

149. The following shall be considered equivalent to paper money: assignations of debt payable to bearer, bank-notes, shares, or bills *ad interim* representing such shares, or receipts as well as certificates of interest,

[1] The change of phraseology is unmeaning.

shares of profits or renewal belonging to such papers, which have been issued by the Empire, the North German Confederation, by a federal state or foreign state, or by a community, corporation, society, or private person authorized to issue such papers.

150. (L.) Any one who depreciates genuine pieces of metallic money appointed for the currency, by cutting or filing or in any other manner, and brings such pieces into circulation as of full weight, or who habitually or in concert with the person who has depreciated such coins, brings them into circulation as of full weight, shall be punished by imprisonment with labour, with which the sentence may include a fine up to 3000 shillings, as well as the forfeiture of civil privileges. The attempt to commit this offence is criminal.

151. (L.) Any one who has procured or manufactured any stamp, seal, puncheon, plate, or other mould, suitable for the preparation of metallic money, paper money, or any papers which are considered equivalent thereto, shall be punished by imprisonment with labour up to two years. (Cf. § 360, iv.)

152. The sentence must include the confiscation of the counterfeit or debased coin, as well as that of the objects designated in § 151, even when the prosecution or condemnation of a definite person does not take place. (Cf. §§ 40, 42.)

NINTH CHAPTER.

PERJURY.

153. (J.) ANY one who falsely swears an oath offered to him, retorted upon him, or administered to him, knowing it to be false, shall be punished by penal servitude up to ten years.

Note.—With regard to the effect on civil privileges

of condemnation under this and the following sections, cf. § 161.

154. (J.) A similar punishment is incurred by the person who corroborates on oath false evidence or a false opinion, knowing them to be false, before a magistrate who is competent to take oaths, or who breaks an oath sworn before his examination by false evidence or a false opinion knowing them to be false.

If the false evidence or opinion is given in criminal proceedings to the prejudice of an accused person, and such person is condemned to death, penal servitude, or any other punishment of imprisonment for more than five years, penal servitude for not less than three years takes place.

155. (J.) It will be considered equivalent to taking an oath if:—

(i.) A member of a religious society, to which the law allows a certain formula of affirmation in the place of the oath, makes a declaration under the formula of affirmation of his religious society.

(ii.) A person who has sworn an oath as party, witness, or expert, makes in a similar capacity an asseveration appealing to the oath already sworn in the same matter, or an expert, who as such is sworn once and for all, makes an asseveration with reference to the oath he has sworn.

(iii.) An official makes an official asseveration appealing to his oath of office.

156. (L.) Any one who makes such an asseveration falsely, knowing it to be false, before a magistrate competent to take an asseveration in the place of an oath, or who makes a false declaration knowing it to be false, appealing to such an asseveration, shall be punished by imprisonment with labour for from one month to three years.

157. If a witness or an expert has been guilty of perjury (§§ 154, 155) or a false asseveration in the place

of an oath, the punishment incurred is to be reduced from a half to a quarter, if:—

(i.) The statement of the truth could draw on the person himself a prosecution for a felony or a misdemeanour.

(ii.) The declarant has made the false declaration in favour of a person, with regard to whom he was permitted to decline to make a declaration, without having been informed of his right to be permitted to decline to make such declaration.

If, in accordance with this section, penal servitude for less than one year is incurred, such penal servitude is to be converted into imprisonment with labour according to § 21.

158. A similar mitigation of punishment takes place, if the person, who has been guilty of perjury or a false asseveration, withdraws the same in the presence of the magistrate who received it, before his information had been lodged or an inquiry commenced against him, and before prejudice at law has arisen against another from such declaration.

159. (L.) Any one who undertakes to suborn another to commit perjury shall be punished by penal servitude up to five years, and any one who undertakes to suborn another to make a false asseveration in the place of an oath, knowing it to be false, shall be punished by imprisonment with labour up to one year.

160. (L.) Any one who suborns another to make a false oath shall be punished by imprisonment with labour up to two years, and the sentence may include the forfeiture of civil privileges; and any one who suborns another to make a false asseveration in the place of an oath shall be punished by imprisonment with labour up to six months. The attempt to commit these offences is criminal.

Note.—A false oath is one which is actually incorrect. In a false oath under this section knowledge is only required on the part of the suborner to constitute criminality, but for perjury under § 159 the knowledge of the person, who is to swear, is also necessary.

161. In every condemnation for perjury, with the exception of cases under §§ 157, 158, the sentence shall include the forfeiture of civil privileges, and besides the permanent incapacity of the person condemned to be examined on oath as witness or expert.

In cases under §§ 156—159 the sentence may include, besides imprisonment with labour, the forfeiture of civil privileges.

Note.—In the first paragraph, the forfeiture of civil privileges and of the capacity to give testimony must be included in the sentence, but if this should be overlooked, such privileges and capacity remain (Leipsic, January 1st, 1880). The first paragraph refers to attempt at and participation in perjury, not to the attempted subornation of § 159 (Berlin, November 4th, 1876).

162. (L.) Any one who deliberately acts contrary to security given by solemn undertaking before the court or to a promise made in an oath of disclosure shall be punished by imprisonment with labour up to two years.

163. If one of the acts designated in §§ 153—156 is committed from negligence, a punishment of imprisonment with labour for one year takes place.

No punishment shall be inflicted, if the declarant withdraws the false declaration in the presence of the magistrate who received it, before information has been lodged or an inquiry commenced against him, and before a prejudice at law has arisen against another from such declaration.

Note.—It has been decided that the oath of disclosure is included under the first paragraph (Leipsic, April 21st, 1882).

TENTH CHAPTER.

FALSE ACCUSATION.

164. (L.) Any one who lodges information with a magistrate accusing some one, contrary to his better knowledge, of committing a criminal act or of infringing his official duty, shall be punished by imprisonment with labour for not less than one month; the sentence on such a person may include the forfeiture of civil privileges.

So long as the proceedings commenced in consequence of the information lodged are pending, the proceedings and the decision with regard to the false accusation shall be suspended.

Note.—Cf. § 69. A private accusation or a proposal to prosecute for insult is information within the meaning of this section (Leipsic, November 11th, 1879, January 1st, 1880). Such an information may constitute an insult (§ 186). (Leipsic, October 25th, 1881.)

165. If a punishment is awarded for false accusation, the injured person must at the same time receive in the judgment the right to make the condemnation publicly known at the cost of the guilty person. The judgment must define the manner and extent of the publication.

A copy of the judgment must be communicated to the accused at the expense of the guilty person.

ELEVENTH CHAPTER.

MISDEMEANOURS RELATING TO RELIGION.

166. (L.) ANY one who gives offence[1] by blaspheming against God publicly in opprobrious language, or any one who covers with opprobrium one of the Christian Churches or any other religious society with corporate rights existing within the federal territory, or their institutions or usages; likewise any one, who is guilty of opprobrious misconduct in a church, or any other place appointed for religious assemblies, shall be imprisoned with labour for a term up to three years.

Note.—This section includes the old Catholics (Berlin, May 24th, 1872), though a different decision was given at Munich (September 15th, 1873), and also the God of the Jews (Leipsic, March 3rd, 1882). Disparagement is not opprobrium within the meaning of this section (Leipsic, December 13th, 1879).

167. (L.) Any one who hinders another by an act of violence or a threat from performing the service of God of any religious society existing in the state, and in like manner any one who deliberately hinders or disturbs the service of God or individual functions of such service of any religious society existing in the state in a church or in any other place appointed for religious assemblies, by creating a confusion or disorder, shall be punished by imprisonment with labour up to three years.

Note.—Heavier punishment shall be inflicted if such disturber be an official. (Cf. § 339.) It has been decided that such disturber need not be actually in the church (Leipsic, February 22nd, 1881).

168. (L.) Any one who unwarrantably removes a

[1] Creates a scandal.

dead body from the custody of the person entitled thereto; and in like manner any one who unwarrantably disturbs or damages a grave, or is guilty of opprobrious misconduct thereto, shall be punished by imprisonment with labour up to two years: the sentence may also include the forfeiture of civil privileges. (Cf. § 367, i.)

TWELFTH CHAPTER.

FELONIES AND MISDEMEANOURS RELATING TO PERSONAL RANK.

169. (L.) Any one who substitutes or deliberately exchanges a child, or any one who in any other way deliberately changes or suppresses the personal rank of another, shall be punished by imprisonment with labour up to three years, and if the act was committed with the intent to make a profit, by penal servitude up to ten years. The attempt to commit this offence is criminal. (Cf. Appendix, Law relating to personal rank.)

170. (L.) Any one who in contracting a marriage fraudulently conceals a legal obstacle from the other party thereto, or any one who fraudulently misleads the other party to conclude a marriage by means of such a deception, as entitles the person deceived to dispute the validity of the marriage, shall, if the marriage is dissolved on one of these grounds, be punished by imprisonment with labour for not less than three months. Prosecution only takes place on the proposal of the party deceived.

THIRTEENTH CHAPTER.

FELONIES AND MISDEMEANOURS AGAINST MORALITY.

171. (L.) Any married person who contracts a fresh marriage before the former marriage has been dissolved, or declared invalid or null, in like manner any unmarried person who enters on a marriage with a married person knowing that such person is married, shall be punished by penal servitude up to five years. If extenuating circumstances exist, imprisonment with labour for not less than six months takes place.

Prescription of the criminal prosecution begins to run from the day on which one of the two marriages is dissolved or declared invalid or null.

Note.—For the punishment of servants connected with the Church, &c. cf. § 338. Malice must be proved on the part of the married person (Leipsic, March 31st, 1881).

172. (L. or A.) Adultery shall be punished by imprisonment with labour up to six months in the case of the guilty married person and the partners in guilt, if the marriage is dissolved on the ground of such adultery. Prosecution only takes place on proposal. (Cf. §§ 64, 69.)

Note.—Prescription begins to run when the sentence dissolving the marriage comes into force; according to French law from the day on which the dissolution is announced. The period for making the proposal begins as soon as the offence is known (Leipsic, March 23rd, 1880).

173. (L.) Carnal knowledge between relations in the ascending and descending line shall be punished, in the former by penal servitude up to ten years, in the latter by imprisonment with labour up to two years.

Carnal knowledge between connections by marriage in the ascending and descending line, and also between brother and sister, shall be punished by imprisonment with labour up to two years.

Together with the punishment of imprisonment with labour the sentence may include the forfeiture of civil privileges.

Relations and connections by marriage in the descending line are not punished, if they have not completed their eighteenth year.

Note.—Relationship in the ascending and descending line includes illegitimate relationship (Leipsic, September 9th, 1880), connections by marriage, brothers and sisters in law, step-parents and step-children, even after the dissolution of a fraudulent marriage (Leipsic, April 7th, 1880). Criminality is not removed by the fact that the marriage of the step-father and step-daughter has taken place (Leipsic, November 10th, 1881).

174. (L.) The following persons shall be punished by penal servitude up to five years:—

(i.) Guardians who commit (*vornehmen*) obscene acts with their wards, adoptive and foster parents who commit [1] obscene acts with their children, clergymen, teachers, and tutors who commit [1] obscene acts with their scholars and pupils who are under age.

(ii.) Officials who commit [1] obscene acts with persons against whom they have to conduct an inquiry, or who are intrusted to their care.

(iii.) Officials, physicians, or other medical men who are employed or engaged in prisons or public institutions appointed for the care of the sick, the poor, or other helpless persons, if they commit [1] obscene acts with the persons admitted into the prison or institution.

If extenuating circumstances exist, the punishment

[1] *Vornehmen. Vornehmen* and *unternehmen* are used in the sense of attempt and effect, except in cases of high treason (§ 83). In this section a literal rendering is out of the question.

of imprisonment with labour for not less than six months takes place.

Note.—Officials in paragraph ii. are the officials mentioned in § 359 (Leipsic, December 22nd, 1881). Officials in (iii.) are not only those mentioned in § 359, but other persons employed; the official translation of the code for Alsace-Lorraine translates freely but correctly "les fonctionnaires, employés, médecins," &c.

175. (L.) Unnatural obscenity committed between persons of the male sex, or between men and beasts, is to be punished by imprisonment with labour; the sentence may include the forfeiture of civil privileges.

Note.—Unnatural obscenity includes only acts similar to carnal knowledge (pæderastia and bestiality), and is less wide than the term obscene acts of §§ 174, 176 (Leipsic, April 23rd, 1880); it does not include onanism between men (Leipsic, May 15th, 1882).

176.[1] Any one shall be punished by penal servitude up to ten years who:—

(i.) (J.) Commits[2] by force obscene acts on a person of the female sex, or compels such person to suffer such obscene acts by threatening immediate danger to life or limb.

(ii.) (J.) Misuses a person of the female sex, who is in a state of absence of volition or of unconsciousness, so as carnally to know her, she not being his wife.

(iii.) (L.) Commits[2] obscene acts with persons under fourteen years of age, or misleads such persons to commit or suffer obscene acts.

If extenuating circumstances exist, imprisonment with labour for not less than six months takes place.

Note.—The Novella of 1876 removed the necessity of a proposal. Under (iii.) the person misused need not co-operate in the act (Leipsic, October 10th, 1881). The person under (i.) may be the offender's wife.

177.[1] (J.) The punishment of penal servitude will be

[1] Novella of 1876. [2] *Vornehmen.*

inflicted on any one who compels a person of the female sex by force or threat of immediate danger to life or limb to allow him carnally to know her, she not being his wife; or on any one who misuses a person of the female sex so as carnally to know her, she not being his wife, after he has for such purpose reduced her to a state of absence of volition or of unconsciousness. If extenuating circumstances exist, the punishment of imprisonment with labour for not less than one year takes place.

Note.—The Novella of 1876 removed the necessity of a proposal to prosecute.

This section (177) gives prominence to the crime of rape, which is included under § 176 (i.) in general terms. It has been decided that the offence is complete with penetration.

178.[1] (J.) If the death of the person injured is caused by one of the acts designated in §§ 176 and 177 the punishment of penal servitude for life or for not less than ten years takes place.

179. (L.) Any one who misleads a person of the female sex to allow him carnally to know her under pretence of marriage, or by promoting or making use of an error, under which she considered the carnal connection to be legitimate, shall be punished by penal servitude up to five years. If extenuating circumstances are present, imprisonment with labour for not less than six months takes place. Prosecution takes place only on proposal.

180. (L.) Any one who habitually or from motives of lucre promotes obscenity by his interposition, or by affording or providing the opportunity, shall be punished by imprisonment with labour for procuring. The sentence may include the forfeiture of civil privileges as well as the permissibility of police supervision.

Note.—Obscenity in the meaning of the section is

[1] Novella of 1876.

not merely carnal connection (Berlin, July 19th, 1882). Keeping a brothel, even with the permission of the police, is criminal (Leipsic, January 29th, 1880). Letting apartments to loose women is also criminal (Leipsic, April 27th, 1880).

181. Procuring, even if it is carried on neither habitually nor from motives of lucre, shall be punished by penal servitude up to five years if:—

(i.) Fraudulent misrepresentations have been employed to assist the obscenity.

(ii.) The guilty person stands to the person, with whom the obscenity is committed, in the relation of father to child, of guardian to ward, of clergymen, tutors, and teachers to the persons who are to be taught or educated by them.

Together with the punishment of penal servitude the sentence of forfeiture of civil rights shall be pronounced, and such sentence may further permit police supervision.

Note.—Paragraph i. includes decoying away to a solitary place, deluding with the hope of a brilliant future, together with the administering of exciting drinks. Paragraph ii. includes step-parents (Leipsic, May 6th, 1882).

182. (L.) Any one who seduces a girl of irreproachable character (*verführen*) who has not completed her sixteenth year to have carnal connection (with himself), shall be punished by imprisonment with labour up to one year. Prosecution only takes place on the proposal of the parents or guardian of the person seduced.

Note.—The illegitimate mother is entitled to make the proposal (Leipsic, December 7th, 1880).

Seduction includes cases in which the girl was ignorant of the nature or quality of the act (Leipsic, March 26th, 1881). The fact of having been deflowered does not always constitute a reproach (Leipsic, May 5th, 1882).

183. (L. or A.) Any one who gives public offence by means of an obscene act shall be punished by imprisonment with labour up to two years, or by a fine up to 150 shillings. Together with the imprisonment with labour the sentence may include the forfeiture of civil privileges.

Note.—Obscene acts include such acts as are not in all places treated as obscene (Leipsic, February 28th, 1880). The question whether expressions by word of mouth, such as songs, are acts in the sense of § 183 is answered in the affirmative by a decision of the Supreme Court at Leipsic, May 6th, 1881, while on the other hand by the old Supreme Court of Berlin, May 5th, 1877, and the Supreme Court of Stuttgart, January 29th, 1877, together with the commentary of Rudorff and Stenglein, it is answered in the negative.

184. Any one who sells, distributes, or otherwise diffuses obscene writings, pictures, or representations, or exposes or exhibits such things in places to which the public has access, shall be punished by imprisonment with labour up to six months.

Note.—A decision at Berlin, October 20th, 1876, holds the confiscation of all obscene writings and pictures lawful, even when no act has been committed contrary to § 184.

FOURTEENTH CHAPTER.

INSULT.

Note.—PERSONS can be prosecuted for insult on a private suit, in so far as prosecution only takes place on proposal, but such prosecution must be preceded by an attempt at reconciliation, except under § 196. Public prosecution will only take place if a public interest is at stake. The court of the lay assessors is competent for private prosecutions, the court of second instance (*Landgericht*, L.) for public prosecutions, but the latter may assign the case to the former.

185. (L. or A.) Insult will be punished by a fine up to 600 shillings, or by arrest, or by imprisonment with labour up to one year, and if the insult be committed by means of an act of violence, by a fine up to 1500 shillings, or by imprisonment with labour up to two years.

Note.—The intent to insult is not necessary, the consciousness that an injury is being offered to a man's honour is sufficient except under § 193 (Leipsic, December 5th, 1879). It is a question of fact whether one, or more than one insult, has been committed (Leipsic, February 9th, 1881). As a rule one insult directed against several persons contains only one independent act (Leipsic, July 14th, 1881). Collective designations (such as Jews) without specification of an individual are not sufficient to constitute criminality (Leipsic, October 6th, 1882).

186. (L. or A.) Any one who asserts or publishes a fact[1] with reference to another person, which is calculated to bring such person into contempt, or to degrade him in public opinion, shall be punished for insult by a fine up to 600 shillings, or by arrest, or by imprisonment with labour up to a year, if such fact is not demonstrably true, or by a fine up to 1500 shillings, or by imprisonment with labour up to two years, if the insult is committed publicly, or by publishing writings, pictures, or representations.

Note.—The fact that the offender believed the insult to be true does not remove criminality (Leipsic, December 1st, 1879). A firm of merchants cannot make a proposal to prosecute, but only the individuals, of which the firm is composed (Leipsic, January 13th,

[1] *Thatsache.*

1880). A letter to the person insulted does not constitute an insult under this section (Leipsic, June 29th, 1881).

187. (L. or A.) Any one who asserts or publishes against his better knowledge an untrue statement[1] with reference to another person, which is calculated to bring such person into contempt or degrade him in public opinion, or endanger his credit, shall be punished for defamatory insult by imprisonment up to two years, and if the defamation is committed publicly, or by the publication of writings, pictures, or representations, by imprisonment for not less than one month. If extenuating circumstances exist, the punishment can be mitigated to one day's imprisonment with labour, or a fine up to 900 shillings may be inflicted.

Note.—Joint stock companies and other commercial societies have right of bringing a criminal action for defamation affecting their credit (Berlin, April 5th, 1877).

188. In cases under §§ 186 and 187 at the request of the person insulted the sentence may include, together with the punishment, a mulct to be paid to the person insulted to the amount of 6000 shillings, if the insult brings with it prejudicial results to the property, profit, or success of the insulted person. A mulct, which has been inflicted, excludes the enforcement of a further claim for compensation.

189. (L. or A.) Any one who covers the memory of a deceased person with opprobrium by the assertion or publication against his better knowledge of an untrue statement,[1] which would be calculated to bring the deceased into contempt, or degrade him in public opinion during his lifetime, shall be punished by imprisonment with labour up to six months. If extenuating circumstances exist, a fine up to 900 shillings may be inflicted. Prosecution takes place only on the pro-

[1] *Thatsache.*

posal of the parents, children, husband, or wife of the deceased.

190. If the fact[1] asserted or published is a criminal act, proof of the truth shall be considered given if the person insulted has been condemned in a valid decision for such act. Proof of the truth is, however, excluded if the person insulted has been acquitted of such act by a valid decision before the assertion or publication.

191. If information of the criminal act is laid before a magistrate with the object of bringing about criminal proceedings, the proceedings and decision with regard to the insult must be suspended till the conclusion is reached that the opening of the inquiry shall not take place, or till the termination of the inquiry that has been commenced.

192. The proof of the truth of the fact[1] asserted or published does not preclude punishment under the regulation of § 185, if the existence of an insult is inferred (*hervorgeht*) from the form of the assertion or publication or from the circumstances, under which it took place.

Note.—The proof of the truth shall not be precluded, even if an insult under § 185 is already established.

193. Contemptuous opinions with regard to scientific, artistic, or professional services, likewise remarks made for the enforcement or defence of rights or for the preservation of vested interests, as well as remonstrances and censure of superiors against their inferiors, information and opinions given in the exercise of his duties by an official, and similar cases, are only criminal in so far as the existence of an insult is inferred from the form of the expression or from the circumstances, under which it took place.

Note.—In cases under § 187 it is not certain whether § 193 is applicable. The old Supreme Court at Berlin decided three times in the affirmative, but the old

[1] *Thatsache.*

Supreme Court at Dresden and the Supreme Imperial Court at Leipsic have decided in the negative; the latter is, therefore, the view which will probably prevail, although one of the decisions (October 10th, 1881) at Leipsic is not clear.

194. The prosecution for an insult only takes place on proposal. The withdrawal of the proposal (§§ 185—193) is permissible.

Note.—Cf. §§ 64, 196, 197, 232. Before the Novella of 1876 the withdrawal of the proposal was permissible in private suits, till the commencement of the execution of the decision. Now the proposal can only be withdrawn up till the time, at which judgment is pronounced. Private accusation for insult can be withdrawn up till the publication of the decision of the court of second instance. The recommencement of an action for insult which has been withdrawn is not permissible. Conditional or limited withdrawal has no effect.

195. If married women or children still under their father's power have been insulted, both the persons insulted and their husbands and fathers have the right to make the proposal for punishment.

196. If the insult is directed against a magistrate, an official, a servant of religion, or a member of the armed authority, while they are engaged in the exercise of, or in relation to their calling, then besides the persons immediately affected their official superiors have also the right to make the proposal for punishment.

197. (L.) There is no need of a proposal, if the insult has been directed against a legislative assembly of the Empire or of a federal state, or against any other political body. Such insult must, however, only be made the subject of a prosecution with the permission of the body which has been insulted.

198. In the case of mutual insults, if a proposal for punishment has been made by one party, the other party is bound, on pain of losing his right, to make the

proposal for punishment at the latest before the conclusion of the proceedings in the first instance, but he is entitled to this, even if at that date the term of three months has expired.

Note.—Cf. § 232. Mutual insults are not those only which are returned on the spot (Berlin, July 5th, 1872), and need not have any real or causal connection (Berlin, October 31st, 1873; Leipsic, June 4th, 1880).

199. If an insult is returned on the spot the judge can declare both parties, or either of them, not liable to punishment.

Note.—"On the spot" does not refer to place according to decisions at Berlin, September 12th, 1873, Dresden, March 3rd, 1873.

200.[1] If a punishment is awarded for an insult committed publicly or through the publication of writings, pictures, or representations, the person insulted must at the same time receive the authorization to make the condemnation publicly known at the cost of the guilty person. The judgment must define the manner in which and the time within which such condemnation is to be made known.

If the insult arose in a newspaper or periodical, the dispositive[2] (*verfügende*) part of the judgment must be made known, on the proposal of the person insulted, by means of the public papers, and certainly, if it is possible, by means of the same newspaper or periodical, and in the same part and with the same type as the impression of the insult.

A copy of the judgment must be sent to the person insulted at the cost of the guilty person.

Note.—In the dispositive part of the judgment the name at least of the person insulted must be contained, otherwise the advertisement is unintelligible and aimless.

[1] Novella of 1876.

[2] The dispositive part of the judgment is that, which contains the tenor without the reasons, on which it is grounded.

The authorization must be pronounced in the dispositive part of the judgment. Except under paragraph ii. the advertisement is not made officially, not even in the cases under § 196 (Berlin, November 28th, 1878).

The judge has to decide the way and the place in the newspaper in which the advertisement is to appear (Leipsic, February 3rd, 1882). The costs are advanced by the person, who makes the proposal, and are only advanced by the Treasury, when a prosecution is made by an official superior under § 196.

A copy must in all cases be sent without a proposal.

FIFTEENTH CHAPTER.

DUEL.

201. (L.) A CHALLENGE to duel with deadly weapons and also the acceptance of such a challenge shall be punished by confinement in a fortress up to six months.

Note.—This includes cases in which the combatants are padded and protected from injury to a great extent.

202. (L.) Confinement in a fortress for from two months to three years takes place if at the time the challenge is made the intent that one of the two parties should lose his life is either expressed or is manifest from the form of the duel chosen.

203. (L.) Such persons as take charge of and deliver a message for a challenge (bearers of challenges) shall be punished by confinement in a fortress up to six months.

204. The punishment of such challenge and the acceptance of the same, and also the punishment of the bearers of the challenge, is not inflicted, if the parties

have of their own free will given up the duel before its commencement.

205. (L.) Duelling shall be punished by confinement in a fortress for from three months up to five years.

206. (J.) Any one who kills his opponent in a duel shall be punished by confinement in a fortress for not less than two years, and if the duel was of such a nature that it must bring about the death of one of the two, by confinement in a fortress for not less than three years.

207. If homicide or bodily injury has been brought about by means of deliberate transgression of the agreed or traditional rules of duelling, the transgressor is to be punished according to the universal regulations relating to the offence of homicide or bodily injury, in so far as a heavier penalty is not incurred according to the preceding enactments.

208.[1] (L. or J.) If the duel has taken place without seconds, the punishment can be raised to half as much again, not, however, to more than fifteen years.

209. Bearers of challenges, who have exerted themselves in earnest to hinder the duel, seconds as well as witnesses, physicians, and surgeons, who have been brought to the duel, are free from punishment.

210. (L.) Any one who intentionally incites another to fight a duel with a third person, especially by showing or threatening contempt, shall, if the duel has taken place, be punished by imprisonment with labour for not less than three months.

[1] Novella of 1876.

SIXTEENTH CHAPTER.

FELONIES AND MISDEMEANOURS AGAINST LIFE.

211. (J.) ANY one who wilfully (*vorsätzlich*) slays a human being, shall be punished for murder with death, if he executed the act with deliberation. (Cf. §§ 44, 49, 80, 216, 217.)

212. (J.) Any one who wilfully slays a human being, shall be punished for manslaughter by penal servitude for not less than five years, if he did not execute the act with deliberation. (Cf. §§ 213, 215.)

213. If the manslayer was excited to anger without any fault of his by a wrongful act, or by serious insult inflicted on him or a relative of his by the person slain, and was by this means carried away to commit the act, or if other extenuating circumstances exist, the punishment of imprisonment with labour for not less than six months takes place. (For relatives cf. § 52.)

214. Any one who in undertaking a criminal act wilfully slays a man with a view to remove an obstacle, which stood in the way of the execution of such act, or with a view to escape being taken in the very act, shall be punished by penal servitude for not less than ten years or by penal servitude for life.

215. (J.) The slaughter of a relation in the ascending line shall be punished by penal servitude for not less than ten years or by penal servitude for life. (Cf. § 212, and for participators § 50.)

216. (L.) If any one has been determined to the slaughter by the express and earnest request of the person slain the sentence must not award less than three years' imprisonment with labour.

217. (J.) A mother, who wilfully slays her illegitimate child at or immediately after birth, shall be punished

by penal servitude for not less than three years. If extenuating circumstances exist, the punishment of imprisonment with labour for not less than two years takes place.

Note.—Cf. §§ 211, 212. Participators are to be punished as murderers according to § 50 (Leipsic, March 2nd, 1881).

218. A woman with child, who wilfully procures abortion or slays the child in the womb, shall be punished by penal servitude up to five years. If extenuating circumstances exist, the punishment of imprisonment with labour for not less than six months takes place.

The same penal regulations are applicable to the man, who with the consent of her, that is with child, has applied or administered to her the means to procure abortion or to slay.

219. (J.) Any one shall be punished by penal servitude up to ten years who shall have for money furnished or applied or administered to a woman, who has procured abortion or killed her child, the means thereto.

Note.—Attempt to procure abortion is only liable under § 118 (Leipsic, February 9th, 1880). A third person who is present is liable as participator (June 24th, 1881).

220. (J.) Any one who wilfully slays or procures the abortion of the offspring of a woman with child without her knowledge or consent shall be punished by penal servitude for not less than two years.

If the death of the woman with child be caused by the act, a punishment of penal servitude for not less than ten years or penal servitude for life takes place.

221. (L.) Any one who exposes a person who is helpless from tender age, infirmity, or sickness, or any one who wilfully abandons such a person in a helpless position, if such person is under his care, or if he has to provide for the lodging, removal, or reception of such

person, shall be punished by imprisonment with labour for not less than three months.

If the act is committed by legitimate parents on their child, imprisonment with labour for not less than six months takes place.

(J.) If a severe bodily injury is caused by the act to a person who has been exposed or abandoned, the punishment of penal servitude up to ten years, and if death is caused by the act, penal servitude for not less than three years takes place.

Note.—For severe bodily injury cf. § 224.

Helpless includes drunken people (Leipsic, January 9th, 1882).

222. (L.) Any one who causes the death of a man by negligence shall be punished by imprisonment with labour up to three years.

If the author was peculiarly bound in virtue of his office, his calling, or his trade to show an attention, which he failed to show, the punishment can be raised to five years' imprisonment with labour.

Note.—'Caused' applies to cases where the offender only joins in the act of another (Leipsic, October 25th, 1881). The duty of paying attention in virtue of one's calling includes the case of inspection of food exposed for sale (Leipsic, December 1st, 1881).

SEVENTEENTH CHAPTER.

BODILY INJURY.

Note.—BODILY injuries arise either from malice or negligence; malicious injuries are either trivial or severe. All injuries due to negligence and all trivial injuries due to malice are only prosecuted on proposal, and it is not requisite first to make an attempt at compromise. These can all be prosecuted privately, public prosecution only taking place, when a public interest is at stake: the former goes before the court of the single judge and lay assessors, the latter before the court of second instance (*Landgericht*), which may transfer the matter to the single judge sitting without assessors.

223. (L. or A.) Any one who deliberately ill-uses the person or injures the health of another shall be punished for inflicting bodily injury by imprisonment with labour up to three years or with a fine up to 1000 shillings.

If the act is committed against a relation in the ascending line, the sentence must award imprisonment with labour for not less than one month.

Note.—This section assumes the unlawfulness of the injury and includes trivial injuries.

223 *a.*[1] (L. or A.) If the bodily injury is inflicted by means of arms, especially a knife or other dangerous implement,[2] or by means of a treacherous surprise or by several persons acting in concert, or by an act involving danger to life, imprisonment with labour for not less than two months takes place.

Note.—This section requires no proposal for prosecution (Leipsic, March 10th, 1880). Dangerous implements include beer glasses but not vitriol (Leipsic, March 31st, 1882).

224. If in consequence of the bodily injury, the injured person loses an important member of the body, the faculty of sight in one or both of his eyes, his hearing, his speech, or the power of generation, or is permanently disfigured in a serious manner, or falls into ill-health, paralysis, or mental debility, penal servi-

[1] Novella of 1876.

[2] Berner notes that the genus 'dangerous implement' is here illogically put under the species 'arms.'

tude up to five years or imprisonment with labour for not less than one year must be awarded.

225. (J.) If any one of the above-mentioned consequences was intended and took place, penal servitude for from two to ten years must be awarded.

226. (J.) If death to the injured person is caused by the bodily injury, penal servitude for not less than three years or imprisonment with labour for not less than three years must be awarded. (Cf. §§ 228, 231.)

227. (L.) If the death or severe injury of a man is caused by an affray or an assault made by several persons, every one, who took part in such affray or assault, must be punished for such participation alone by imprisonment with labour up to three years, in case he was not involved therein without fault of his own. (Cf. § 367, x.)

If one of the above-mentioned consequences must be ascribed to several injuries, which have caused such consequences not individually but by their concurrence, every one, to whose charge one of such injuries is laid, must be punished by penal servitude up to five years. (Cf. § 73, ii.)

228.[1] If extenuating circumstances exist, then the sentence shall, in cases under the second paragraph of § 223, and § 223 *a*, take the form of imprisonment with labour up to three years, or a fine up to 1000 shillings; in cases under § 224 and the second paragraph of § 227, imprisonment with labour for not less than three months.

229. Any one who deliberately administers to another, with the intent of injuring his health, poison or other substances calculated to destroy the health, shall be punished by penal servitude up to ten years.

If a severe bodily injury is caused by such act, penal servitude for not less than five years must be awarded, and if death has been caused by the act, penal servitude

[1] Novella of 1876.

for not less than ten years or penal servitude for life must be awarded.

Note.—Poison is from the meaning of the word calculated to destroy health, and no proof of this need be brought (Leipsic, June 30th, 1881).

230. (L. or A.) Any one who has caused the bodily injury of another through negligence, shall be punished by a fine up to 900 marks or by imprisonment with labour up to two years.

(L.) If the author was especially bound in virtue of his office, calling, or trade to show the attention, which he failed to show, the punishment can be raised to three years' imprisonment with labour.

231. In all cases of bodily injury there can at the request of the injured party be awarded a mulct to be inflicted on the offender up to the amount of 6000 shillings.

The award of a mulct precludes the enforcement of a further claim for damages.

The persons condemned are responsible for the mulct as joint debtors.

232.[1] The prosecution of trivial malicious injuries to the body and all bodily injuries due to negligence (§§ 223, 230) takes place only on proposal, so far as the bodily injury was not inflicted concurrently with a transgression of the duty of office, calling, or trade.

If the misdemeanour is committed against a relative the proposal may be withdrawn.

The regulations contained in §§ 195, 196, 198 are applicable here also.

Note.—For relatives cf. § 52. Where injuries have been mutually inflicted, the counter prosecution is permissible till the conclusion of the final speeches in the court of the first instance. § 198 does not extend to cases, in which insult and injury can be set off one against the other.

[1] Novella of 1876.

233. If trivial bodily injuries are repaid with the same, if insults are repaid with trivial bodily injuries, or the latter with the former, on the spot, the judge can award a punishment milder in kind and amount, or none at all, to both or one of the accused. (Cf. § 199.)

Note.—Under §§ 223, 340 no such reckoning takes place (Leipsic, October 28th, 1879, July 4th, 1882).

EIGHTEENTH CHAPTER.

FELONIES AND MISDEMEANOURS AGAINST PERSONAL LIBERTY.

234. (J.) ANY one who gets into his power a human being by treachery, threat, or force, with the intent of exposing him in a helpless condition, or bringing him into slavery, thraldom, or foreign military or naval service, shall be punished by penal servitude for kidnapping.

235. (L.) Any one who takes away a minor by treachery, threat, or force from his parents or guardians shall be punished by imprisonment with labour, and (J.) if the act is committed with the intent of using the minor to beg, or from motives of lucre, or for immoral purposes or employments, by penal servitude up to ten years.

236. (J.) Any one who carries off a female against her will by treachery, threat, or force, for immoral purposes (*um sie zur Unzucht zu bringen*) shall be punished by penal servitude up to ten years, and if the abduction was committed with the intent to bring the woman so carried off to marriage, by imprisonment with labour. Prosecution only takes place on proposal.

237. (L). Any one who carries off an unmarried female, being a minor, with her consent, without, however, the consent of her parents or her guardian, for immoral purposes or for marriage, shall be punished by imprisonment with labour. Prosecution only takes place on proposal.

238. If the abductor has married the person abducted, prosecution only takes place after the marriage has been declared invalid. (Cf. §§ 69, 236, 237.)

239. (L.) Any one who deliberately and unlawfully shuts up another human being, or deprives him in any other way of his liberty, shall be punished by imprisonment with labour.

Note.—This does not include taking away the clothes of persons, who are bathing (Leipsic, April 26th, 1882).

(J.) If liberty has been withdrawn for more than a week, or if a severe bodily injury has been caused to the person, who has been deprived of his liberty, by the withdrawal of his liberty or by the treatment experienced during such withdrawal, penal servitude up to ten years must be awarded. If extenuating circumstances exist, the punishment of imprisonment with labour for not less than one month takes place.

(J.) If the death of the person who has been deprived of his liberty, is caused by the withdrawal of his liberty or by the treatment experienced by him during the same, penal servitude for not less than three years must be awarded. If extenuating circumstances exist, the punishment of imprisonment with labour for not less than three months takes place.

240.[1] (L.) Any one who compels another unlawfully by force or threatening with a felony or misdemeanour to commit, suffer, or forbear an act, shall be punished by imprisonment with labour up to one year, or by a fine up to 600 shillings. The attempt to commit this offence is criminal.

[1] Novella of 1876.

Note.—The Novella of 1876 removed the necessity of a proposal.

For the whole section cf. §§ 114, 126, 241, 243, 254.

241.[1] (L. or A.) Any one who threatens another with the commission of a felony shall be punished by imprisonment with labour up to six months or with a fine up to 300 shillings. (Cf. §§ 126, 240, 253, 254.)

Note.—The Novella of 1876 removed the necessity of a proposal. It is indifferent, who is to commit the crime (Leipsic, May 1st, 1882).

NINETEENTH CHAPTER.

THEFT AND EMBEZZLEMENT.

Note.—For certain trivial acts of pilfering cf. § 370. Trivial cases of theft from field and forest are dealt with by the legislation of the individual states. (Introductory Law, § 2.)

242. (L. or A.) Any one who takes away any movable thing not being his own from another, with the intent of unlawfully appropriating it, shall be punished for theft by imprisonment with labour. The attempt to commit this offence is criminal.

Note.—The court of the lay assessors is competent in questions of theft, when the value of the property stolen does not exceed twenty-five shillings, otherwise the court of second instance (*Landgericht*), which can, however, assign the case to the lower court. Theft is complete when the thing is taken away (Leipsic, April 12th, 1881).

243. (L.) Penal servitude up to ten years must be awarded if—

(i.) Objects dedicated to the service of God are stolen from a building appointed for the service of God.

[1] Novella of 1876.

(ii.) Theft is committed from a building or enclosed space by breaking in, entering, or breaking open cases (*Behältnisse*).

(iii.) The theft is effected by the application of false keys or other implements, not intended for opening in a regular manner, for the opening of a building or the approaches to an enclosed space, or for the opening of doors or cases in the interior of such room or space.

(iv.) Theft is committed in a public road, a street or public place, a water-way or railroad, or in a post-office or the yards belonging thereto, or in a railway station, from luggage or other objects, which are to be forwarded, by means of cutting away or loosening the fastening or safety band, or by the application of false keys or other implements not intended for opening in a regular manner.

(v.) The thief or a participator in the theft carries arms at the time of committing the act.

(vi.) Several persons co-operate in the theft, who have bound themselves together for the continual commission of robbery or theft.

(vii.) The theft is committed at night-time in an inhabited building, into which the thief has crept with intent to steal, or in which he has concealed himself with like intent, even if at the time of the theft inhabitants are not present in the building. The enclosed space, which belongs to an inhabited building, and the buildings of every kind within such a space, as well as ships, which are inhabited, shall be considered as inhabited buildings.

If extenuating circumstances exist, the punishment of imprisonment with labour for not less than three months takes place.

Note.—It is a moot point what constitutes night-time. It was held to be the local time of going to bed at Dresden, September 15th, 1871, Jena, September 27th, 1871, and Mannheim, January 26th, 1878; but at

Leipsic, December 23rd, 1880, it was held to be the time of darkness between sunset and sunrise.

244. (L.) Any one who has been punished in German territory as thief, robber, or like a robber, or as a receiver of stolen goods, and has thereafter again committed one of these acts and been punished for such act, shall, if he commit a simple theft (§ 242) be punished by penal servitude up to ten years, if he commit a serious theft (§ 243), by penal servitude for not less than two years. If extenuating circumstances exist, then in the case of simple theft the punishment of imprisonment with labour for not less than three months takes place, in case of serious theft, the punishment of imprisonment with labour for not less than one year.

Note.—For relapse cf. §§ 245, 249, 252, 255, 258. Punishments for theft imposed by the police are also the basis of relapse and cases of abetting and participation as well (Leipsic, January 12th, 1881, March 3rd, 1882). Each of the former punishments must have been wholly or partially suffered or remitted (Leipsic, May 29th, 1880).

245. The regulations of § 244 are applicable even if the former punishments were only partially suffered, or were wholly or partially remitted, but are excluded if ten years have elapsed between the suffering or remission of the last punishment and the commission of the fresh theft.

246. (L. or A.) Any one who unlawfully appropriates any movable property not being his own, which he has in his possession or keeping, shall be punished for embezzlement by imprisonment with labour up to three years, and if the thing was intrusted to him, by imprisonment with labour up to five years. If extenuating circumstances exist a fine up to 900 shillings can be inflicted. The attempt to commit this offence is criminal.

Note.—For embezzlement by officials cf. §§ 350, 351.

The pledging of other persons' property, which has been let to the pledger with the will and capability of redemption, is not embezzlement (Leipsic, April 24th, 1880).

247.[1] Any one who is guilty of theft or embezzlement against relatives, guardians, or tutor, or any one who steals or embezzles things of trifling value from a person, to whom he stands in the relation of apprentice, or in whose household community he is a servant, is only to be prosecuted on proposal. The withdrawal of the proposal is permissible.

A theft or embezzlement committed by relations in the ascending line against relations in the descending line, or by one of a married pair against the other, is free from punishment.

These regulations are not applicable to participators or favorers (*Begünstiger*), who do not stand in one of the above-mentioned personal relations.

Note.—For this last paragraph cf. § 50 and § 257.

248. Together with the punishment of imprisonment with labour awarded for theft or embezzlement, the sentence may include the forfeiture of civil privileges. Together with the punishment of penal servitude awarded for theft, police supervision may also be permitted by the sentence.

TWENTIETH CHAPTER.

ROBBERY AND EXTORTION.

249. (J.) Any one who takes away from another any movable thing not being his own with violence to the person, or with the application of threats with imme-

[1] Novella of 1876.

diate danger to life or limb, with the intent to unlawfully appropriate such movable thing, shall be punished by penal servitude for robbery. If extenuating circumstances exist, the punishment of imprisonment with labour for not less than six months takes place.

250. (J.) Penal servitude for not less than five years shall be awarded if:—

(i.) The robber or one of the participators in the robbery carries weapons at the commission of the act.

(ii.) Several persons co-operate in the robbery, who have bound themselves together for the continual commission of robbery or theft.

(iii.) The robbery was committed on a public road, a street or railway, a public place, on the high seas, or on a water-way.

(iv.) The robbery was committed at night-time in an inhabited building (§ 243, vii.) into which the offender had crept or made entry by force, or in which he had concealed himself with similar intent.

(v.) The robber has been already once punished as a robber or like a robber in German territory. The regulations of § 245 are applicable in this case also.

If extenuating circumstances exist, the punishment of imprisonment with labour for not less than one year takes place.

251. (J.) The robber shall be punished by penal servitude for not less than ten years or by penal servitude for life, if a human being has been tortured in the robbery, or if a severe bodily injury or death has been caused to such person by the violence used upon him.

252. (J.) Any one who, when taken in the act of theft, uses violence against a person, or employs threats with immediate danger to life or limb to maintain himself in the possession of the stolen property, must be punished like a robber.

253. (L.) Any one who, to procure for a third person

an unlawful advantage in property, compels another by violence or threat to commit, suffer, or forbear an act, must be punished for extortion by imprisonment with labour for not less than one month. The attempt to commit this offence is criminal. (Cf. §§ 240, 339.)

254. (L.) If the extortion is committed by threatening with murder, arson, or causing an inundation, penal servitude up to five years must be awarded. (Cf. §§ 126, 241.)

255. (J.) If the extortion is committed by violence against a person, or with the application of threats of immediate danger to life or limb, the author is to be punished like a robber.

256. Together with the punishment of imprisonment with labour awarded for extortion, the sentence may include the forfeiture of civil privileges, and together with the punishment of penal servitude awarded for robbery and extortion, the sentence may permit police supervision.

TWENTY-FIRST CHAPTER.

FAVORING (BEGÜNSTIGUNG) AND RECEIVING.

257. (L. or A.) ANY one who after the commission of a felony or a misdemeanour knowingly renders aid to the author or participator to withdraw the same from punishment, or to secure him the advantages of the felony or misdemeanour, must be punished for favoring by a fine up to 600 shillings, or by imprisonment with labour up to one year, and if he renders this assistance for his own advantage, by imprisonment with labour. The punishment must, however, not be more severe in kind and amount than that, with which the act itself is threatened.

Favoring is free from punishment, if the same was afforded to the author or a participator by a relative with the purpose of withdrawing him from punishment.

Favoring is to be punished as assistance, if it was promised before the commission of the act. This provision is applicable to relatives also.

258. Any one who is guilty of favoring for the sake of his own advantage shall be punished as a receiver if the person favored has been guilty of—

(i.) (L. or A.) A simple theft or an embezzlement, by imprisonment with labour.

(ii.) (L.) A serious theft, a robbery, or an offence which is to be punished like robbery, by penal servitude up to five years.

If extenuating circumstances exist, the punishment of imprisonment with labour for not less than three months takes place.

These penal regulations are also applicable if the receiver is a relative.

259. (L or A.) Any one who to his own advantage secretes, purchases, receives in pawn, or who otherwise takes into his possession or co-operates in the sale by others of things, of which he knows or must assume from the circumstances that they have been acquired by means of a criminal act, shall be punished as a receiver by imprisonment with labour.

Note.—It is not necessary that the receiver should know the exact kind of criminal act, and the details of such act (Leipsic, April 4th, 1880). The words, "must assume from the circumstances," imply gross carelessness of an extraordinary nature (Leipsic, April 28th, 1880).

260. Any one who practises receiving habitually or as a trade shall be punished by penal servitude up to ten years.

261. Any one who has been punished in German territory for receiving once, and also for receiving committed a second time thereafter, shall be punished by

penal servitude for not less than two years, if the receiving committed afresh relates to a serious theft, robbery, or an offence, which is to be punished like robbery. If extenuating circumstances exist, the punishment of imprisonment with labour for not less than one year takes place.

If the receiving relates to another criminal act, penal servitude up to ten years must be awarded. If extenuating circumstances exist, the punishment of imprisonment with labour for not less than three months takes place.

The regulations contained in § 245 are applicable here also.

262. Together with the punishment of imprisonment with labour, the sentence may include the forfeiture of civil privileges, and with every condemnation for receiving the sentence may permit police supervision.

TWENTY-SECOND CHAPTER.

FRAUD AND BREACH OF TRUST.

263. (L. or A.) ANY one who in the intent to procure for himself or a third person an unlawful advantage in property by causing or confirming a mistake by means of misrepresentation of untrue or distortion or suppression of true statements (*Thatsachen*), shall be punished for fraud by imprisonment with labour, with which the sentence may include a fine up to 3000 shillings as well as the forfeiture of civil privileges. If extenuating circumstances exist, the fine may be inflicted alone. The attempt to commit this offence is criminal.

Any one who commits a fraud against relatives, guardians, or tutors must only be prosecuted on proposal. The withdrawal of the demand is permissible.

Note.—The necessity of a proposal for the prosecution of those, who had defrauded persons in whose service they were, was removed by the Novella of 1876.

The court of lay assessors is competent in questions where the damage does not exceed twenty-five shillings, otherwise the court of second instance, which can, however, assign the matter to the court of lay assessors.

The damage to property within the meaning of this section includes the withdrawal of gain, of which there is a certain prospect (Leipsic, December 12th, 1881), fraudulent borrowing (Leipsic, December 11th, 1880), cheating in bills at taverns (Leipsic, January 3rd, 1881), clandestine entry into railway carriages (Leipsic, June 20th, 1881), mendacious begging (July 4th, 1881), realizing claims, which have been assigned to others, by the assignor (Leipsic, July 12th, 1881), false allegation of the existence of a rule of law (October 3rd, 1881).

264. (L.) Any one who has been punished in German territory once and again thereafter a second time for fraud committed shall be punished by penal servitude up to ten years for fraud committed thereafter and at the same time with a fine of from 150 to 6000 shillings. If extenuating circumstances exist, imprisonment with labour for not less than three months takes place, with which at the same time a fine up to 3000 shillings may be inflicted. The regulations contained in § 245 are applicable here also.

265. (J.) Any one who with fraudulent intent sets fire to an object insured against the danger of fire, or causes a ship which is insured as such, or for its cargo or freight, to sink or run ashore, shall be punished by penal servitude up to ten years, and at the same time with a fine of from 150 up to 6000 shillings. (Cf. §§ 306—308, 323.) If extenuating circumstances exist, imprisonment with labour for not less than six months takes place, with which the sentence may include a fine up to 3000 shillings.

266. (L.) The following persons shall be punished for breach of trust by imprisonment with labour, with which the sentence may include the forfeiture of civil privileges:—

(i.) Guardians, curators, trustees, sequestrators, official receivers, executors, administrators of foundations[1] if they intentionally act to the prejudice of the persons or things intrusted to their charge.

(ii.) Persons acting under a power of agent (*Bevollmächtigte*), who intentionally make arrangements with regard to rights or other property belonging to the person, who gave the power of agent to the disadvantage of the same.

(*Note.*—This includes members of the directory or committee of supervision of a society of shareholders. For 'agent' as opposed to 'attorney' (*Prokurist*), cf. the Commercial Code.)

(iii.) Land surveyors, auctioneers, brokers, vouchers for property, managers, weighers, measurers, sorters, workmen, stowers, and other persons bound by the authorities to the exercise of their trade, if they intentionally act in the business intrusted to them to the prejudice of those persons whose business they are looking after.

If the breach of trust is committed to procure an advantage in property for oneself or for another, then together with the imprisonment with labour a fine up to 3000 shillings can be inflicted.

[1] *E. g.* for charitable or educational purposes.

TWENTY-THIRD CHAPTER.

FORGERY OF DOCUMENTS.

267. (L.) ANY one who with unlawful intent forges or fraudulently prepares and uses for the purpose of deception a German or foreign public document, or a similar private document which is of importance for the proof of rights or legal relations, shall be punished for the forgery of a document by imprisonment with labour.

Note.—The character of documents in general and of public documents in particular, as well as the proof of the importance of private documents, are matters of fact for the jury to decide.

The code of civil procedure defines public documents as "documents which are drawn up in the prescribed form by a public magistrate (*Behörde*) within the scope of his official competence, or by a person invested with public credit within the department of business assigned to him."

Forged telegrams (Leipsic, May 5th, 1880, March 6th, 1883) and marks on tin plates (*Blechmarken*) (Leipsic, January 31st, 1881) are within this section.

268. A forgery of a document committed with the intent to procure for oneself or another an advantage in property, or to cause damage to another, shall be punished if :—

(i.) (L.) The document is a private document, by penal servitude up to five years, with which the sentence may include a fine up to 3000 shillings.

(ii.) (J.) The document is a public document, by penal servitude up to ten years, with which the sentence may include a fine of from 150 up to 6000 shillings.

If extenuating circumstances exist, imprisonment with labour takes place, a punishment which must not fall below a term of one week in the case of forgery of a private document, and not below a term of three months in the case of the forgery of a public document With the imprisonment the sentence may include a fine up to 3000 shillings.

269. It shall be considered as equivalent to the fraudulent preparation of a document, if any one gives a documentary content to a paper provided with the signature of another without the will or contrary to the direction of that other by filling up such paper.

270. It shall be considered equivalent to the forgery of a document, if any one with the intent to deceive makes use of a false or forged document knowing it to be false or forged.

271. (L.) Any one who maliciously causes declarations, negotiations, or matters of fact, which are of importance for the proof of rights or legal relations, to be attested as having been delivered or having occurred while they never have been delivered or never have occurred at all, or, if at all, in another manner or by a person in a capacity, which did not belong to him, or by another person, shall be punished by imprisonment with labour up to six months or by a fine up to 300 shillings. (Cf. § 348.)

272. (J.) Any one who commits the above-mentioned act with the intent to procure for himself or another an advantage in property or to cause damage to another shall be punished by penal servitude up to ten years, with which the sentence may include a fine of from 150 to 6000 shillings. (Cf. § 349.) If extenuating circumstances exist, the punishment of imprisonment with labour takes place, with which the sentence may include a fine up to 3000 shillings.

273. (L.) Any one who knowingly makes use of a false attestation of the kind mentioned in § 271 for the purpose of deception shall be punished according to the regulation in that paragraph contained, and if the intent

was directed to procure for himself or another an advantage in property, or to cause damage to another, such an one shall be punished according to the directions of § 272.

274. (L.) Any one shall be punished by imprisonment with labour, and may further be fined up to 3000 shillings, who:—

(i.) Destroys, damages, or suppresses a document, which does not belong to him at all, or which does not belong exclusively to him, with the intent to cause damage to another.

(ii.) Takes away, destroys, makes unrecognizable, displaces, or sets in a false position a boundary stone or any other mark for indicating a boundary or a flood-mark, with the intent to cause damage to another. (Cf. §§ 133, 348, 349.)

275. (L.) Any one shall be punished by imprisonment for not less than three months who:—

(i.) Knowingly makes use of false or forged stamped paper, false or forged stamp marks, blank stamped forms, impressions of stamps, postal or telegraphic franking marks, or stamped letter covers.

(ii.) [1] Any one who prepares counterfeit stamped paper, counterfeit stamp marks, blank stamped forms, or impressions of stamps for playing cards, passes, or other such printed or written papers; likewise any one who prepares counterfeit postal or telegraphic franking marks or stamped letter covers, with the intent to employ them as genuine.

(iii.) Any one who forges genuine stamped paper, genuine stamp marks, blank stamped forms, impressions of stamps, postal or telegraphic franking marks or stamped letter covers, with the intent to employ them as of a higher value.

Note.—This section includes foreign stamp marks (Leipsic, June 20th, 1882). 'Forges,' cf. p. 160, *supra*.

276. (A.) Any one who knowingly employs for docu-

[1] Novella of 1876.

ments, on which there is a stamp duty, stamped paper, stamp marks, or blank stamped forms, which have been already once used, likewise impressions of stamps, which have served to indicate taxation which has taken place, shall be punished by a fine up to 600 shillings, besides the punishment which is incurred by evading the stamp tax.

277. (L.) Any one who draws up a certificate in the capacity of physician or any other qualified medical capacity, which does not belong to him, or in the name of such persons without being entitled thereto, about the state of his own health or that of others, or falsifies a genuine certificate of such a nature and makes use thereof to deceive a magistrate or an insurance society, shall be punished by imprisonment with labour up to one year.

278. (L.) Physicians and other qualified medical men, who draw up an incorrect certificate with regard to the state of health of a person, for use before a magistrate or an insurance society, against their better knowledge, shall be punished by imprisonment with labour for from one month to two years.

279. (L.) Any one who makes use of a certificate of the kind mentioned in §§ 277, 278, to deceive a magistrate or an insurance society with regard to the state of his health or that of another, shall be punished by imprisonment with labour up to one year.

280. Together with the punishment of imprisonment with labour, awarded according to the regulations of §§ 267, 274, 275, 277—279, the sentence may include the forfeiture of civil privileges.

TWENTY-FOURTH CHAPTER.[1]

BANKRUPTCY.

(IMPERIAL Bankruptcy Law of February 10th, 1877.)

209. (J.) Debtors, who have suspended payment or in respect of whose property proceedings in bankruptcy have been instituted, shall be punished with penal servitude for fraudulent bankruptcy, if they have with the intent to prejudice their creditors :—

(i.) Concealed or made away with portions of property.

(ii.) Recognized or published debts or legal obligations wholly or partly fabricated.

(iii.) Neglected to keep commercial books, which they were bound by law to keep. (Cf. Commercial Code, Article 28.[2])

(iv.) Destroyed or concealed their commercial books, or so kept or altered them, that such books do not convey a clear idea (*Uebersicht*) of the condition of the property.

If extenuating circumstances exist, the punishment of imprisonment with labour for not less than three months takes place.

Note.—The concurrence of different acts (i.—iv.) does not form a plurality of delicts or real concurrence within the meaning of § 74, nor can there be concurrence of fraudulent and simple bankruptcy (§ 210). Leipsic, November 3rd, 1879, March 17th, 1882.

210. (L.) Debtors, who have suspended payment or with regard to whose property proceedings in bankruptcy

[1] §§ 281-3 were replaced by §§ 209-14 of the Bankruptcy Law of 1877, according to § 3 of the law which introduced the criminal code. Cf. *supra*, p. 176.

[2] A translation of the Commercial Code with a commentary by the author of the present work is in the press.

have been commenced, shall be punished by imprisonment with labour for simple bankruptcy, if they have :—

(i.) Employed excessive sums or become indebted by means of expenditure, gambling, or trading on differences in goods or Stock Exchange papers.

(ii.) Neglected to keep commercial books, which they were bound by law to keep, or have concealed, destroyed, or kept such books in such a disorderly manner, that they do not convey a clear idea of the condition of the property.

(iii.) Contrary to the regulations of the commercial code, neglected to draw a balance of their property within the time prescribed. (Cf. Commercial Code, Art. 29.)

211. (L.) Debtors, who have suspended payment or with regard to whose property proceedings in bankruptcy have been instituted, shall be punished by imprisonment with labour up to two years, if they, although they knew their insolvency, have with a view to favor a creditor above the rest guaranteed such creditor a security or satisfaction, to which he had no claim in such manner or at such time.

Note.—The favored creditor can be abettor to the misdemeanour mentioned in this section, but he does not become an assistant thereto by merely receiving the money.

212. (J.) Any one shall be punished by penal servitude up to ten years who :—

(i.) Has concealed or made away part of his property in the interest of a debtor, who has suspended payment, or with reference to whose property proceedings in bankruptcy have been instituted.

(ii.) Has in the course of the proceedings enforced fabricated claims in his own name, or by means of suborned persons, in the interest of such a debtor with a view to procure an advantage in property for himself or for another.

If extenuating circumstances exist, the punishment of imprisonment with labour or a fine up to 6000 shillings takes place.

213. (L.) A creditor, who has obtained a voucher or promise of special advantages from the common debtor or from other persons on the understanding that he shall vote in a certain way at divisions of the creditors, shall be punished by a fine up to 3000 shillings or by imprisonment with labour up to one year.

214. The penal regulations of §§ 209—211 are applicable against the members of the committee of a society of shareholders or registered association (*Genossenschaft*), and against the liquidators of a commercial society, or a registered association which has suspended payment, or with regard to the property of which proceedings in bankruptcy have been instituted, if such persons have committed the acts threatened with punishment in such capacity.

TWENTY-FIFTH CHAPTER.

CRIMINAL SELFISHNESS AND BREACH OF SECRETS BELONGING TO OTHERS.

284. (L.) Any one who makes a trade of a game of chance, shall be punished by imprisonment with labour up to two years, with which the sentence may include a fine of 300 to 600 shillings as well as the forfeiture of civil privileges.

If the person condemned is a foreigner, the local police magistrates are authorized to banish him from the federal territory. (Cf. § 361.)

Note.—Bookmakers who keep a business office are liable under this section (Leipsic, October 13th, 1880).

285. (L. or A.) The occupier of a public place of

meeting, who allows games of chance there or aids in the concealment of such games, shall be punished with a fine up to 1500 shillings.

Note.—The concealment in rooms, which are not public, is criminal, it being indifferent whether the object is gain or amusement (Leipsic, February 28th, 1882).

286. (L.) Any one who arranges public lotteries without the permission of the authorities shall be punished by imprisonment with labour up to two years or by a fine up to 3000 shillings.

Raffles publicly arranged for movable or immovable things must be considered equivalent to lotteries.

287. This article is replaced by Article 14 of the law to protect trade-marks of November 30th, 1874. "Any one who wittingly and unlawfully marks wares or their cases with a trade-mark protected under this law, or with the name or firm of a German producer or trader, or who wittingly brings into circulation or exposes for sale such wares being unlawfully marked, shall be punished by a fine from 150 to 3000 shillings, or by imprisonment with labour up to six months, and is bound to compensate the injured person. Criminal prosecution only takes place on proposal.

Note.—The proposal to prosecute may not be withdrawn. (Cf. *infra*, Appendix, Law relating to Trade-Marks.)

288. (L. or A.) Any one who alienates or makes away with component parts of his property, when threatened with an execution, with the intent to frustrate the satisfaction of his creditors, shall be punished by imprisonment with labour up to two years. Prosecution only takes place on the proposal of the creditor.

Note.—Alienation may include letting on lease (Leipsic, February 17th, 1882). (Cf. § 137.)

289. (L.) Any one who with unlawful intent takes away his own movable property, or the movable

property of another for the benefit of the proprietor from the usufructuary, the mortgagee, or the person, who has a right of using or detaining the property, shall be punished by imprisonment with labour up to three years, or by a fine up to 900 shillings. Together with the sentence of imprisonment with labour, the sentence may include the forfeiture of civil privileges. The attempt to commit this offence is criminal. Prosecution only takes place on proposal. The directions of the second and third paragraphs of § 247 are applicable here also.

290. (L.) Public pawnbrokers, who make use of objects taken in pawn without authorization, shall be punished by imprisonment with labour up to one year, with which a fine up to 900 shillings may be awarded.

291. (L.) Any one who unlawfully appropriates ammunition, which has been shot away at the practice of the artillery, or any one who unlawfully appropriates leaden balls from the receptacles at the shooting places for the troops, shall be punished by imprisonment with labour up to one year, or a fine up to 900 shillings.

292.[1] (A.) Any one who hunts at places, at which he is not entitled to hunt, shall be punished with a fine up to 300 shillings, or by imprisonment with labour up to three months. If the offender is a relative of the person entitled to hunt, prosecution only takes place on proposal. The withdrawal of the proposal is permissible. (Cf. § 368, x.)

Note.—The Novella of 1876 limited the necessity of a proposal to relatives. Game in enclosures is the subject of common theft (Leipsic, December 12th, 1879).

293. (L. or A.) The punishment can be raised to a fine of as much as 600 shillings, or to imprisonment with labour for as long as six months, when the game is beset (*nachstellen*) not with firearms or hounds, but with snares, nets, traps, or other contrivances, or

1 Novella of 1876.

when the misdemeanour is committed during the legal close time, in woods, at night-time, or by several persons in company.

Note.—Here also, if the offender is a relative of the person entitled to hunt, a proposal is necessary (Leipsic, January 10th, 1873). Night-time is after dark and before light (Leipsic, December 23rd, 1880).

294. (L.) Any one who, without being entitled to hunt, practises hunting as a trade shall be punished by imprisonment with labour for not less than three months: the sentence may also include the forfeiture of civil privileges, and may further permit police supervision.

295. Together with the punishment incurred by the hunting misdemeanour, the sentence must include the confiscation of the arms, hunting-tools, and hounds which the offender took with him on his unlawful hunting expedition, as well as of the snares, nets, and traps, and other contrivances, without distinction whether they belong to the person condemned or not.

296.[1] (L.) Any one who unlawfully fishes or catches crabs at night-time, by torchlight, or by the use of noxious or explosive materials, shall be punished by a fine up to 600 shillings, or by imprisonment with labour up to six months. (Cf. § 370, iv.)

Note.—The Novella of 1876 removed the necessity of a proposal.

296 *a.*[1] Foreigners, who fish in German waters, without authorization shall be punished with a fine up to 600 shillings, or by imprisonment with labour up to six months. Together with the fine or the imprisonment with labour, the sentence must include the confiscation of the catching implements, which the offender had with him, when he fished without authorization, likewise of the fish contained in the vessel, without distinction whether the implements and fish belong to the person condemned or not.

[1] Novella of 1876.

297. A traveller or member of the crew, who without the foreknowledge of the captain, likewise a captain who without the foreknowledge of the owner, takes on board objects, which endanger the ship or the cargo, in that they may cause the seizure or confiscation of the ship or cargo, shall be punished by a fine up to 1500 shillings, or by imprisonment with labour up to two years.

298. A sailor who absconds with his pay, or who has concealed himself, to withdraw himself from the service he has undertaken, shall be punished by imprisonment with labour up to one year, without distinction whether the offence has been committed in Germany or in foreign territory.

299. (A.) Any one who maliciously and without authorization opens a closed letter or other closed document not intended for his cognizance, shall be punished by a fine up to 300 shillings, or by imprisonment with labour up to three months. Prosecution only takes place on proposal. (Cf. §§ 354, 355, 358.)

300. (L. or A.) Solicitors (*Rechtsanwalte*), advocates, notaries, counsel in criminal cases, physicians, surgeons, midwives, apothecaries, and their assistants, shall be punished by a fine up to 1500 shillings, or by imprisonment with labour up to three months, if they reveal without authorization secrets, which are intrusted to them in virtue of their office, position (*Stand*), or trade. Prosecution only takes place on proposal.

301. (L.) Any one shall be punished by imprisonment with labour up to six months, or by a fine up to 1500 shillings, who, from motives of lucre and by trading on the thoughtlessness or inexperience of a minor, causes the issue by such minor to himself of acknowledgments of debt, bills of exchange, receipts, deeds of suretyship, or any other document containing an engagement (*Verpflichtung*), or even only the verbal communication of a promise to pay. Prosecution only takes place on proposal.

302. (L.) Any one shall be punished by imprisonment with labour up to one year, or a fine up to 3000 shillings, who from motives of lucre, and by trading on the thoughtlessness or inexperience of a minor, causes a promise to be made by such minor to himself, under a pledge of honour, or on word of honour, on oath, or under similar assurances or asseverations, of payment of a sum of money or the fulfilment of an obligation arising from a legal relation, and directed to the guarantee of things having a money value. Together with the punishment of imprisonment with labour, the sentence may include the forfeiture of civil privileges.

The same punishment is incurred by the man who permits the transfer to himself of a claim, of which he knows that the settlement has been promised by a minor in the above-mentioned manner. Prosecution takes place only on proposal.

302 *a*. (L.) Any one shall be punished for usury by imprisonment with labour up to six months, and at the same time by a fine up to 3000 shillings, who, profiting by the necessity, thoughtlessness, or inexperience of another, causes the guarantee to himself or a third person, of advantages in property either for a loan, or in the case of delaying the enforcement of a money claim, if such advantages exceed the usual rate of interest in such a manner, that according to the circumstances of the case, they stand in striking disproportion to the service rendered. The sentence may also include the forfeiture of civil privileges.

Note.—§§ 302 *a*, *b*, *c*, *d*, on usury, are due to the law of May 24th, 1880, and came into force on June 14th, 1880.

The chief marks of usury under this section are, subjectively, profiting by necessity, thoughtlessness, and inexperience; objectively, an unusual rate of interest and a disproportion between service and advantage.

according to the circumstances of the case (Leipsic, May 25th, 1881).

302 *b*. (L.) Any one who conceals the usurious advantages in property (§ 302 *a*) to himself or a third person, or who causes a promise of such advantages to be made mutually, or by pledging honour, or on the word of honour, or on oath, or under similar assurances or asseverations, shall be punished by imprisonment with labour up to one year, and by a fine up to 6000 shillings. The sentence may further include the forfeiture of civil privileges.

302 *c*. The same punishments (§§ 302 *a*, 302 *b*) are incurred by the man, who acquires a claim of the above-mentioned nature, with knowledge of the circumstances of the case, and either further alienates the same, or enforces such usurious advantage in property.

302 *d*. (L.) Any one who practises usury as a trade or habit, shall be punished by imprisonment with labour for not less than three months, and at the same time by a fine of from 150 up to 15,000 shillings. The sentence must also include the forfeiture of civil privileges. (Cf. § 32.)

Note.—This section exceeds the highest amount of a fine so far under the code, viz. 6000 shillings.

To constitute usury as a trade instances may be reckoned, which occurred before the enactment of this code (Leipsic, February 2nd, 1882), but not to constitute usury as a habit (February 24th, 1882).

TWENTY-SIXTH CHAPTER.

DAMAGE TO PROPERTY.

303.[1] (L. or A.) ANY one who maliciously and unlawfully damages or destroys property belonging to another,

[1] Novella of 1876.

shall be punished by a fine up to 1000 shillings, or by imprisonment with labour up to two years.

The attempt to commit this offence is criminal. Prosecution only takes place on proposal. If the misdemeanour is committed against a relative, the withdrawal of the proposal is permissible.

304. (L. or A.) Any one who maliciously and unlawfully damages or destroys objects of veneration of a religious society existing in the state, or things dedicated to divine service, or tombs, public monuments, objects of art, science, or trade preserved in public collections or publicly exhibited, or objects which serve for public use or for the beautification of public roads, places, or pleasure-grounds, shall be punished by imprisonment up to three years, or by a fine up to 1500 shillings. Together with the punishment of imprisonment with labour, the sentence may include the forfeiture of civil privileges. The attempt to commit these offences is criminal.

305. (L.) Any one who maliciously and unlawfully destroys either wholly or partially a building, a ship, a bridge, a dam, a road that has been constructed, a railway or other edifice, the property of others, shall be punished by imprisonment with labour for not less than one month. The attempt to commit this offence is criminal.

TWENTY-SEVENTH CHAPTER.

FELONIES AND MISDEMEANOURS INVOLVING DANGER TO THE PUBLIC.

306. (J.) Any one shall be punished for arson by penal servitude, who maliciously sets on fire:—

(i.) A building appointed for meetings for divine service.

(ii.) A building, a ship, or a hut, which serves for the habitation of human beings.

(iii.) A room, which serves temporarily for the residence of human beings, and especially at the time, at which they are wont to reside in it. (Cf. §§ 265, 307 and foll., 325.)

307. (J.) Arson (§ 306) shall be punished by penal servitude for not less than ten years, or by penal servitude for life if :—

(i.) The fire caused the death of a human being, because he was in the room, which was set on fire at the time of the act.

(ii.) The arson was committed with the intent of committing murder or robbery, or to excite a riot under cover of such arson.

(iii.) The incendiary has removed or rendered useless apparatus for extinguishing fire, in order to prevent or make difficult the extinguishment of the fire. (Cf. § 325; Introductory Law § 4.)

308. (J.) Any one shall be punished for arson by penal servitude up to ten years, who maliciously sets on fire buildings, ships, huts, mines, magazines, storehouses which stand on public places intended therefor, stores of agricultural products, or of building materials, or fuel, crops in the field, woodlands, or turf-moors, if these objects are the property of another, or even if they are special property of the incendiary, but from their condition and position are calculated to communicate the fire to one of the rooms designated in § 306, i.—iii., or one of the above designated objects, being the property of another. If extenuating circumstances exist, the punishment of imprisonment with labour for not less than six months takes place.

Note.—If one of the acts of arson mentioned in §§ 306, 307 was intended, then in the second case of § 308 the punishment of attempt to commit the former takes place according to § 73. (Cf. also §§ 265, 325.)

309. (L.) Any one who through negligence brings about a fire of the kind mentioned in §§ 306—308, shall be punished by imprisonment with labour up to one year, or by a fine up to 900 shillings, and if the death of a human being has been caused by the fire, by imprisonment with labour for from one month to three years.

310. If the offender extinguished the fire before such fire was discovered, and before more damage was done than was effected by the mere setting on fire, he is free from punishment. (Cf. § 46, ii.)

311. The total or partial destruction of a thing by the use of powder or other explosive materials must be considered equivalent to setting on fire. (Cf. § 325.)

312. (J.) Any one who maliciously brings about an inundation, accompanied by common danger to human life, shall be punished by penal servitude for not less than three years, and if the death of a human being has been caused by the inundation, by penal servitude for not less than ten years or by penal servitude for life. (Cf. § 325; Introductory Law, § 4.)

313. (J.) Any one who maliciously brings about an inundation with common danger to property, shall be punished by penal servitude.

(L.) If, however, the intent of the offender only aimed at the protection of his property, imprisonment with labour for not less than one year must be awarded. (Cf. § 325.)

314. (L.) Any one who through negligence brings about an inundation, with common danger to life or property, shall be punished by imprisonment up to one year, and if the death of a man has been caused by the inundation, by imprisonment with labour for from one month up to three years.

315. (J.) Any one who maliciously damages the grounds or means of traffic or other appurtenances of a railway, or causes such hindrance on the railroad, by

false signs or signals, or in any other way in such a manner as to endanger the traffic, shall be punished by penal servitude up to ten years.

If a severe bodily injury has been caused by the act, penal servitude for not less than five years takes place, and if the death of a human being has been caused, penal servitude for not less than ten years or penal servitude for life.

Note.—The section does not refer to tramways (Berlin, May 14th, 1873). (Cf. §§ 224, 325; I. L., § 4.)

316. (L.) Any one who negligently places the traffic on a railway in danger by one of the above-mentioned acts, shall be punished by imprisonment with labour up to one year, and if the death of a human being has been caused by the act, by imprisonment with labour for from one month to three years.

A similar punishment is incurred by the persons, who are appointed to the management of railway journeys, and to the supervision of the permanent way and carrying on of the traffic, if they by the neglect of the duties incumbent upon them place a train in danger.

317. (L.) Any one who maliciously commits against a telegraphic institution, which serves a public purpose, acts, which prevent or destroy the use of such institution, shall be punished by imprisonment with labour up to three years.

318. (L.) Any one who negligently commits against a telegraphic institution, which serves the public purpose, acts, which prevent or destroy the use of such institution, shall be punished by imprisonment with labour up to one year, or by a fine up to 900 shillings.

A similar penalty is incurred by those persons, who are appointed for the supervision and service of the telegraphic institutions and their appurtenances, if they by neglect of their duties prevent or destroy the use of the institution.

[1] Novella of 1876.

319.[1] If any of the officers mentioned in §§ 316 and 318 are condemned for the acts designated in §§ 315—318, such officer can at the same time be declared incapable for employment in the railway or the telegraph service, or in certain branches of these services.

320. (L.) The manager of a railway company as well as the manager of a telegraphic institution, which serves for public purposes, who does not at once effect the removal of the person condemned, on the communication to him of the valid decision, shall be punished by a fine up to 300 shillings, or by imprisonment with labour up to three months.

Similar punishment is incurred by any one, who has been declared incapable for the railway and telegraph service, if he allows himself to be reappointed at a railway or telegraphic institution, as well as by those, who have reappointed him, although they knew that he had been declared incapable.

321.[1] (L.) Any one shall be punished by imprisonment with labour for not less than three months, who maliciously destroys or damages aqueducts, sluices, weirs, dykes, dams, or water-works, or bridges, ferries, roads, or fences, or apparatus which serve to contain water, or for working mines, or for lightning conductors, or for the entry or exit of the workmen, or disturbs the water-way in navigable streams, rivers, or canals, and by means of one of these acts causes danger to the life or health of others. (Cf. § 325.)

(L.) If a severe bodily injury has been caused by one of these acts, penal servitude up to ten years takes place, and (J.) if the death of a human being has been caused, penal servitude for not less than five years.

322. (J.) Any one who maliciously destroys, makes away with, or renders useless a fire-signal appointed for the security of navigation, or any other signal exhibited for this object, or any one who extinguishes

[1] Novella of 1876.

such a fire-signal, or, contrary to his duty of service, does not exhibit the same afresh, or exhibits a false signal, which is calculated to make navigation insecure, especially any one who lights at night-time on the shore level a fire, which is calculated to endanger navigation, shall be punished by penal servitude up to ten years.

If the stranding of a ship has been caused by such act, penal servitude for not less than five years takes place, and if the death of a human being has been caused thereby, penal servitude for not less than ten years or penal servitude for life.

323. (J.) Any one who maliciously effects the stranding or sinking of a ship, and thereby causes danger to the life of another, shall be punished by penal servitude for not less than five years, and if the death of a human being has been caused by the act, by penal servitude for not less than ten years, or by penal servitude for life. (Cf. § 325.)

324. (J.) Any one who maliciously poisons reservoirs, or wells of water, which serve the use of others, or objects, which are intended for public sale or use, or any one who mixes with such objects, substances, of which it is known that they are calculated to destroy human health; further, any one who knowingly and without mentioning their character sells, exposes for sale, or otherwise brings into circulation, such poisoned things, or such things so mixed with dangerous substances, shall be punished by penal servitude up to ten years; and if the death of a human being has been caused by the act, by penal servitude for not less than ten years, or penal servitude for life. (Cf. Appendix VIII.; I. L., § 4.)

325. Together with the punishment of penal servitude, awarded according to the regulations of §§ 308, 311, 312, 313, 315, 321, 324, the sentence may permit police supervision.

326. (L.) If one of the acts designated in §§ 321—324 has been committed from negligence, imprisonment

with labour up to one year must be awarded, if damage has been caused by the act, and imprisonment with labour for from one month to three years, if the death of a human being has been caused thereby.

327. (L. or A.) Any one who knowingly infringes the rules of isolation or supervision, or the prohibition of importation issued by the competent magistrates, to avoid the importation or spread of a contagious disease, shall be punished by imprisonment with labour up to one year.

(L.) If in consequence of this infringement a human being has been attacked by contagious disease, imprisonment with labour for from three months to three years takes place.

328. (L. or A.) Any one who knowingly infringes the rules of isolation or supervision, or the prohibition of importation issued by the competent magistrates, to avoid the importation or spread of cattle plagues, shall be punished by imprisonment with labour up to one year.

(L.) If in consequence of this infringement cattle have been attacked by the plague, the punishment of imprisonment with labour for from one month to two years takes place.

329. (L.) Any one who fails through malice to fulfil at the appointed time, or in the manner previously agreed, contracts for delivery, concluded with a magistrate, for the needs of the army or navy at the time of a war, for the necessaries of life, or to avert or remove distress, shall be punished by imprisonment with labour for not less than six months. The sentence may also include the forfeiture of civil privileges.

If negligence is the cause of the non-fulfilment of the contract, imprisonment with labour up to two years must be awarded, if damage has been caused by the act.

The same punishments are applicable to sub-contractors, middlemen, and agents of the contractor, who, knowing the object of the delivery, cause the non-delivery through malice or negligence.

330. (L.) Any one who, in the management or erection of a building, acts contrary to the universally recognized rules of the art of building in such a manner, that danger to others arises therefrom, shall be punished by a fine up to 900 shillings, or by imprisonment with labour up to one year.

Note.—This includes acts of omission (Leipsic, January 4th, 1883).

TWENTY-EIGHTH CHAPTER.

FELONIES AND MISDEMEANOURS IN OFFICE.

Note.—Participation by a non-official is criminal (Leipsic, June 22nd, 1880).

331. (L.) An official, who receives, demands, or permits a promise of presents or other advantages for an act, which belongs to his office, and which is not in itself an infringement of his duty, shall be punished by a fine up to 300 shillings, or by imprisonment with labour up to six months.

Note.—The person who gives such presents, is free from punishment.

332. (L.) An official, who receives, demands, or permits a promise of presents or other advantages for an act, which involves an infringement of the duties of the office or service, shall be punished for corruption by penal servitude up to five years. If extenuating circumstances exist, the punishment of imprisonment with labour takes place.

333. Any one who offers, promises, or guarantees to an official or a member of the armed forces presents or other advantages, to determine him to commit an act

involving an infringement of the duty of his office or the service, shall be punished for corruption by imprisonment with labour; the sentence may also include the forfeiture of civil privileges. If extenuating circumstances exist, a fine up to 1500 shillings may be inflicted.

334. (J.) A judge, arbitrator, juryman, or lay assessor who demands, receives, or permits a promise of presents or other advantages, to manage or decide a lawsuit (*Rechtssache*), the management or decision of which falls to him, in favour or to the prejudice of a party in the cause, shall be punished by penal servitude.

The person who offers, promises, or guarantees, to a judge, arbitrator, juryman, or lay assessor presents or advantages for the above-mentioned ends shall be punished by penal servitude. If extenuating circumstances exist, the punishment of imprisonment with labour takes place.

335. In the cases of §§ 331, 334, declaration must be made in judgment that the thing received or the value of the same is forfeited to the state.

336. (L.) An official or arbitrator, who is deliberately guilty of a perversion of justice in the management or decision of a lawsuit in the favour or to the prejudice of a party, shall be punished by penal servitude up to five years.

337. This section is replaced by § 67 of the law concerning the attestation of personal rank (February 6th, 1875). "A clergyman or other servant of religion, who proceeds to the solemnization of a marriage, before it has been proved to him that the marriage has been concluded before the registrar (*Standesbeamte*), shall be punished by a fine up to 300 shillings, or by imprisonment with labour up to three months." (Cf. Appendix IX.)

338. A servant of religion or an official registrar of personal rank, who, knowing that a person is married, concludes a new marriage for such person, shall be

punished by penal servitude up to five years. (Cf. § 171; Appendix IX.)

339. An official, who unlawfully compels any one to do, suffer, or forbear, an act by misuse of his official power, or by threat of a definite misuse of the same, shall be punished by imprisonment with labour. The attempt to commit this offence is criminal.

In cases under §§ 106, 107, 167, and 253, the punishment therein threatened takes place if the act is committed by an official, even though without force or threat, but through misuse of his official power or a threat of a definite misuse of the same.

340. An official, who maliciously commits or permits the commission of a bodily injury in exercise or in dereliction of his office shall be punished by imprisonment with labour for not less than three months. If extenuating circumstances exist, the punishment can be mitigated to one day's imprisonment with labour, or a fine up to 900 shillings can be inflicted.

(J.) If the bodily injury is a severe one, penal servitude for not less than two years must be inflicted. If extenuating circumstances exist, imprisonment with labour for not less than three months takes place. (Cf. § 224.)

341. (L. or A.) An official, who maliciously undertakes or permits the undertaking of an arrest, or preliminary apprehension and seizure, or act of coercion, or lengthens the period of a withdrawal of liberty, without being entitled to do so, shall be punished according to the directions of § 239, but with imprisonment with labour for three months at the least. (Cf. § 358.)

342. (L.) An official, who commits a breach of the house peace (§ 123), in exercise or dereliction of his office, shall be punished by imprisonment with labour up to one year, or with a fine up to 900 shillings.

343. (L.) An official, who applies or permits the application of coercive measures in an inquiry, to extort

confession or declaration, shall be punished with penal servitude up to five years.

344. (J.) An official, who maliciously proposes or decrees the opening or continuation of an inquiry to the prejudice of a person, of whose innocence he is aware, shall be punished by penal servitude.

345. (J.) A similar punishment is incurred by the official, who maliciously permits the execution of a sentence, of which he knows that it ought not to be executed at all, or not in that manner or to that extent.

(L.) If the act is committed through negligence, the punishment of imprisonment with labour, confinement in a fortress up to one year, or a fine up to 900 shillings takes place.

346. (L.) An official, who in virtue of his office has to co-operate in the exercise of the corrective power (*Strafgewalt*), or in the execution of a sentence, shall be punished by penal servitude up to five years, if he omits the prosecution of a criminal act with the intent unlawfully to withdraw any one from lawful punishment, or if he commits an act, which is calculated to effect an acquittal or a punishment not in conformity with the law, and does not conduct the execution of the sentence pronounced, or executes a milder sentence than the sentence awarded. If extenuating circumstances exist, the punishment of imprisonment with labour for not less than one month takes place.

347. (L.) An official, who maliciously permits the escape, or maliciously effects, or furthers the liberation of a prisoner, whose supervision, escort, or custody is intrusted to him, shall be punished by penal servitude up to five years. If extenuating circumstances exist the punishment of imprisonment with labour for not less than one month takes place.

If the escape has been furthered or facilitated by negligence, the punishment of imprisonment with labour

U

up to six months, or a fine up to 600 shillings is inflicted. (Cf. § 121.)

348. (L.) An official, who is authorized to receive public documents, and who maliciously within his competency either makes a false attestation, or false entry in a public registry or book of a matter of fact of legal importance, shall be punished by imprisonment with labour for not less than one month. (Cf. §§ 271, 272, 349.)

The same punishment is incurred by an official, who maliciously destroys, makes away with, damages, or forges, a document, which is intrusted to him or to which he has access in virtue of his office. (Cf. §§ 133, 349.)

Note.—Documents generally are within the meaning of this section, and not merely those, which are mentioned in § 261 (Leipsic, Oct. 13th, 1882).

349. (J.) If any of the acts designated in § 348 is committed with the intent to procure an advantage in property for oneself or another, or to inflict damage on another, penal servitude up to ten years and at the same time a fine of from 150 to 3000 shillings are to be awarded. (Cf. §§ 271, 272.)

350. (L.) An official, who embezzles money or other things, which he has received or has in custody in his official capacity, shall be punished by imprisonment with labour for not less than three months. The sentence may also include the forfeiture of civil privileges. The attempt to commit this offence is criminal. (Cf. §§ 50, 246.)

351. (J.) If the official has with reference to the embezzlement kept incorrectly, forged, or suppressed the accounts, registers, or books appointed for the entry or control of the receipts or expenditure, or drawn incorrect conclusions or abstracts from these accounts, registers, or books, or inserted incorrect supplements in them, or if he has with reference to the embezzlement placed false indications of their money value on

barrels, bags, and packets, penal servitude up to ten years must be awarded.

If extenuating circumstances exist, the punishment of imprisonment with labour for not less than six months takes place.

352. (L.) An official, advocate, notary, or other legal assistant, who has to levy dues or other compensation for official acts to his own benefit, shall be punished by a fine up to 300 shillings or by imprisonment with labour up to one year, if he levies dues or compensation, for which he knows that the payer is not liable at all or only to a smaller amount. The attempt to commit this offence is criminal. (Cf. § 358.)

353. (L.) An official, who has to levy taxes, dues, or other payments for a public treasury, shall be punished by imprisonment with labour for not less than three months, if he levies payments, for which he knows that the payer is not liable at all or only to a smaller amount, and fails to bring the whole or part of the amount unlawfully raised to the treasury.

A similar punishment is incurred by the official, who maliciously and unlawfully makes deductions on official expenditure in money or natural products from the receiver, and enters the expenditure in the accounts as made in full. (Cf. § 358.)

353 *a.*[1] (L.) An official in the service of the Foreign Office of the German Empire who violates the official secrecy by unlawfully communicating to others the contents of documents (*Schriftstücke*), which are intrusted to him, or to which he has access in virtue of his office, or instructions given him by his superior or the contents of the same, shall be punished by imprisonment with labour or by a fine up to 5000 shillings, in so far as a severer punishment is not incurred under other regulations.

A similar punishment is incurred by an official

[1] Novella of 1876.

intrusted with a foreign mission or an official employed in such mission, who maliciously acts contrary to the instructions given him officially by his superior, or who in the intent to mislead his superior in his official acts reports to him untrue or distorted statements (*Thatsachen.*)

354. A postal official, who opens or suppresses the letters or packets intrusted to the post in other cases than those, for which the law has provided, or who knowingly permits another to commit such an act or knowingly renders him assistance thereto, shall be punished by imprisonment with labour for not less than three months.

Note.—Under letters post-cards are included (Leipsic, Dec. 8th, 1879).

The postal law of Oct. 28th, 1871, declares in § 5 "the secrecy of letters is inviolable; the necessary exceptions in criminal inquiries and in bankruptcy and civil suits must be fixed by an imperial law. Till the issue of an imperial law those exceptions shall be defined by the laws of the several states." (Cf. Appendix VI.)

355. Telegraphic officials or other persons intrusted with the supervision and service of a telegraphic institution serving public objects, who forge despatches intrusted to a telegraphic institution, or who open or suppress such despatches in other cases than those, for which the law has provided, or unlawfully inform a third person of their contents, or knowingly allow another to commit such an act or knowingly render him assistance thereto, shall be punished by imprisonment with labour for not less than three months. (Cf. § 358.)

356. (L.) An advocate, attorney, or any other legal assistant, who contrary to his duty serves both parties in the same lawsuit by counsel and assistance in regard to the matters intrusted to him in virtue of his official capacity, shall be punished by imprisonment for not less than three months.

(L.) If such a person acts in agreement with the

opposite party to the prejudice of his client, the punishment of penal servitude up to five years takes place.

357. A superior official, who maliciously misleads or undertakes to mislead his subordinates to a criminal act in their official capacity, or knowingly permits such a criminal act on the part of his subordinates, incurs the punishment, with which such criminal act is threatened.

The same regulation is applicable to an official, to whom the supervision or control of the official business of another has been intrusted, so far as the criminal act committed by this last-mentioned official relates to the business belonging to such supervision or control.

358. Together with the punishment of imprisonment with labour inflicted according to the direction of §§ 331, 339, 340, 341, 352—355, 357, the sentence may further include the forfeiture of the capacity of holding public offices for the space of from one to five years.

Note.—A punishment of imprisonment with labour for three months (§ 32) is not necessary here.

359. Under officials within the meaning of the criminal law are to be understood all persons in the service of the Empire or in the immediate or mediate service of a federal state appointed for life or for a period, or only provisionally, without distinction whether they have taken the oath of service or not, likewise notaries, but not advocates and attorneys (*Anwalte*).

TWENTY-NINTH CHAPTER.

MINOR OFFENCES.

Note.—Attempt and assistance and favor (§§ 43, 48, 257) are here free from punishment. This holds good in the subsidiary penal laws unless such laws contain directions to the contrary.

The court of the single judge and lay assessors is as a rule competent for all minor offences; but cf. the code of criminal procedure, §§ 100, 113, 211, 231, 232, 447 and foll., 453.

360. Any one shall be punished by a fine up to 150 shillings or with arrest:—

(i.) Who takes or publishes sketches of fortresses or individual works of a fortress, without especial permission.

(ii.) Who secretly or contrary to the prohibition of the authorities[1] collects stores of arms or ammunition outside the exercise of his trade.

(iii.) Who emigrates while he is a reserve man on furlough, or a member of the military or naval militia, or a substitute reserve man of the first class, without having given notice of his impending emigration to the military authorities.[1]

(iv.) Who prepares without a written order from the authorities[1] stamps, seals, puncheons, plates or other moulds, which could serve for the preparation of metal or paper money, or of such papers as, according to § 149, are considered equivalent to paper money, or of stamped paper, stamp marks, blank stamped forms, stamped impressions, public certificates and attestations, or who delivers the aforesaid to any other than the authorities.[1] (Cf. §§ 151, 275, 276.)

(v.) Who without written orders from the authorities[1] undertakes the impression of the stamps, seals, puncheons, plates, or forms mentioned in iv., or to print specimens for the public papers, attestations, and certificates there mentioned, or delivers impressions to any one other than the authorities.[1]

(vi.) Who prepares or publishes cards recommending goods, advertisements, or other printed matter or copies, which resemble in form or decoration paper money or the papers which according to § 149 are considered

[1] *Behörde.*

equivalent to paper money, or who prepares stamps, puncheons, plates, or other moulds, which could serve for the preparation of such printed matter or copies.

(vii.)[1] Who uses without authorization the copy of the Imperial arms, or of the arms of one of the federal princes or states.

Note.—The Imperial Eagle can be used by all German manufacturers as a mark for goods and on labels, but not in the form of an escutcheon.

(viii.) Who wears without authorization a uniform official dress, official emblem, an order or distinction, or assumes a title, dignity, or predicate of nobility, likewise any one who uses a name, which does not belong to him, in answer to a competent official.

(ix.) Who, contrary to legal regulations and without the approval of the state authorities,[2] establishes funds for dowries, deaths, or widows, institutions for insurance, or other similar societies or institutions intended to make payments in capital or annuities in return for a payment of purchase-money or of contributions of money in the event of certain conditions or at the end of certain periods.

(x.) Who, when summoned to give help by the police magistrates or their deputies at accidents or occasions of public danger or necessity, renders none, although he could have satisfied the demand without considerable personal danger.

(xi.) Who improperly creates a disturbing noise or is guilty of gross misbehaviour.

(xii.)[1] Who as pawnbroker, or second-hand dealer, in the exercise of his trade acts contrary to the regulations issued in reference to such trade, especially any one who exceeds the rate of interest appointed by local law or the ordinance of competent magistrates.

(xiii.) Any one who spitefully tortures or cruelly

[1] Novella of 1876. [2] *Behörde.*

ill-treats beasts either publicly or in a manner to create scandal.

(xiv.) Any one who without authorization holds games of chance on a public road, street, or place, or place of assembly.

In cases under i., ii., iv., v., vi., and xiv. the sentence may include, together with the fine or arrest, the confiscation of such sketches of fortresses or works of fortresses, of stores, of arms or ammunition, of stamps, seals, puncheons, plates, or other moulds, of impressions or copies, of the money on the gaming-table, or in the bank, without distinction whether they belong to the person condemned or not. (Cf. §§ 40, 42.)

361. Any one will be punished by arrest :—

(i.) Who, after he has been placed under police supervision, acts contrary to the restrictions put upon him in consequence of the same. (Cf. §§ 38, 39.)

(ii.) Who, after he has been banished from the Imperial territory or the territory of a federal state, returns without permission. (Cf. §§ 39, 284, 362.)

(iii.) Who wanders about as a vagrant.

(iv.) Who begs or trains or sends out children to beg, or omits to prevent persons, who are under his power and supervision and belong to his household, from begging.

(v.) Who gives way to gambling, drink, or idleness to such an extent, that he falls into a condition, in which the assistance of others must be called in by means of the magistrates, to maintain him or to maintain those whom he is in duty bound to support.

(vi.) [1] A female, who is placed under police supervision for pursuing immorality as a trade, if she acts against the police regulations issued for the security of the public health in this respect, public order, and public decency, or who practises immorality as a trade without being placed under such supervision.

(vii.) Any one who, when he receives support from the

[1] Novella of 1876.

public funds for the poor, refuses from aversion to work to perform the work suited to his powers, which has been assigned him by the authorities.

(viii.) Who after the loss of the employment he has hitherto held, has not procured himself employment elsewhere within the time appointed by the competent magistrates, and cannot prove that he could not have obtained such employment notwithstanding the efforts he has made.

(ix.) [1] Any one who omits to prevent children or other persons under his power, who are committed to his supervision and belong to his household, from committing theft, as well as from committing criminal infringements of custom and tax laws, or the laws for the protection of forests or crops, hunting or fishing.

The regulations of these laws with regard to the liability for the fines incurred by the offender or other payments of money are not affected hereby. In cases under ix., instead of arrest a fine up to 150 shillings can be inflicted.

362. The persons condemned according to the regulations of § 361, iii.—viii., can be employed on works, which are suited to their capacities and relations within and without the penal establishment, so far as they are (in the latter case) kept separate from other labourers who are free.

With the condemnation to arrest the sentence may direct that the condemned person is to be assigned to the local police magistrates after the punishment has been completed. The local police magistrates receive thereby the authorization, either to place the condemned person for as much as two years in a workhouse or to employ him on works of public usefulness. In cases under § 361, iv., this is however only permissible, if the condemned person has in the last three years been several times condemned for this minor offence in a

[1] Novella of 1876.

valid decision, or if such person has begged with threats or with arms.

If a foreigner has been assigned by sentence to the local police magistrates, instead of being placed in a workhouse he may be banished from the federal territory.

Note.—Local police magistrates means the superior police magistrates of each federal state. (Cf. §§ 16, 18, 361, ii.)

363.[1] Any one who with a view to deceive the magistrates or private persons, for the purpose of the better success of himself or another, falsely prepares or forges passes, military discharges, police books, or other such papers of legitimation, service or work books, or other such evidence, which has to be exhibited according to special regulations, as well as evidence of character or capacity, or any one who knowingly makes use of such a false or forged document, shall be punished by arrest or a fine up to 150 shillings.

A similar punishment is incurred by the person who uses for the same ends, such documents, being genuine, and issued for another, as if they had been issued for himself, or who gives up to another for the object in view documents issued for himself.

364. Any one shall be punished by a fine up to 150 shillings, who knowingly alienates or offers for sale stamped paper, which has been once used, after removing wholly or partially the writing marks set thereon, or stamped marks, blank stamped forms which have been once used, or stamped impressions of the kind mentioned in § 276, which have been cut off or in some other way separated.

Note.—This section does not refer to exposing for sale postage and telegraphic stamps.

365. Any one who stays in a public-house or a public place of amusement beyond the time prescribed by the police, notwithstanding that the landlord, his deputy, or

[1] Novella of 1876.

a police officer has invited him to leave, shall be punished by a fine up to fifteen shillings.

The landlord, who suffers his guests to stay beyond the time prescribed by the police, shall be punished by a fine up to sixty shillings or by arrest up to fourteen days.

366. Any one shall be punished by a fine up to sixty shillings or by arrest up to fourteen days—

(i.) Who acts contrary to the regulations issued against disturbance on Sundays and Feast-days.

(ii.) Who rides or drives at excessive speed in cities or villages, or drives or rides horses with danger to the public on public streets or places in towns or villages.

(iii.)[1] Who wantonly hinders the passage of others on public roads, streets, places, or water-ways.

(iv.) Who drives in towns with sleighs without a firm pole or without large or small bells.

(v.) Who without taking the necessary measures for security drives beasts or allows them to stand in towns or villages, roads, streets, or places, or other localities where they can do harm by running away, kicking, or in any other manner.

(vi.) Who sets dogs at men.

(vii.) Who throws stones or other hard bodies or refuse at men or horses or other beasts of draught or burden, against houses, buildings, enclosures, or into gardens.

Note.—This includes cases in which the man aimed at is not hit (Leipsic, January 31st, 1881).

(viii.)[1] Any one who puts out or hangs out objects without suitable fastening, through the overturning or fall of which any one can be hurt, over public streets or water-ways, or places thereon where men are wont to carry on traffic, or who pours or throws out things in such a manner, that any one may be injured or befouled thereby.

(ix.)[1] Who puts out, lays down, or leaves on the

[1] Novella of 1876.

ground on public roads, streets, places, or water-ways objects, by means of which free traffic may be hindered.

(x.) [1] Who transgresses the police regulations issued for the maintenance of security, convenience, cleanliness, and quiet, on public roads, streets, places, or water-ways.

366 *a.*[1] Any one who transgresses the police regulations issued for the protection of the banks, (*Dünen*) and the shores of the sea and of rivers, as well as the plantations and approaches of the same, shall be punished by a fine up to 150 shillings or by arrest.

367. Any one shall be punished by a fine up to 150 shillings or by arrest:—

(i.) Who without the knowledge of the magistrates buries or makes away with a dead body, or who without authorization takes away a part of a dead body from the custody of the person entitled thereto. (Cf. § 168.)

(ii.) Who acts contrary to the police regulations with regard to premature burial.

(iii.) Who without the permission of the police prepares, exposes for sale, sells, or otherwise hands over to another poison or medicine, in so far as the trade therein is not uncontrolled.

(iv.) Who without the prescribed permission prepares gunpowder or other explosive materials, or fireworks.

(v.) [1] Who does not observe the ordinances issued for the keeping or forwarding of poisonous wares, gunpowder, or fireworks, or for the keeping, forwarding, delivery, or use of blasting or other explosive materials, or for the use of the authorization to prepare or expose for sale these substances and also medicines.

(vi.) Who keeps wares, materials, or other stores, which easily ignite of themselves or easily catch fire, in places or receptacles where their ignition can be dangerous, or who keeps materials, which cannot lie together without danger of ignition, without separating them.

[1] Novella of 1876.

(vii.) Who exposes for sale or sells adulterated or tainted drink or food, especially meat containing trichiniæ. (Cf. Appendix XI.)

(viii.)[1] Who without the permission of the police places spring-guns, traps, or foot-snares, in places inhabited or frequented by human beings, or who shoots in such places with firearms or other shooting implements, or burns fireworks.

(ix.) Who exposes for sale or wears contrary to legal prohibition arms for striking, cutting, or shooting, which are concealed in sticks or canes or in a similar manner.

(x.)[1] Who in an affray, into which he was not drawn without fault of his, or in an assault, makes use of arms, especially of a knife or any other dangerous implement.

Note.—The attack need not be made by several persons (Leipsic, Nov. 29th, 1872). (Cf. § 227.)

(xi.) Who without the permission of the police keeps dangerous wild beasts, or allows wild or malignant beasts to wander at large, or in respect of them omits the precautions necessary to avoid damage.

(xii.) Who in the public streets, roads, or places, in yards, houses, and generally in places to which men resort, leaves wells, cellars, pits, openings or declivities uncovered or unguarded in such a manner, that danger to others can arise thereby.

(xiii.) Who in spite of the demand of the police omits to repair or pull down buildings, which threaten to fall.

(xiv.) Who takes in hand the erection or repair of buildings, wells, bridges, sluices, or other structures without taking the precautions for safety directed by the police or otherwise requisite.

(xv.) Who as architect, builder, mason carries out or causes to be carried out a building or repairs, for which the approval of the police is necessary without such approval, or with arbitrary deviation from the building

[1] Novella of 1876.

plan approved by the magistrates. (For xiii.—xv. cf. § 350.)

In the cases of vii.—ix. this sentence may include, together with the fine or the arrest, the confiscation of the adulterated or tainted drinks or food, likewise of the spring-guns, traps, foot-snares, as well as the forbidden arms, without distinction whether they belong to the person condemned or not. (Cf. §§ 40, 42.)

368. Any one shall be punished by a fine up to sixty shillings or by arrest up to fourteen days:—

(i.) Who acts contrary to the police regulations with regard to the closing of vineyards.

(ii.) Who omits to remove caterpillars according to the regulations of law and of the police.

(iii.) Who without the permission of the police erects a new fireplace or transfers to another place one already existing.

(iv.) Who omits to take care that the fireplaces in his house are kept in repair and secure against fire, or that the chimneys are cleaned at the proper time.

(v.) Who enters barns, stalls, lofts, or other rooms, which serve for the storing of inflammable things with uncovered fire or light, or approaches the same with uncovered fire or light.

(vi.) Who lights a fire in dangerous places in woods or heaths, or in dangerous proximity to buildings or inflammable objects.

(vii.) Who shoots with firearms or lets off fireworks in dangerous proximity to buildings or inflammable objects.

(viii.) Who does not keep the apparatus for extinguishing fire prescribed by the police at all or not in a serviceable condition, or omits to follow other regulations of the police with regard to fire.

(ix.) Who unwarrantably walks, drives, rides, or drives cattle over gardens, or vineyards, or, before the harvest is finished, over meadows or sown fields, or over such fields, meadows, pastures, or pleasure-grounds as are provided with a fence, or the entry of which is forbidden by a notice of warning, or on a private road closed by a notice of warning.

(x.) Who without the approval of the person entitled to hunt, or any other such warranty, is found in the hunting district of another, off the public road appointed for the common use, equipped for hunting although not actually hunting.

(xi.) Who unwarrantably takes the eggs or young of wild birds that are game or of singing birds.

369. The following persons shall be punished by a fine up to 100 shillings or by arrest up to four weeks:—

(i.) Locksmiths, who without the order of the authorities or the approval of the tenant of a dwelling, prepare keys to rooms or receptacles in such dwelling, or open locks in the same, or who without the approval of the master of the house or his representative, prepare house keys or deliver master keys or picklocks without the permission of the police magistrates.

Note.—Dwelling includes flats and lodgings.

(ii.) Tradesmen, in whose houses are found measures, weights, and scales suitable for use in their trade, which are not provided with the legal gauge-stamp or which are false, or tradesmen who are guilty of any other infringement of the police regulations as to weights and measures.

(iii.) Tradesmen, who work with fire, if they do not follow the regulations which are issued for the fixing and guarding of the fireplaces, and also as to the manner and time, at which they are to use the fire.

In case of ii., together with the fine or arrest the sentence must include the confiscation of the unlawful weights, measures, scales, or other such implements for measuring. (Cf. §§ 40, 42.)

370.[1] Any one shall be punished by a fine up to 150 shillings or by arrest:—

[1] Novella of 1876.

(i.) Who unwarrantably injures the landed property of another, a public or private road, or a boundary ridge, by digging or ploughing it up.

(ii.) Who unwarrantably digs from public or private roads earth, stone, or turf, or from landed property which belongs to another earth, loam, sand, gravel, marl, cuts sods, or peat (*Bülten*), removes turf, stone, minerals, for the taking of which a grant or concession or permission of the magistrates is not necessary, or similar objects.

(iii.) Who buys or takes in pawn uniform or arms from a sub-officer of the servant class, or a common soldier of the army or navy, without the written permission of the officer in command.

(iv.) Who unwarrantably fishes for fish or crabs. (Cf. § 296.)

Note.—The necessity of a proposal was removed by the Novella of 1876.

(v.) Who purloins nourishment or food of inconsiderable value or in small quantities for immediate consumption.

Purloining committed by relations in the ascending line against relations in the descending line, by one member of a married pair against another, is free from punishment.

Note.—It is indifferent whether the purloining takes place under aggravating or extenuating circumstances (Munich, December 3rd, 1875). Fuel and fodder for cattle are not within the meaning of this section, and flowers are not (Leipsic, October 24th, 1880), but seed potatoes so long as they are eatable (February 2nd, 1880).

(vi.) Who removes corn or other objects intended or suitable for the feeding of cattle, against the will of the proprietor, to feed the cattle of the same therewith.

In cases under v., vi. prosecution only takes place on proposal. The withdrawal of the proposal is permissible.

APPENDIX.

I.

THE competency of the courts in criminal cases according to the law for the constitution of the law courts for Germany (January 27th, 1877). Articles 27—29, 72—76, 80, 123, 136.

I. DISTRICT COURTS (*Amtsgerichte*).

Note.—These courts consist of a judge and two lay assessors, except in cases of theft in field and forest, and in minor offences if the public prosecutor permits and the accused confesses when the judge sits alone; hence they are also called the courts of the lay assessors.

27. The courts of the lay assessors are competent :—

(i.) For all minor offences. (Cf. the code, §§ 1, 360—370.)

(ii.) For those misdemeanours which are only threatened with imprisonment with labour for three months at the utmost, or with a fine of 600 shillings at the utmost, either alone or together with arrest, or in combination with each other, or in combination with confiscation, except the misdemeanour defined in § 320 of the criminal code, and that defined in § 74 of this law. (Cf. the code, §§ 123 (i.), 148, 276, 292, 299.)

(iii.) For those insults and bodily injuries, which are only to be prosecuted on proposal, if the prosecution takes place by way of private action. (Cf. the code, §§ 185—187, 189, 194, 223, 230, 232.)

(iv.) For the misdemeanour of theft in cases under § 242 of the criminal code, if the worth of the object stolen does not exceed five-and-twenty shillings.

(v.) For the misdemeanour of embezzlement in cases under § 246 of the criminal code, if the value of the money embezzled does not exceed five-and-twenty shillings.

(vi.) For the misdemeanour of fraud in cases under § 263, if the damage does not exceed five-and-twenty shillings.

(vii.) For the misdemeanour of damage to property in cases under § 303 of the criminal code, if such damage does not exceed five-and-twenty shillings.

(viii.) For the misdemeanour of favor and the misdemeanour of receiving in cases under § 258 (i.) and § 259 of the criminal code, if the act, to which the favor or receiving relates, is within the competency of the court of lay assessors.

28. If the competency of the court of lay assessors is conditioned by the value of a thing or by the amount of damage, and it is proved in the main proceedings that the value or damage amounts to more than five-and-twenty shillings, the court has only to declare its incompetency in cases, in which the suspension of the inquiry seems to be demanded by other reasons.

29. To the courts of lay assessors further belong those criminal questions, the treatment and decision of which is assigned to them according to the directions of the fifth chapter by the criminal division of the provincial courts.

II. Provincial courts (criminal division).

72. The courts of the criminal division are competent for those decisions relating to the preliminary inquiry and its results, which are to be issued by the court according to the regulations of the code of criminal procedure. They decide complaints against the directions of the judge of inquiry and the district judge,

as well as against those of the court of lay assessors. The regulations relating to the competency of the court of the Empire are not affected hereby.

The criminal division further settles the business assigned to the provincial courts in the ordinance for criminal procedure.

Note.—The provincial courts are divided into a civil and a criminal division.

73. The courts of the criminal division are competent as having cognizance :—

(i.) Of the misdemeanours, which do not belong to the competency of the courts of lay assessors.

(ii.) Of those felonies, which are threatened with penal servitude for five years at the utmost, alone or in combination with other punishments. This regulation is not applicable in the cases of §§ 86, 100, and 106 of the criminal code. (Cf. the criminal code, §§ 159, 171, 173, 174, 179, 181, 218, 224, 227, 254, 258 (ii.), 268 (i.), 321, 332, 336, 338, 343, 346, 347, 356.)

(iii.) Of the felonies of persons, who at the time of the deed had not yet completed their eighteenth year. (Cf. the criminal code, § 57.)

(iv.) Of the felony of obscenity in cases under § 176 (iii.) of the criminal code.

(v.) Of the felonies of theft in cases under §§ 243, 244 of the criminal code.

(vi.) Of the felony of receiving in cases under §§ 260, 261 of the criminal code.

(vii.) Of the felony of fraud in cases under § 264 of the criminal code.

74. The courts of the criminal division are further exclusively competent as having cognizance :—

(i.) Of acts committed contrary to the law of October 25th, 1867, with regard to the nationality of merchant ships, &c.

(ii.) Of the acts, which are criminal under Articles 206, 249, and 249 *a.* of the law of June 11th, 1870, with regard to companies, in which the shareholders only risk their shares, and companies, in which some shareholders have a limited and some an unlimited liability.

(iii.) Of acts committed contrary to the regulations of §§ 1—3 of the law of June 8th, 1871, with regard to paper bills payable to the bearer with premiums.

(iv.) Of the acts which are criminal under § 67 and § 69 of the law of February 6th, 1875, with regard to the attestation of personal rank, &c.

(v.) Of the acts which are criminal under § 59 of the Bank Law of March 14th, 1875.

75. The court of the criminal division can at the opening of the main proceedings, on the proposal of the public prosecutor, assign the management of the case to the courts of lay assessors, in so far as such courts are not already competent, if it can be assumed from the circumstances of the case that no other and higher punishment would be awarded than that mentioned in § 27, ii. (*supra*), and no higher fine than 600 shillings, in the following misdemeanours:[1]—

(i.) Resistance to the power of the state in cases under §§ 113, 114, 117, paragraph i., and 120 of the criminal code.

(ii.) Against the public order in cases under § 123, paragraph iii., and § 137 of the criminal code.

(iii.) Against morality in cases under § 183 of the criminal code.

(iv.) Insult and bodily injury in cases where prosecution only takes place on proposal. (Cf. §§ 185-7, 189, 194, 223, 230, 232 of the criminal code.)

(v.) Bodily injury in cases under § 223 *a.* of the criminal code.

(vi.) Theft in cases under § 242 of the criminal code.

(vii.) Embezzlement in cases under § 246 of the criminal code.

[1] These paragraphs are marked L. or A.

(viii.) Favoring. (Cf. § 257.)

(ix.) Receiving in cases under § 258 (i.) and § 259 of the criminal code.

(x.) Fraud in cases under § 263 of the criminal code.

(xi.) Criminal selfishness in cases under §§ 288, 298 of the criminal code.

(xii.) Damage to property in cases under §§ 303, 304 of the criminal code.

(xiii.) Misdemeanours involving danger to the public in cases under § 327, paragraph i., § 328, paragraph i. of the criminal code.

(xiv.) Those misdemeanours, which are only threatened with imprisonment with labour for six months at the most, or with a fine of 1500 shillings at the most, alone or in combination with each other, or in combination with confiscation, except the misdemeanours defined in §§ 128, 271, 296 *a.*, 301, 331, and 347 of the criminal code, and the misdemeanour defined in § 74 of the law. (Cf. criminal code, §§ 116, 134, 136, 145, 160, 172, 184, 241, 285, 293, 296, 300, 320.)

(xv.) Acts committed contrary to the regulations with regard to the levying of public taxes and dues, the punishment of which consists in multiplication of the amount of the tax or other payment embezzled.

Complaint (*Beschwerde*) cannot take place.

If in case of xv. a magistrate of the administration has brought a public accusation, he has the right of proposing an assignment to the court of the lay assessors, in the same manner as the public prosecutor has.

Note.—The courts of the lay assessors can in all cases assigned as above deviate from the assumption of the court of the criminal division, and inflict a higher punishment than three months' imprisonment with labour and 600 shillings.

76. The courts of the criminal division are further competent as having cognizance of the management

and decision with regard to the legal remedy of appeal against the decisions of the court of the lay assessors.

III. JURY COURTS.

80. The jury courts are competent for the felonies which do not belong to the competency of the criminal division or the court of the Empire.

IV. SUPERIOR PROVINCIAL COURTS.

123. The superior provincial courts are competent for:—

(i.) The management and decision with regard to the legal remedies.

(ii.) Revision of the decision of the courts of the criminal division on appeal.

(iii.) Revision of the decisions of the court of the criminal division as a court of first instance, in so far as the revision is exclusively based on the infringement of a rule of local law contained in one of the laws of the particular state.

(iv.) The complaint against decisions of criminal judges in the first instance, so far as the court of the criminal division is not competent, and against decisions of the court of the criminal division on complaint and on appeal. (Cf. §§ 72, 76, 183.)

V. THE COURT OF THE EMPIRE.

136. In criminal cases the court of the Empire is competent:—

(i.) For inquiry and decision in the first and last instance in cases of high treason and treason, in so far as these felonies are directed against the Emperor or the Empire. (Cf. §§ 80—93 of the code.)

(ii.) For the management and decision with regard to the legal remedies of revision against decisions of the courts of the criminal division in the first instance so far as the superior provincial court is not competent, and against decisions of the jury courts. (Cf. § 123 of the code.)

The court of the Empire is competent as a court of

appeal in criminal proceedings for acts committed contrary to the directions with regard to the levying of dues and taxes, which are to be paid into the Imperial treasury, and for the management and decision with regard to the legal remedy of revision against decisions of the courts of the criminal division, so far as the decision of the court of the Empire is demanded by the public prosecutor on sending in the minutes to the court of revision.

II.

INTRODUCTORY LAW FOR ALSACE-LORRAINE.

1. THE appended criminal code for the German Empire comes into force in Alsace-Lorraine on October 1st, 1871.

The regulations of this code, in which mention is made of the Federal states and their relations are to be applied to Alsace-Lorraine and its corresponding relations.

2. With October 1st, 1871, all criminal regulations, in so far as they refer to matters which are the subject of the criminal code for the German Empire, are repealed.

There remain in force the particular directions with regard to matters, which are not touched by the criminal code, namely, criminal acts in violation of the laws relating to the press, the post, the customs, fishery, hunting, fields and forests, with regard to the misuse of the right of forming societies and assemblies, and with regard to thefts of wood from forests, and neglect of school.

3. If reference is made in the local laws to criminal regulations, which are repealed by the criminal code for the German Empire, the corresponding regulations of the latter take the place of the former.

4. The felonies threatened with penal servitude for life in §§ 81, 88, 90, 307, 311, 312, 315, 322, 323, and 324 of the criminal code for the German Empire are to be punished with death, if they are committed in a part of the Empire, which is declared in a state of siege, or at the seat of war during a war which has broken out against the German Empire.

5. From the 1st of October, 1871, those forms of punishment must alone be inflicted, which are contained in the criminal code for the German Empire.

If the penalty of death, *travaux forcés, déportation,* or *réclusion* are threatened in the local laws, penal servitude must be awarded ; if *détention,* confinement in a fortress ; if *dégradation civique,* imprisonment with labour with or without the forfeiture of civil privileges; if *emprisonnement* or *prison* is threatened, imprisonment with labour, but if the punishment threatened does not exceed six weeks in length, arrest must be awarded. If in the local laws labour in the parish or in the forest is threatened instead of imprisonment with labour or a fine, it may be awarded under this law.

6. Prescription in civil suits arising from criminal acts comes into force in the very same periods, which are appointed for the prescription of the criminal prosecution in the criminal code for the German Empire.

7—10 are repealed.

11. The division of criminal acts into felonies, misdemeanours, and minor offences set forth in § 1 of the criminal code holds good also for those criminal acts, to which other criminal laws than the present criminal code are to be applied. If the punishment is designated in such laws, as at pleasure, the act is a minor offence.

12. Inquiry and decision are made—

With regard to minor offences, by the police courts.

With regard to misdemeanours, by the correctional divisions of the provincial courts.

With regard to felonies, by the jury courts.

The main trial for simple theft, simple receiving (§ 261 of the criminal code, paragraph ii.), and fraud is to be assigned, in cases of repeated relapse in so far as there are no extenuating circumstances, by means of the senate for indictments to the correctional courts, which must not declare themselves incompetent because there are no extenuating circumstances.

With regard to all felonies and misdemeanours of such persons, as have not completed their eighteenth year at the time of the act, judgment is given by the correctional divisions, so far as the case is not to be relegated to the jury court because of *connexité*. It is left to the discretion of the judge whether the reprimand should be administered by writing or by word of mouth.

LAW AMENDING THE INTRODUCTORY LAW OF THE GERMAN CRIMINAL CODE FOR ALSACE-LORRAINE OF JULY 7TH, 1873.

The police courts inquire and decide with regard to the criminal acts designated in Articles 192, 194, 195 of the *Code forestier* according to the law of June 18th, 1859, and also those designated in Articles 196, 197, 199 of the *Code forestier*, even in cases in which the punishments threatened in the articles designated, or in combination with Article 201 of the *Code forestier*, consist in a fine of more than 150 shillings, or in a term of imprisonment of more than six weeks.

13. The enactment of Article 341 of the *Code d'Instruction Criminelle* is only to be applied to the cases threatened with punishment by the criminal code, when the criminal code expressly permits extenuating circumstances.

14. The existing procedure remains in force for the punishment of neglect of school.

15. All persons condemned for one and the same felony or misdemeanour are to be condemned jointly to

pay the costs, to make repayment, and to give such compensation as the sentence may award.

If the sentence includes confiscation or a fine, but at the same time repayment and compensation, the last-mentioned have the preference, if the property of the person condemned is not sufficient to defray all these expenses.

16. The directions issued during the war with regard to the competency of the martial courts, as well as the material penal regulations relating to the felonies and misdemeanours assigned to such courts, remain in force so long as they are not repealed by Imperial ordinances.

III.

VACCINATION LAW OF APRIL 8TH, 1874.

1. THE following persons must undergo vaccination :—

(i.) Every child before the expiration of the calendar year, which follows the year in which it was born, in so far as it has not according to medical evidence gone through the natural small-pox.

(ii.) Every scholar of a public institute or private school, with the exception of Sunday and evening schools, within the year in which the scholar has completed his twelfth year, in so far as he has not, according to medical evidence, gone through the natural small-pox in the last five years or been vaccinated with success.

5. Every vaccinated child must be brought before the vaccinating physician at the earliest on the sixth, at the latest on the eighth, day after the vaccination.

7. For every vaccinating district a list of the children to be vaccinated under § 1, i. shall be issued by the

competent magistrate before the beginning of the vaccination season. The principals of the different institutes must prepare a list of the children actually vaccinated under § 1, i. The vaccinating physician shall notify in the list whether the vaccination was completed with or without success, or if and why such vaccination was either wholly or provisionally omitted.

After the end of the calendar year the lists are to be delivered to the magistrates. The mode of delivery of the lists shall be arranged by the Federal Council.

8. Besides the vaccinating physicians, physicians alone are authorized to undertake vaccination.

They must keep lists of the vaccinations carried out in the form prescribed in § 7, and lay them before the competent magistrates at the end of the year.

10. With regard to each vaccination a vaccination certificate shall be issued by the physician after its effect has been proved. In the vaccination certificate, together with the Christian name and surname of the child vaccinated and the day and year of its birth, attestation shall be given either that the legal obligation has been satisfied by the vaccination, or that the vaccination must be repeated in the following year.

In the medical evidence, by which the entire or provisional liberation from vaccination (§§ 1, 2) must be proved, attestation shall be given on what grounds and for how long the vaccination must remain unperformed, giving the description of the person prescribed for the vaccination certificate.

12. Parents, foster-parents, and guardians are bound on official demand to prove by means of the prescribed certificate that the vaccination of their children or children committed to their charge has been performed or omitted for a lawful reason.

13. The principals of those institutes, the scholars of which are under the obligation to be vaccinated, must settle whether the legal vaccination has taken place

by demanding the prescribed certificates on admitting scholars. The principals must take care that pupils, who fall under the obligation of being vaccinated under §§ 1, 2, while they are attending the institute satisfy such obligation. If a vaccination has been omitted without lawful reason, the principal must insist on a subsequent performance of the same. They are bound to lay a catalogue of the scholars, for whom no proof of vaccination has been brought, before the competent magistrates four weeks before the end of the school year.

14. Parents, foster-parents, guardians who omit to keep the proof which they are bound to do under § 12, shall be punished with a fine up to twenty shillings.

Parents, foster-parents, and guardians, whose children and wards remain unvaccinated, or are not brought before the physician after vaccination (§ 5) without lawful reason and in spite of official demand, shall be punished with a fine up to fifty shillings or with arrest up to three days.

15. Physicians and principals of schools, who do not fulfil the duties laid upon them by § 8, paragraph ii., § 7, and § 13, shall be punished with a fine up to 100 shillings.

16. Any one who unwarrantably undertakes vaccinations shall be punished with a fine up to 150 shillings or with arrest up to fourteen days.

17. Any one who acts with negligence in performing a vaccination shall be punished by a fine up to 500 shillings or by imprisonment with labour up to three months, in so far as no severer punishment is incurred under the criminal code.

IV.

PRESS LAW (MAY 7TH, 1874).

I. INTRODUCTORY REGULATIONS.

1. The freedom of the press is only subject to those limitations, which are prescribed or permitted by the present law.

2. The present law is applicable to all the products of the book printing press, as well as to all other multiplications of writings and symbolical representations with or without writing, and of musical works, with text or explanations, effected by mechanical or chemical means and designed for publication. That which is hereafter directed with regard to prints holds good for all the products designated above.

3. Publication in the meaning of this law includes further putting up, setting out, or exposing such articles in places where knowledge may be had of them by the public.

4. No withdrawal of the authorization independently to carry on any trade whatsoever connected with the press, or otherwise to publish or sell prints, can take place either under judicial or administrative law. For the rest the regulations of the trade law hold good for the carrying on of the trade of the press.

5. Those persons who, according to § 57 of the trade law, ought to be refused a certificate of legitimation can be prohibited by the police of the place from publicly publishing prints, such publication not being their trade. Acts committed against such prohibition shall be punished according to § 148 of the trade law.

II. ORDER OF THE PRESS.

6. Every print appearing, where this law is in force, must contain the name and address of the printer, and, if it is designed for the book trade or for publication in

other ways, the name and dwelling of the publishing bookseller, or in cases where the print is sold directly the name of the author or editor. In the place of the name of the printer or publishing bookseller it is enough to give the firm, which is entered in the commercial register. (Cf. The Commercial Code, § 12.)

The prints, which serve only the objects of trade and traffic, of home and social life, are excluded from this regulation, such as formulæ, tickets of price, visiting cards, and the like, as well as voting tickets for public elections, so far as they contain nothing more than the object, time, and place of the election and the designation of the persons to be elected.

Note.—Offences against § 6 do not give ground for the application of § 41 of the criminal code (Leipsic, March 8th, 1882).

7. Newspapers and periodicals which appear in monthly or shorter periods, whether regular or not, (periodical prints within the meaning of the law,) must further contain on every number and every piece or part the name and residence of the responsible editor.

The denomination of several persons as responsible editors is only permissible in cases, where it can be distinctly seen from the form and tenor of the denomination, for which part of the print each of the persons named is editor.

8. Responsible editors of periodical prints must only be persons, who are within the jurisdiction of the Empire, in the possession of civil privileges, and have their place of abode or usual residence within the German Empire.

9. The publishing editor must send a copy of each number (part, piece) of a periodical print to the police magistrate of the place of issue, free of charge so soon as the distribution and sending off commences, in return for a certificate which is to be immediately delivered to him. This regulation is not applicable to prints

which serve exclusively the objects of science, art, trade, or industry.

10. The responsible editor of a periodical print, which admits advertisements, is bound to admit the official notifications communicated to him by public magistrates at their request, on the payment of the usual charge for insertion, in one of the next two numbers of the paper.

11. The responsible editor of a periodical print is bound to admit a correction of the facts communicated in the last number, on the request of a public magistrate or private person who has been implicated, without interpolations or omissions, if the correction is signed by the sender, has no criminal content, and confines itself to a statement of matters of fact. (The punishment of the editor under § 19 does not remove the obligation to insert the correction. Berlin, September 13th, 1877.)

The impression must take place in the number, which follows next after the receipt of the missive and which is not already finished for the press, and above all, in the same part of the print and with the same type as the impression of the article which is to be corrected. The admission takes place free of charge, in so far as the reply does not exceed the space of the communication which is to be corrected; for the lines beyond this amount the usual charge for insertion must be paid.

12 and 13 lay down exceptions in favour of the prints issued by the magistrates and the Parliaments, as well as for the correspondence which is sent to editors alone.

14. If condemnation has twice taken place within the space of a year on the ground of §§ 41 and 42 of the criminal code against a number (piece, part,) of a periodical print, which appears outside German territory, the Imperial Chancellor can forbid the further publication of the print for as much as two years by public

notification within two months from the time when the last judgment came into legal force.

The prohibitions issued hitherto in the individual federal states on the ground of the local legislation against foreign prints are hereby repealed.

15. In times of danger of war publication with regard to movements of troops or means of defence can be forbidden by the Imperial Chancellor by means of a public notification.

16. Public invitations by means of the press to raise the amount of fines inflicted for a criminal act and costs, as well as public certificates, by means of the press, of the receipt of contributions to such objects, are forbidden.

The amount received in consequence of such invitations, or the value of the same, is to be declared confiscated to the fund for the poor at the place of collection.

17. Indictments or other official documents of criminal proceedings must not be published through the press, till such documents have been made known in public at the trial or the proceedings have reached their close.

18. The following offences shall be punished by a fine up to 1000 shillings, or by arrest, or by imprisonment with labour up to six weeks:—

(i.) Infringements of the prohibitions contained in §§ 14, 15, 16, and 17.

(ii.) Infringements of the regulations of §§ 6, 7, and 8, committed by means of false accounts with the knowledge of their incorrectness.

The same punishment is also incurred by the publishing editor of a periodical print, if he knowingly allows another person to be falsely named as editor.

19. The following offences shall be punished by a fine up to 150 shillings or by arrest:—

(i.) Infringements of §§ 6, 7, and 8, which are not met by § 18, ii.

(ii.) Infringements of § 9.

(iii.) Infringements of §§ 10 and 11.

In cases under iii. prosecution only takes place on proposal, and the sentence must at the same time order the admission of the article sent into the next following number. If this demand has been unlawfully refused in good faith, the offender must be absolved from punishment and costs, and merely the later admission must be ordered.

III. RESPONSIBILITY FOR THE CRIMINAL ACTS COMMITTED THROUGH THE PRESS.

20. Responsibility for acts, the criminality of which is founded on the contents of a print, is determined according to the existing universal criminal laws.

If the print is periodical, the responsible editor is to be punished as author, unless the assumption of his authorship is excluded by special circumstances.

Note.—The ignorance of the editor of the criminal content need not rest either on negligence or malice (Leipsic, April 4th, 1882).

21. If the contents of a print constitute a criminal act, the responsible editor, the publishing editor, the printer, and the person who has distributed the print as a trade, or published it in any other public way (publisher), shall, in so far as they are not liable to punishment under § 20, as author or participator, be punished for negligence by a fine up to 1000 shillings, or by arrest or by confinement in a fortress, or by imprisonment with labour up to one year, if they do not prove the application of the care conformable to their duties or circumstances, which made the application of such care impossible.

Punishment is however excluded in the case of the persons named, if they prove before the publication of the first judgment, that a person who is within the jurisdiction of a German federal state was the author or the contributor, with whose approbation the publication took place; or, if it is a question of a non-periodical print, if they prove that such a person was the editor of such print or one of the persons named before them in the above list; or, in case such person is dead, they must prove that he was within the jurisdiction of a German federal state at the time of the publication. With regard to the publishing editor of foreign prints, punishment is further excluded if such print has reached him by way of the book trade.

IV. PRESCRIPTION.

22. The criminal prosecution of such crimes and misdemeanours, as are committed by means of the publication of prints, as well as such other misdemeanours as are threatened with punishment in this law, falls under prescription in six months.

V. CONFISCATION.

23. A confiscation of prints without an order from a judge only takes place—

(i.) If a print does not correspond with the regulations of §§ 6 and 7, or is published contrary to the regulations of § 14.

(ii.) If an act be committed contrary to a prohibition issued on the ground of § 15 of this law by means of a print.

(iii.) If the contents of a print constitute one of the acts threatened with punishment in §§ 85, 95, 111, 130, or 184 of the German criminal code, but only in cases under §§ 111 and 130 if there is imminent danger that if the confiscation is delayed the invitation or incitement will immediately result in a felony or misdemeanour.

24. The competent court has to decide with regard to the confirmation or annulling of the provisional confiscation. This decision must be proposed by the public prosecutor within twenty-four hours after the order of confiscation, and be issued by the court within twenty-four hours after receiving the proposal.

If the police magistrate has arranged the confiscation without an order from the public prosecutor, the former must despatch an account of the transaction to the latter without delay, and at the latest within twelve hours. The public prosecutor must either order the removal of the confiscation by means of a mandate, which can be immediately executed, or propose the judicial confirmation within twelve hours after receiving the account of the transaction.

If on the expiration of the fifth day after the order of confiscation, the confirmatory judicial decision has not reached the magistrate who ordered the confiscation, the confiscation becomes void and the individual pieces must be restored.

25. There is no legal remedy against the decision of the court, which annuls the provisional confiscation.

26. The provisional confiscation, which has been confirmed by a court of law, must be again annulled, if criminal proceedings have not been opened in the chief matter within two weeks of the confirmation.

27. The confiscation of prints only includes the copies, where such prints are found for the purpose of publication. Such confiscation may extend to the plates and type which serve for multiplying the print. In the case of prints in the narrower sense, the paragraph must on the proposal of the person concerned be deposited instead of being confiscated.

In cases of confiscation the passages of the writing, which give cause to such confiscation, must be designated, and the laws, which have been infringed, must be cited. Separable parts of the print (supplements to a newspaper, &c.) which contain nothing criminal, are to be excluded from the confiscation.

28. While the confiscation lasts the publication of the print under confiscation, or the reprint of the passage which gave cause for the confiscation, is not permitted.

Any one who, with the knowledge that the confiscation has taken place, acts contrary to the regulation shall be punished by a fine up to 500 shillings or by imprisonment with labour up to six months.

§§ 29, 30 contain regulations with regard to the relation of the press law to certain special enactments in the Imperial and local laws.

31. This law comes into force on July 1st, 1874. Its introduction into Alsace-Lorraine is reserved for an especial law.

V.

LAW FOR THE PROTECTION OF TRADE-MARKS (NOVEMBER 30TH, 1874).

1. TRADESMEN whose firm is entered in the commercial register can give notice at the competent court of marks which are to be used on their goods or on the cases of their goods to distinguish them from the goods of other tradesmen, with a view to the entry of such marks in the commercial register of the place where their chief establishment is situated.

Note.—Firm is used as the official signature of his own name used by every person as opposed to familiar abbreviations or nicknames.

14. Any one who wittingly and unlawfully marks wares or their cases with a trade-mark protected under this law, or with the name or firm of a German producer or trader, or who wittingly brings into circulation or exposes for sale such wares being unlawfully marked, shall be punished by a fine of from 150 to 3000 shillings, or by imprisonment with labour up to six months, and is bound to compensate the injured person. Prosecution only takes place on proposal.

15. In the place of any compensation under this law the sentence can at the request of the injured person

include together with the punishment a mulct to be paid him up to the amount of 5000 shillings. For this mulct the persons condemned thereto are liable as joint debtors. An imposed mulct excludes the enforcement of a further claim for compensation.

16. The court decides at its free discretion, after weighing all the circumstances, whether damage has arisen and how far such damage extends.

17. If a condemnation ensues in virtue of § 14, then at the proposal of the person injured the sentence must include the destruction of the marks on the goods and cases in the possession of the persons condemned, or if the removal of the mark is not otherwise possible, the destruction of the cases or of the goods themselves.

If the condemnation ensues in the criminal proceedings, the injured person must be authorized to make the condemnation publicly known at the expense of the person condemned. The manner in which and the time within which the publication must be made must be determined in the judgment.

18. The protection guaranteed according to the contents of this law to the proprietor of a trade-mark, a name, or a firm, is not excluded by the fact that the trade-mark, name, or firm are used with changes which could be perceived by the use of special attention.

20. The regulations of this law apply to trade-marks of tradesmen who do not possess a commercial establishment in German territory, as well as to the names or firms of foreign producers or traders, if in the state in which their establishment is situated German trade-marks, names, and firms enjoy protection, according to a notice made in the Imperial Gazette under the following rules:—

(i.) The notice of a trade-mark must be given at the Commercial Court at Leipsic, with the declaration that the notifier submits himself to the jurisdiction of the court named for suits based on this law.

(ii.) Together with the notice evidence must be given that in the foreign state the requisites are fulfilled under which the notifier can there claim a protection for the mark.

(iii.) The notice entitles the notifier to the mark only so far and so long as the notifier is protected in the use of the mark in the foreign state.

Note.—Mutual protection of trade-marks, names, and firms according to this section exists with France, Spain, the United States, Portugal, Russia, Sweden and Norway, Great Britain, Italy, Belgium, Luxemburg, Brazil, Denmark, Austria-Hungary, Switzerland, Roumania.

VI.

LAW AGAINST THE GENERALLY DANGEROUS EFFORTS OF SOCIAL DEMOCRACY (OCTOBER 21ST, 1878).

1. SOCIETIES, which aim at the subversion of the existing political or social order by social democratic, socialist, or communist efforts, must be forbidden.

The same holds good of societies in which social democratic, socialist, or communist efforts, directed at the subversion of the existing political or social order, come to light in a manner endangering the public peace, and especially the harmony of the several classes of the population. Unions of any kind are equivalent to societies.

2. Registered societies are dealt with in cases under § 1, paragraph ii. by § 35 of the law of July 4th, 1868, with regard to the position at private law of companies for acquisitive and economical purposes.

Registered provident societies are dealt with under

like circumstances by § 29 of the law with regard to registered provident societies of April 7th, 1876.

3. Independent (*i. e.* not registered) societies with a common fund, which aim at the mutual support of their members according to their statutes, are in cases under § 1, paragraph ii., not to be forbidden, but to be placed under an extraordinary state control.

If several independent societies of the above-mentioned kind are united, then if in one of them the efforts designated in § 1, paragraph ii. come to light, the separation of this society from the union can be ordered and a control instituted over such society.

In like manner if the efforts designated come to light in a branch society, the control must be limited to such branch.

4. The magistrates intrusted with the control are authorized—

(i.) To be present at all sittings and meetings of the society.

(ii.) To summon and conduct general meetings.

(iii.) To inspect the books, records, and balance of cash, as well as to demand information as to the relations of the society.

(iv.) To forbid the execution of decisions, which are calculated to promote the efforts designated in § 1, paragraph ii.

(v.) To intrust suitable persons with the care (*Wahrnehmung*) of the duties of the committee or other leading organs.

(vi.) To take into custody and administer the funds of the society.

5. If the general meeting of the committee, or any other leading organ of the society, acts contrary to the orders issued by the controlling magistrates within their competency, or if the efforts designated in § 1, paragraph ii. come to light in the society, even after the institution of the control, the society can be prohibited.

6. The police magistrates of the several states are competent to issue the prohibition and the order of control. The Imperial Chancellor has the right of prohibiting foreign societies.

The prohibition is in all cases to be published in the Imperial Gazette, the prohibition issued by the local police magistrates in the paper of the place or district appointed for the official notices of the magistrates.

The prohibition is effective for the whole of the federal territory, and includes all branches of the society and every pretended new society which really sets itself up as the old. (Cf. *infra*, §§ 17, 21.)

7. By virtue of such prohibition the funds of the society, as well as all objects designed to aid the objects of the society, are to be confiscated by means of the magistrates.

After the prohibition has become finally valid the administrative magistrates, who are to be appointed by the local police magistrates, must intrust the winding up of the business of the society (liquidation) to suitable persons and carefully superintend the same, and also publish the names of the liquidators.

The place of the decision of the general meeting, for which provision is made in the laws or statutes, is taken by the decision of the administrative magistrates.

The assets of the society are to be applied according to the statutes of the society under the universal legal regulations without prejudice to the legal claims of third persons and of members of the society.

The date at which the prohibition becomes finally valid, is to be regarded as the date of the dissolution or closing of the society. Complaint against the orders of the magistrates can only be made to the supervising magistrates.

8 The prohibition issued by the local police magistrates, as well as the order of control, is to be made known to the committee of the society so far as such

committee exists in German territory by a written mandate containing the reasons therefor. Against such prohibition the committee has the right to complain. (Cf. § 26, *infra.*)

The complaint must be laid within a week of the delivery of the mandate before the magistrate, who issued such mandate. The complaint has no effect in delaying execution.

9. Assemblies, in which social democratic, socialist, or communist efforts directed to the subversion of the existing political or social order come to light, are to be dissolved.

Assemblies, of which the assumption that they are designed to further the efforts mentioned in the first paragraph is justified by facts, are to be prohibited.

Public festivities and excursions are equivalent to assemblies. (Cf. § 17, *infra.*)

10. The police magistrates are competent to prohibit and dissolve such meetings.

Complaints can only be made to the supervising magistrate.

11. Prints in which social democratic, socialist, or communist efforts for the subversion of the existing political or social order, are manifested in a manner endangering the public peace, and especially the harmony of the several classes of the population, are to be prohibited.

In the case of periodical prints the prohibition can be extended to further issue, as soon as the prohibition of one number has taken place under this law.

12. The local police magistrates are competent to issue the prohibition, the local police magistrates of the district in which the paper appears, in the case of papers issued periodically in German territory. The prohibition of the further publication of a periodical, which appears outside German territory, is in the power of the Imperial Chancellor.

The prohibition is to be made known in the manner

prescribed in § 6, paragraph ii., and is effectual for the whole territory of the Federation.

13. The prohibition of a print when issued by the local police magistrates, is to be made known to the printer or publisher; the prohibition of a printed paper, which does not appear periodically, is to be made known to the author therein named, in so far as such persons are in German territory, by means of a written mandate containing reasons for such prohibition.

The printer, publisher, or author has the right of complaint against the mandate. (Cf. § 26.)

The complaint must be laid within a week of the delivery of the mandate before the magistrate who has issued the same. The complaint has no effect in delaying execution.

14. On the ground of the prohibition the copies of such print, which are found in places where they are lying ready for publication, are to be confiscated. The confiscation can extend to the plates and type, which serve for the multiplication of the copies; in the case of prints in the narrower sense, instead of the confiscation of the composition the same must be deposited in the custody of the court on the proposal of the person concerned. The confiscated prints, plates, and type must be rendered unserviceable after the prohibition has become finally valid. Complaint can only be made to the supervising magistrate.

15. The police magistrate is authorized to confiscate provisionally prints of the kind mentioned in § 11, as well as plates and type serving for their multiplication, even before the issue of a prohibition. The confiscated print is to be delivered to the local police magistrates within twenty-four hours. The last-named must either at once direct the annulling of the confiscation or issue the prohibition within a week. If the prohibition be not issued within this period, the confiscation becomes null and the individual copies, plates, and type must be given up. (Press Law, § 24.)

16. The collection of contributions for the furtherance of social democratic, socialist, or communist efforts for the subversion of the existing political or social order, as well as public invitation to make such contributions, is to be forbidden by the police. The prohibition is to be made publicly known. The complaint can only be made to the supervising magistrates. (Press Law, § 16.)

17. (A.) Any one who takes part in a forbidden society as member, or is active in the interest of such society, shall be punished by a fine up to 500 shillings or by imprisonment with labour up to three months. (§ 6.)

A similar punishment is incurred by the man, who takes part in a forbidden meeting or who does not immediately retire after the police have broken up a meeting.

(L.) Against those persons who take part in the meeting as president, manager, director, agent, speaker, or treasurer, or who invite persons to the meeting, a sentence of imprisonment with labour from one month to one year is to be passed.

18. (L.) Any one who places rooms at the service of a forbidden society or a forbidden meeting, shall be punished by imprisonment with labour for from one month to one year.

19. (L. or A.) Any one who publishes, continues, or reprints a forbidden print or a print, which has been laid under provisional confiscation, shall be punished by a fine up to 1000 shillings, or by imprisonment with labour up to six months. (Cf. §§ 11, 12, 15.)

Note.—Under print photographs are included (Leipsic, June 6th, 1881).

20. (A.) Any one who acts contrary to a prohibition issued according to § 16, shall be punished by a fine up to 500 shillings, or by imprisonment with labour up to three months. Further, the amount received in consequence of the forbidden meeting or the invitation, or the value of such amount, is to be declared con-

fiscated to the fund for the poor of the place of the meeting.

21. Any one who commits one of the acts forbidden in §§ 17, 18, 19, without knowledge of but after the publication of the prohibition in the Imperial Gazette, is to be punished with a fine up to 150 shillings or with arrest.

Similar punishment is incurred by the man, who acts contrary to a prohibition issued according to § 16 after the publication of the prohibition. The final direction of § 20 is applicable in such cases.

22. Persons who make a business of agitation for the efforts defined in § 1, paragraph ii., can, if they are condemned for acting against §§ 17—20, be sentenced to have their place of residence circumscribed, together with the punishment of imprisonment.

On the ground of this sentence the local police can prohibit the person condemned residing in definite districts or places, but not from residing in his place of domicile, unless he has not yet been there six months. Foreigners can be banished by the local police magistrates from the federal territory. Complaint can only be made to the supervising magistrate.

(L.) Offences under this section shall be punished by imprisonment with labour for from one month to one year.

23. Under the presuppositions mentioned in § 22, paragraph i., keepers of inns and tap-houses, persons who retail brandy or spirits, book printers, booksellers, keepers of lending libraries and reading-rooms, can, besides the punishment of imprisonment, be forbidden by the sentence to ply their trades.

24. Persons who make it their business to further the efforts designated in § 1, paragraph ii., or who have been lawfully condemned to punishment under a regulation of this law, can be refused by the local police the authorization required for publicly publishing prints whether as a trade or not, and the authorization for trading with

prints as a pedlar. Complaint can only be made to the supervising magistrate.

N.B.—The authorization for trading as a bookseller with a permanent establishment cannot be withdrawn (Leipsic, May 10th, 1882).

25. (L. or A.) Any one who acts contrary to a sentence given on the ground of § 23, or a mandate issued on the ground of § 24, shall be punished by a fine up to 1000 shillings, or by arrest or by imprisonment with labour up to six months.

26. For the decision of the complaints raised in the cases under §§ 8 and 13 a commission shall be formed. The Federal Council shall choose four members from its midst, and five from the members of the highest courts of the Empire or the individual federal states.

These five members shall be chosen for the period that this law remains in force, and the period of their remaining in judicial office. The Emperor shall name the president and his deputy from the number of the members.

27. The commission shall give its decisions, when five members are present, of whom at least three must belong to the judicial division. Before the decision as to complaints, the person implicated must have an opportunity of giving reasons for his complaint verbally or in writing. The commission is authorized to take evidence fully, especially by hearing witnesses and experts on oath, or to cause evidence to be taken by means of a request to a magistrate of the Empire or a federal state.

With regard to the obligation to appear as witness or expert, as well as with regard to the punishments to be awarded in case of disobedience, the regulations of the civil laws of procedure apply which are in force at the place where the commission or the magistrate, to whom the request is addressed, is sitting.

The decisions take place at the discretion of the

commission, and there is no appeal. For the rest the order of business in sittings of the commission will be settled by regulations to be proposed by the commission and referred for confirmation to the Federal Council.

28. The following orders can be issued by the central magistrates of the federal states for districts and places, which are threatened with danger to the public security by the efforts designated in § 1, paragraph ii., so far as they are permissible under the laws of the several states and subject to the approval of the Federal Council, for the space of one year at the most:—

(i.) That meetings must only take place with the previous approval of the police magistrates. This limitation does not extend to meetings convoked for the purpose of electing representatives for the Parliament of the Empire or for those of the several states.

(ii.) That the distribution of prints on public roads, streets, places, or any other public spots must not take place.

(iii.) That persons, from whom danger to the public security or order is to be apprehended, may be forbidden to reside in certain districts or localities.

(iv.) That the possession, carrying, importation, and sale of arms can be forbidden, limited, or subjected to certain conditions.

Account must immediately be given to the Imperial Parliament, that is, at the next meeting thereof, with regard to each order issued on the ground of the preceding regulations.

The orders issued are to be published in the Imperial Gazette, and in the manner prescribed for the mandates of the local police.

(L. or A.) Any one who acts contrary to such orders, or to the mandates issued on the ground of such orders, with knowledge or after the public notification has been made, shall be punished by a fine up to 1000 shillings, or by arrest, or by imprisonment with labour up to six months.

29. The central police authorities of the Federation shall make known what magistrates in each state are to be understood under the term local police magistrates and police magistrates.

30. This law comes into force on the day of publication, and remains in force till March 31st, 1881.

Note.—A supplementary law as to the authentic interpretation and period of validity of the law of October 21st, 1878, passed in 1880, added the following provisions :—

(1) The regulation made in § 28 (iii.) of the law of October 21st, 1878, is elucidated in the following manner—to wit, that such regulation is not applicable to members of the Imperial Parliament or of a legislative assembly who are residing at the place of meeting of such body during its sittings. Complaint against the mandates issued on the ground of § 28 of the above-mentioned law can only be made to the supervising magistrates.

(2) The period, through which the law against the commonly dangerous efforts of social democracy of October 21st, 1878, is to remain in force, shall hereby be extended to September 30th, 1884, thus altering § 30 of that law.

In 1884 the Socialist Law was extended for three years more.

VII.

LAW WITH REGARD TO THE POSTS OF THE GERMAN EMPIRE (OCTOBER 28TH, 1871). (EXTRACT.)

ESPECIAL PRIVILEGES OF THE POST.

18. No distraint is allowed against ordinary and extraordinary posts, couriers, and expresses (*Estafetten*). Further, no distraint may be enforced against the postillion who returns with the team which has been used (*ledig*). Persons who act contrary to this regulation incur a fine of from one to sixty shillings.

19. Every conveyance must give way to the ordinary and extraordinary posts, couriers, and expresses on the usual signal being given. Persons who act contrary to this regulation incur a fine of from one to thirty shillings.

23. The watchers at gates, the officials at gates, bridges, and barriers, are bound to open the gates and turnpikes with the utmost speed as soon as the postillion gives the usual signal. In like manner the ferrymen must make the passage for the same purpose without delay. Persons who act contrary to this regulation incur a fine of from one to thirty shillings.

PENAL REGULATIONS WITH REGARD TO FRAUDS ON POST AND POSTAGE.

27. The following persons shall be punished by a fine of four times the amount of the postage evaded, but never of less than three shillings:—

(i.) Any one who for a payment forwards or transmits letters or political newspapers contrary to the regulations of §§ 1, 2, otherwise than through the post.

If the transmission is effected in packets sealed, sewn up, or otherwise closed, the transmitter only incurs the punishment if he could have known the prohibited nature of the packet.

Note.—Under §§ 1, 2 the post receives the privilege to transmit for money closed letters and newspapers with political contents which appear more than once a week, an exception being made in the case of such packets sent from *one* consignor by means of express messengers or bearers.

(ii.) Any one who applies a mark freeing the article sent from the payment of the postage to a packet (*Sendung*) which is liable for postage, or who wrongly packs up such a packet in another packet which is forwarded postage free on the application of a prescribed sign.

(iii.) Any one who uses a postage stamp to frank a packet after such stamp has been depreciated. The universal criminal laws shall determine how far a more serious punishment is incurred in this case for the effacement of the obliterating mark which has also taken place.

(iv.) Any one who delivers letters or other objects to an official of the post or postillion to take with him with a view to evading the postage dues.

In the cases defined in sub-sections ii. and iii. the punishment is incurred with the delivery of the packet to the post.

28. On the first relapse the punishment (§ 27) shall be doubled, and on further relapses quadrupled.

A person is said to have relapsed if, after he has been punished by a court of law or by the administrative officials (§§ 34, 35) for the frauds defined in § 27, he commits such a fraud again. The increase of the punishment for relapse takes place even if the former punishment was only partially expiated, but is excluded if three years have elapsed since the expiation or remission of the last punishment up to the commission of the new fraud.

29. Any one who wittingly travels with the post

without being registered, with the intent of defrauding the postal treasury of the passenger's fare, shall be punished by a fine of four times the amount of the fare evaded, but never of less than three shillings.

30. Besides the punishment, the postage which would have been levyable for the transmission of the objects by the post must be paid in cases under § 27, and the fare evaded must be paid in cases under § 29. In cases under § 27 (i.) the consignor and the transmitter are jointly liable for the postage.

31. The length of the term of arrest which takes the place of a fine which cannot be levied must be settled by the judge, and must not exceed six weeks.

32. The postal authorities and officials who discover a fraud are authorized to seize the letters and objects found on that occasion which are the subject of the minor offence, and to retain them wholly or partially till either the postal dues, the fine, and the costs have been paid, or security has been given for them.

33. The fines mentioned in §§ 27—29 are to be paid into the treasury for impoverished postal officials, or into the poor-box.

VIII.

THE IMPERIAL MILITIA LAW (MAY 2ND, 1874). (EXTRACT.)

33. Any one who omits to make the announcements prescribed according to § 31 for the correction of the primary lists, and all persons bound to serve who do not appear punctually at the times to be appointed by the reserve officials, are to be punished with a fine up to thirty shillings, or with arrest up to three days, in

so far as they have not thereby incurred a severer punishment.

If the omission is brought about by circumstances, the removal of which did not lie in the power of the person bound to make the announcement or appear, the above-mentioned consequences do not take place.

69. Soldiers of the supplementary reserve of the first class who withdraw themselves from the control imposed upon them by reason of the law, shall be punished with a fine up to sixty shillings or with arrest.

IX.

LAW RELATING TO THE ATTESTATION OF PERSONAL RANK AND THE CONCLUSION OF MARRIAGE (FEBRUARY 6TH, 1875).

ATTESTATION OF BIRTH.

17. NOTICE must be given of every birth of a child within a week to the class official (*Standesbeamte*) of the district in which the confinement has taken place.

18. The following persons are bound to make the announcement:—

(i.) The legitimate father.
(ii.) The midwife who was present at the confinement.
(iii.) The physician who was present at the same.
(iv.) Every other person who was at hand at the same.
(v.) The mother as soon as she is capable.

The persons however who are named later in the above list are only bound by this duty if one of the persons named before is not present, or if such person is hindered from giving notice.

19. The notice must be given by the persons bound thereto by word of mouth, or by means of another person having knowledge thereof of his own.

20. In cases of birth which take place in public institutes for confinement, midwifery, sickness, imprisonment, as well as in barracks, the duty of giving notice falls exclusively to the head of the institute or the official who has been authorized by the competent magistrate. A written notice in an official form is sufficient.

21. The class official is bound to convince himself in a suitable manner of the correctness of the notice if he has reason for doubt.

22. The entry of the birth must contain :—

(i.) The christian and surname, rank or trade, and abode of the notifier.

(ii.) Place, day, and hour of the birth.

(iii.) Sex of the child.

(iv.) Christian name of the child.

(v.) Christian names, surnames, religion, rank or trade, and abode of the parents.

Where two or more children are born at the same time the entry must be made separately for each child, and with such detail that the succession of the different births is clear.

If the christian names of the child are not yet settled at the time the notice is given, notice must be given of such names afterwards, and at the most within two months after the birth. The entry of such names is made on the margin of the first entry.

23. If a child is still-born or died at birth, notice must be given at the latest on the next day. The entry must then be made only in the register of deaths, with the entries prescribed in § 22, i.—iii. and v.

24. Any one who finds a new-born child is bound to give notice of the fact to the local police authorities at the latest on the following day. The police authorities must make the necessary inquiries and give notice to the class official of the district of the result with a view to entry in the register of births.

The entry must contain the time, place, and circumstances of the discovery, the condition and distinctive marks of the clothes and other objects found with the child, the bodily characteristics of the child, its presumptive age, its sex, the magistrate, institute, or person with whom the child was lodged, and the name which was given to the child.

ATTESTATION OF DEATHS.

56. Notice must be given of every death on the following week-day to the class official of the district in which the death took place.

57. It is the duty of the head of the family, and if such head does not exist or is prevented from giving notice, of the person in whose house or lodging the death has taken place, to give the notice.

58. §§ 19—21 apply also with regard to the notice which must be given of deaths.

If an official inquiry is held with regard to a death, the entry is made on the ground of the written communication of the competent official.

ATTESTATION OF THE PERSONAL RANK OF PERSONS WHO ARE AT SEA.

61. Births and deaths which take place on ships during a voyage at sea must be attested in the day-book according to the directions of this law at the latest on the day following the birth or death by the captain of the ship, with the assistance of two of the officers of the ship or other credible persons. In cases of death the presumptive cause of death must be set down at the same time.

62. The captain must deliver two copies of the document attested by himself to the first sailors' office to which such delivery can be made.

One of these copies must be preserved at the sailors' office, the other must be forwarded to the class official in whose district the parents of the child or of the deceased person were domiciled or were last domiciled, with a view to an entry being made in the register.

63. If the captain is dead or is prevented from so doing, the mate (*Steuermann*) must fulfil the duties imposed on the captain in §§ 61, 62.

64. As soon as the ship has entered the German harbour in which it concludes its voyage, the day-book must be laid before the competent magistrate who has the supervision of class officials of the harbour district.

Such magistrate must forward an attested copy of the class documents entered in the day-book to the class official, in whose register the case must be entered (§ 62) for the purpose of checking the entries.

CONCLUDING REGULATIONS.

67. A clergyman or other servant of religion who proceeds to the religious solemnities of the conclusion of a marriage before it has been proved to him that the marriage has been concluded before the class officials, shall be punished by a fine up to 300 shillings or by imprisonment with labour up to three months.

68. Any one who does not discharge the duty of giving notice prescribed in §§ 17—20, 22—24, 56—58, shall be punished by a fine up to 150 shillings or by arrest.

The criminal prosecution does not take place if the notice has been given at the right time, although not by the persons first bound to give such notice.

The class officials are further authorized to compel by means of fines the persons who are bound to give notice or perform other acts to discharge these duties: such fines must not exceed the amount of fifteen shillings for each individual case.

69. A class official who solemnizes a marriage neglecting the directions given in this law shall be punished by a fine up to 600 shillings.

X.

LAW RELATING TO THE STAMP DUTIES ON PLAYING CARDS (JULY 3RD, 1878).

1. PLAYING cards are under the regulations of this law subject to a stamp duty payable into the Imperial Treasury which amounts to $3\frac{1}{2}d.$ (30 pf.) for every pack of cards of thirty-six sheets or less, of *6d.* (50 pf.) for every other pack of cards.

10. Playing cards which, contrary to the regulations of this law, are not provided with the necessary stamp are liable to confiscation, no matter to whom they belong, and no matter whether a definite person is prosecuted or not.

Any one who exposes for sale, sells, distributes, or acquires cards which, contrary to the regulations of this law, are not provided with the necessary stamp, or who plays with or wittingly has in his possession such cards, incurs for each pack a penalty of thirty shillings.

Innkeepers and other persons who entertain guests have incurred the same penalty if unstamped cards are played with in their houses and grounds, and it is not proved that this has taken place without their knowledge.

§§ 11 and foll. contain penal regulations against importers, traders, and manufacturers.

XI.

LAW RELATING TO THE TRAFFIC IN ARTICLES OF FOOD AND ENJOYMENT (NAHRUNGSMITTELN, GENUSSMITTELN) AND OBJECTS OF GENERAL USE (MAY 14TH, 1879).

1. THE traffic in articles of subsistence and enjoyment, as well as toys, carpets, colours, eating, drinking,

and cooking utensils, and petroleum, is subject to supervision under this law.

2. The police officials are authorized to enter the rooms in which objects of the kind defined in § 1 are exposed for sale during the usual business hours, or while the rooms are opened for traffic.

3. They are authorized on giving a receipt to take samples at their choice of the objects of the kind defined in § 1 which are in the above-mentioned rooms, or which are sold or exposed for sale in public localities and markets, places and streets, or which are being hawked about, with a view to examine such objects.

At the request of the proprietor part of the samples must be officially wrapped up or sealed up and left behind. Compensation must be given for the sample taken at the rate of the usual price of sale.

3. The police officials are authorized in the case of persons who have been condemned to a punishment of imprisonment in virtue of §§ 10, 12, 13 of this law, to make re-examinations (*Revisionen*) in the rooms in which objects of the kind defined in § 1 are exposed for sale, or which serve for keeping or producing of such objects with a view to sale, during the time mentioned in § 2.

This authorization begins as soon as the judgment is legally valid, and ceases when three years have elapsed from the day on which the punishment of imprisonment was completed, fell under prescription, or was remitted.

4. The competency of the magistrates and officials to take the measures defined in §§ 2 and 3 depends on the lawful regulations of the local legislatures.

Local regulations which give the police wider powers than the regulations enacted in §§ 2 and 3 are not affected hereby.

5. Regulations can be issued by Imperial ordinance with the consent of the Federal Council for the protection of health which forbid :—

(i.) Definite ways of producing, keeping, and packing articles of food and enjoyment which are intended for sale.

(ii.) Selling and exposing for sale as a trade of articles of food and enjoyment of a definite kind, or under a name which does not correspond to their true nature.

(iii.) Selling and exposing for sale with a view to slaughter of beasts which are suffering from definite diseases, as well as the selling and exposing for sale of the flesh of beasts which were afflicted with certain diseases.

(iv.) The employment of certain materials and colours in the manufacture of objects intended for clothes, toys, carpets, eating, drinking, and cooking utensils, as well as selling and exposing for sale as a trade objects which have been produced contrary to this prohibition.

(v.) Selling and exposing for sale as a trade petroleum of a definite nature.

Note.—Imperial ordinances were issued on May 5th, 1882, March 3rd, 1883, with regard to the employment of poisonous colours; and an Imperial ordinance was issued on February 24th, 1882, with regard to selling petroleum and exposing petroleum for sale.

6. Imperial ordinances can be issued for the Empire with the consent of the Federal Council to forbid or limit the production, sale, or exposure for sale of objects intended for the adulteration of articles of food or enjoyment.

7. The Imperial ordinances issued in virtue of §§ 5, 6 must be laid before the Imperial Parliament if it is assembled, otherwise at the next meeting of the Imperial Parliament. Such ordinances must be repealed so far as the Imperial Parliament demands their repeal.

8. Any one who infringes the ordinances issued in virtue of §§ 5, 6 shall be punished by a fine up to 150 shillings or by arrest.

The regulations of the local laws must not threaten a heavier punishment.

9. Any one who, contrary to the regulations of §§ 2—4, refuses to permit the entry into the rooms, the taking of a sample, or the re-examination there mentioned, shall be punished by a fine of from 50 to 150 shillings or by arrest.

10. Any one shall be punished by imprisonment with labour up to six months, and a fine up to 1500 shillings, or with one of these punishments:—

(i.) Who adulterates articles of food or enjoyment with a view to deceive in commerce or trade.

(ii.) Who wittingly sells articles of food or enjoyment which are spoilt, counterfeit, or adulterated without mentioning that fact, or who exposes such articles for sale under a designation calculated to deceive.

11. If the act designated in § 10 (ii.) has been committed from negligence, a fine up to 150 shillings or arrest takes place.

Cf. the criminal code, § 367 (vii.), which is not repealed.

12. Any one shall be sentenced to be imprisoned with labour, and if the court shall see fit to forfeit his civil privileges:—

(i.) Who maliciously produces objects which are intended to serve others as articles of food or enjoyment in such a manner that the enjoyment of the same is calculated to injure human health; likewise any one who wittingly sells, exposes for sale, or otherwise brings into circulation as articles of food or enjoyment objects the enjoyment of which is calculated to injure human health.

(ii.) Who maliciously produces articles of dress, toys, carpets, eating, drinking, and cooking utensils, in such a manner that the use of such articles in the manner which is directed or which could have been foreseen is calculated to injure human health; in like manner any one who wittingly sells, exposes for sale, or otherwise brings such objects into circulation.

The attempt to commit this offence is criminal.

If a serious bodily injury or the death of a human being has been caused, penal servitude up to five years takes place.

Note.—It has been decided that bringing into circulation includes making a present of or using the article in one's own household (Leipsic, December 13th, 1880, October 27th, 1882), and the knowledge that such article was being used as an article of food (March 11th, 1881). Further, under such articles is included unripe fruit which is eatable and has only been cooked (Leipsic, June 4th, 1881).

13. If in cases under § 12 the use or enjoyment of the object was calculated to destroy human health, and if this quality was known to the offender, penal servitude up to ten years takes place; and if the death of a human being has been caused by the act, penal servitude for not less than ten years or penal servitude for life.

The sentence may further permit police supervision.

Note.—Cf. the criminal code, § 367 (vii.). The want of police regulations with regard to the examination of pork does not exclude criminality under § 14 of this law and §§ 222—230 of the criminal code (Leipsic, February 15th, 1882).

14. If one of the acts designated in §§ 12, 13 has been committed from negligence the court must inflict a fine up to 1000 shillings or imprisonment with labour up to six months; and if the act has caused injury to the health of a human being, imprisonment with labour up to one year, but if the death of a human being has been caused, imprisonment for from one month to three years.

15. In cases under §§ 12—14 the sentence must include the confiscation of objects produced, sold, or

exposed for sale, or otherwise brought into circulation contrary to the regulations designated, without distinction whether they belong to the person condemned or not; in cases under §§ 8, 10, 11 the sentence may include confiscation.

Note.—The regulations of § 15 with regard to confiscation are exhaustive, and § 42 of the criminal code is not applicable under this law.

16. The court may direct in the judgment or criminal injunction that the sentence be made publicly known at the cost of the guilty person.

The court must on the proposal of an accused person who has been acquitted direct that the acquittal be officially published.

The state treasury bears the costs in so far as such costs have not been imposed on the informer.

The judgment must define how the publication is to take place.

17. If there is a public institution for the technical examination of articles of food and enjoyment for the place, the fines imposed in virtue of this law are payable to the fund which bears the costs of the maintenance of the institution so far as they are not payable to the state.

XII.

AN ENUMERATION OF THE MORE IMPORTANT IMPERIAL LAWS WHICH CONTAIN PENAL REGULATIONS CONCURRENT WITH THE CRIMINAL CODE, OR WHICH RELATE TO CRIMINAL LAW.

1. LAW relating to the levying of a duty on salt of October 11th, 1867. (Not formally speaking an Imperial law.)

2. Law relating to flag of the Empire (Federation) of November 25th, 1867.

3. Law relating to the interest permissible under contracts (repeal of the penalties for usury) of November 11th, 1867.

4. Law relating to the levying of a duty on the manufacture of brandy in the lands of the Hohenzollern family of May 5th, 1868, the supplementary law of November 15th, 1874, and law of July 8th, 1868.

5. Law relating to societies (*Genossenschaften*) for industrial and economical purposes of July 4th, 1868.

6. Law relating to the taxation of brandy in the different states belonging to the North German Confederation of July 8th, 1868.

7. Law regulating weights and measures for the North German Confederation of August 17th, 1868, and supplements of March 3rd, 1870, December 7th, 1873, and orders of the Imperial Chancellor issued on this subject on August 16th, 1871, and July 25th, 1875.

8. Gauge law of July 16th, 1869, with supplements of the commission.

9. Law relating to the Rinderpest of April 7th, 1869, together with the instructions issued, May 29th, 1869.

10. Law relating to the introduction of stamps for telegrams, May 16th, 1869.

11. Laws relating to the stamp duty on bills of exchange for the North German Confederation of June 10th, 1869, and instructions issued, July 16th, November 11th, 1881.

12. The trade ordinance for the North German Confederation of June 21st, 1869. The law introducing the above into Bavaria, June 12th, 1872. Laws relating to the alteration of the trade ordinance of March 7th, 1876, March 8th, 1876, July 17th, 1878, July 15th, 1880, July 18th, 1881.

13. Law relating to the taxation of sugar of June 20th, 1869.

14. The law of the Customs Union of July 1st, 1869.

15. Law amending the taxation of sugar, May 2nd, 1870.

16. Law relating to the rights of authors to writings, pictures, musical compositions, and dramatic works, of June 11th, 1870.

17. Law relating to Commandit share societies and share societies of June 11th, 1870.

18. Imperial law with regard to bills payable to the bearer with premia of June 8th, 1871, together with the instructions issued by the Imperial Chancellor on June 6th, July 1st, July 7th, 1871.

19. Postal law for the German Empire, October 28th, 1871; supplementary law of December 20th, 1875. Postal law of March 8th, 1879; supplementary law of March 12th, 1883.

20. Law relating to the limitations of landed property in the vicinity of fortresses of December 21st, 1871.

21. Law relating to the levying of the tax on brewing of May 31st, 1872, and supplementary law of December 23rd, 1876.

22. Military criminal code for the German Empire, with introductory law of June 6th, 1872.

23. Law relating to sailors for the German Empire of December 27th, 1872.

24. Law relating to the duty of German merchant ships to take on board sailors who are in distress at sea, December 27th, 1872.

25. Law relating to the registration and denomination of merchant ships of June 28th, 1873, and directions of the Imperial Chancellor, November 13th, 1873.

26. Mint law of July 9th, 1883.

27. Vaccination law of April 8th, 1874.

28. Military law for the Empire of May 2nd, 1874; supplementary law of May 6th, 1881. Militia law of September 28th, 1875, and supplementary law of August 31st, 1880.

29. Law to prevent the unauthorized exercise of offices in the Church of May 4th, 1874.

30. Law relating to the press of May 7th, 1874.

31. Law relating to ships going ashore of May 17th, 1874.

32. Trade-mark law of November 30th, 1874.

33. Regulations for the railroads of Germany of January 4th, 1875.

34. Law relating to the attestation of personal rank and the solemnization of marriage of February 6th, 1875.

35. Law relating to the exercise of military control, &c. of February 15th, 1875.

36. Bank law of March 14th, 1875.

37. Law relating to the rights of authors with regard to artistic productions of January 9th, 1876.

38. Law relating to the protection of photographs against unauthorized imitation of January 10th, 1876.

39. Law relating to the author's right in patterns and models of January 11th, 1876.

40. Law relating to the removal of contagious materials in the transports of cattle on railways of February 25th, 1876.

41. Law relating to registered provident societies of April 4th, 1876.

42. Law relating to the close time for the capture of seals of December 4th, 1876.

43. Imperial bankruptcy law of February 10th, 1877.

44. Patent law of May 25th, 1877.

45. Law relating to the infringement of prohibitions issued to avoid the Rinderpest of May 21st, 1878.

46. Law relating to the stamp duty on playing cards of July 3rd, 1878.

47. Law against the commonly dangerous efforts of social democracy of October 21st, 1878.

48. Law relating to the traffic in articles of food, &c. of May 14th, 1879.

49. Law relating to the tax on tobacco of July 16th, 1879.

50. Law relating to the freedom of brandy from taxation when used for the objects of trade, July 19th, 1879.

51. Law relating to the statistics of the traffic in goods of July 20th, 1879.

52. Law relating to the avoidance and suppression of cattle plagues. Instructions of the Federal Council of February 12th, 1881, and amendment thereof, April 24th, 1882.

53. Law relating to notices to be made at Consulate with reference to ships of March 25th, 1880, with supplement, July 28th, 1880.

54. Law relating to voyages with freight along the coast, May 22nd, 1881, and the Imperial ordinance and the proclamation by the Imperial Chancellor of December 29th, 1881.

55. Law relating to the levying of the Imperial stamp duties of July 1st, 1881, with directions for its enforcement, July 7th, 1881.

56. Law relating to the designation of the contents of vessels used in taverns.

INDEX.